Friedrich Nietzsche is one of the most influential thinkers of the past 150 years and *On the Genealogy of Morality* (1887) is his most important work on ethics and politics. A polemical contribution to moral and political theory, it offers a critique of moral values and traces the historical evolution of concepts such as guilt, conscience, responsibility, law and justice. This is a revised and updated edition of one of the most successful volumes to appear in Cambridge Texts in the History of Political Thought. Keith Ansell-Pearson has modified his introduction to Nietzsche's classic text, and Carol Diethe has incorporated a number of changes to the translation itself, reflecting the considerable advances in our understanding of Nietzsche in the twelve years since this edition first appeared. In this new guise, the Cambridge Texts edition of Nietzsche's *Genealogy* should continue to enjoy widespread adoption, at both undergraduate and graduate level.

CAMBRIDGE TEXTS IN THE
HISTORY OF POLITICAL THOUGHT

FRIEDRICH NIETZSCHE
On the Genealogy of Morality

CAMBRIDGE TEXTS IN THE HISTORY OF POLITICAL THOUGHT

Series editors

RAYMOND GEUSS
Professor of Philosophy, University of Cambridge

QUENTIN SKINNER
Regius Professor of Modern History in the University of Cambridge

Cambridge Texts in the History of Political Thought is now firmly established as the major student textbook series in political theory. It aims to make available to students all the most important texts in the history of western political thought, from ancient Greece to the early twentieth century. All the familiar classic texts will be included, but the series seeks at the same time to enlarge the conventional canon by incorporating an extensive range of less well-known works, many of them never before available in a modern English edition. Wherever possible, texts are published in complete and unabridged form, and translations are specially commissioned for the series. Each volume contains a critical introduction together with chronologies, biographical sketches, a guide to further reading and any necessary glossaries and textual apparatus. When completed the series will aim to offer an outline of the entire evolution of western political thought.

For a list of titles published in the series, please see end of book

FRIEDRICH NIETZSCHE

On the Genealogy of Morality

EDITED BY
KEITH ANSELL-PEARSON
Department of Philosophy,
University of Warwick

TRANSLATED BY
CAROL DIETHE

CAMBRIDGE
UNIVERSITY PRESS

CAMBRIDGE UNIVERSITY PRESS
Cambridge, New York, Melbourne, Madrid, Cape Town, Singapore, São Paulo, Delhi

Cambridge University Press
The Edinburgh Building, Cambridge CB2 8RU, UK

Published in the United States of America by Cambridge University Press, New York

www.cambridge.org
Information on this title: www.cambridge.org/9780521691635

In the translations, introduction and editorial matter
© Cambridge University Press 1997

First published 1997
Revised Student edition first published 2007
Fourth printing 2009

Printed in the United Kingdom at the University Press, Cambridge

A catalogue record for this publication is available from the British Library

ISBN 978-0-521-87123-5 hardback
ISBN 978-0-521-69163-5 paperback

Contents

Acknowledgements and a note on the text

Carol Diethe is responsible for the translation of all the material featured in this book with the exception of the supplementary material taken from the Cambridge University Press editions of *Human, All too Human* (volumes one and two), pp. 123–32 and *Daybreak*, pp. 133–44, and translated by R. J. Hollingdale.

The notes which accompany the text were prepared by Raymond Geuss, who profited from editorial material supplied in the editions of G. Colli and M. Montinari (Berlin/New York, de Gruyter, 1967–88) and Peter Putz (Munich, Goldman, 1988).

The essay 'The Greek State' was originally intended by Nietzsche to be a chapter of his first published book, *The Birth of Tragedy* (1872); together with the essay 'Homer's Contest' and three other essays – on the topics of truth, the future of education, and Schopenhauer – it formed part of the 'Five prefaces to five unwritten books' Nietzsche presented to Cosima Wagner in the Christmas of 1872. The German text of the two essays, newly translated here, can be found in volume 1 of *Nietzsche. Sämtliche Werke: Kritische Studienausgabe* (Berlin/New York, de Gruyter, 1988), pp. 764–78 and pp. 783–93.

Nietzsche's own italicization and idiosyncratic punctuation have been retained in the text.

A note on the revised edition

This second, revised edition features a new introduction by the editor and a revised and updated guide to further reading. The translation has been extensively modified in an effort to present the reader with a more accurate and reliable text. The editor and translator wish to thank those scholars who brought errors in the original translation to their attention and made suggestions for refining the text, in particular Christa Davis Acampora and Duncan Large. Ultimately, we made our own decisions and sole responsibility for the text remains with us. Keith Ansell-Pearson wishes to thank Richard Fisher of Cambridge University Press for supporting the idea of a second, revised edition of the text, and Christa Davis Acampora, Carol Diethe and Raymond Geuss for looking over versions of the introduction and providing helpful comments. Carol Diethe wishes to thank Jürgen Diethe for his considered comments.

Note by the translator: Anyone who has read Nietzsche in the original will be aware of his polished style, and will have admired his capacity to leap from one idea to another with *finesse*, to sprinkle foreign words into his text, to emphasize words with italics, or to coin a string of neologisms while rushing headlong through a paragraph until, finally, he reaches the safe landing of a full stop. Humbling though the experience often was, I have tried to keep faith with Nietzsche's punctuation and to capture as much of his style as was possible in translation while still holding on to the demands of accuracy. For accuracy in translating Nietzsche is increasingly important. When the first edition came out in 1994, I felt I could render a term like 'blue-eyed' as 'naïve', as in the phrase 'naïvely mendacious', which now appears as 'blue-eyed mendacious' in the text (III, 19).

Now, however, there are several dictionaries collating Nietzsche's terms, and the method adopted in the recently published first volume of de Gruyter's *Nietzsche Wörterbuch* (Vol. I, A–E) includes information on the frequency of Nietzsche's use of a given term. For example, there is an entry for 'blue', and we are told that Nietzsche used it seventy-two times. In view of this scrutiny of Nietzsche's vocabulary, one feels duty-bound to be as literal as possible, and the translation has been checked and tightened with this aspect of Nietzsche research in mind.

Nietzsche used foreign words liberally, and these usually appear in italics in the text, though not always, as when Nietzsche actually used an English word in his text, such as 'contiguity' or, more surprisingly, 'sportsman' and 'training', quite modern words at that time (III, 17, 21).

Some of Nietzsche's terms are given in German after a word to clarify the translation of a key word, or a word translated in a seemingly anarchic way; hence *Anschauung* (normally used for 'view' or 'opinion') appears after 'contemplation' to confirm that it is Schopenhauer's aesthetic term under discussion. Often, of course, the context dictates that some words are translated differently within the text. One example is *Freigeist*, translated as 'free-thinker' on page 19 and 'free spirit' on page 77. In Nietzsche's day, the free-thinker was usually an enlightened but still religious person, probably with liberal views. When, on page 19, Nietzsche refers to his interlocutor as a democrat (a term of abuse for Nietzsche), we can safely assume that he has the free-thinker in mind. Yet Nietzsche saw himself as a free spirit, and praised the Buddha for breaking free from his domestic shackles; for this reason, 'free spirit' is used on p. 77, and this is the best translation for *Freigeist* when – as more usually – Nietzsche used it in a positive sense.

Much trickier was the wordplay Nietzsche introduced when explaining that Christian guilt (*Schuld*) stems from a much earlier concept of debt (also *Schuld*). In sections 20–2 of the Second Essay, it is only possible to know which meaning Nietzsche had in mind by the surrounding references to 'moralizing' (where we are fairly safe with 'guilt') or 'repayment' (where 'debt' is necessary). It is not always quite as neat as this sounds, and on a few occasions (pages 62 and 63), 'debt/guilt' is used to indicate that Nietzsche is changing gear.

On one occasion, where Nietzsche describes Napoleon as a synthesis of *Unmensch* and *Übermensch* (p. 33), the German words are given *first* and the English translation is in brackets: a high-risk strategy in any translation. The reason for this is an experience I had when teaching undergraduates who did not know any German, but who wanted to know more about Nietzsche's 'slogans': eternal return, the will to power and especially the *Übermensch* – variously translated as 'superman' or 'overman', though the German term is now in widespread use. Although Walter Kaufmann in his translation of *On the Genealogy of Morals* provided an excellent description of Napoleon as 'this synthesis of the inhuman and superhuman', I could not convince my students that this text contained any reference to the *Übermensch*. Kaufmann's index had no such entry, and nobody grasped that the word 'superhuman' – elegant as it was alongside 'inhuman' – actually translated *Übermensch*. Once the decision had been taken to place the German word in the text 'proper', we felt we had to pay *Unmensch* the same compliment, especially as Nietzsche intends his readers to reflect on the two types of human being, *Mensch*.

Finally, a word about the title. When I first heard about a book by Nietzsche called *Zur Genealogie der Moral*, I assumed the translation would be *On the Genealogy of Morality*, since for me, *die Moral* meant ethics as a formal doctrine, in other words, morality in a grand and abstract sense which naturally comprised morals. I am more relaxed on the matter now, but still feel that to talk about morality as a singular entity and phenomenon is truer to Nietzsche's meaning. Everyone concerned with this book has had that consideration in mind, and a primary concern was to make Nietzsche *accessible*.

Introduction: on Nietzsche's critique of morality

Introduction to Nietzsche's text

Although it has come to be prized by commentators as his most important and systematic work, Nietzsche conceived *On the Genealogy of
Morality* as a 'small polemical pamphlet' that might help him sell more
copies of his earlier writings.[1] It clearly merits, though, the level of attention it receives and can justifiably be regarded as one of the key texts of
European intellectual modernity. It is a deeply disturbing book that
retains its capacity to shock and disconcert the modern reader. Nietzsche
himself was well aware of the character of the book. There are moments
in the text where he reveals his own sense of alarm at what he is discovering about human origins and development, especially the perverse
nature of the human animal, the being he calls 'the sick animal' (*GM*,
III, 14). Although the *Genealogy* is one of the darkest books ever written,
it is also, paradoxically, a book full of hope and anticipation. Nietzsche
provides us with a stunning story about man's monstrous moral past,
which tells the history of the deformation of the human animal in the
hands of civilization and Christian moralization; but also hints at a new
kind of humanity coming into existence in the wake of the death of God
and the demise of a Christian-moral culture.

On the Genealogy of Morality belongs to the late period of Nietzsche's
writings (1886–8). It was composed in July and August of 1887 and published in November of that year. Nietzsche intended it as a 'supplement'

---

[1] Letter to Peter Gast, 18 July 1887, in *Selected Letters of Friedrich Nietzsche*, ed.
Christopher Middleton (London and Chicago: University of Chicago Press, 1999),
p. 269.

to and 'clarification' of *Beyond Good and Evil*, said by him to be 'in all essentials' a critique of modernity that includes within its range of attack modern science, modern art and modern politics. In a letter to his former Basel colleague Jacob Burckhardt dated 22 September 1886, Nietzsche stresses that *Beyond Good and Evil* says the same things as *Zarathustra* 'only in a way that is different – very different'. In this letter he draws attention to the book's chief preoccupations and mentions the 'mysterious conditions of any growth in culture', the 'extremely dubious relation between what is called the "improvement" of man (or even "humanisation") and the enlargement of the human type', and 'above all the contradiction between every moral concept and every scientific concept of *life*'. *On the Genealogy of Morality* closely echoes these themes and concerns. Nietzsche finds that 'all modern judgments about men and things' are smeared with an over-moralistic language; the characteristic feature of modern souls and modern books is to be found in their 'moralistic mendaciousness' (*GM*, III, 19).

In *Ecce Homo* Nietzsche describes the *Genealogy* as consisting of 'three decisive preliminary studies by a psychologist for a revaluation of values'. The First Essay probes the 'psychology of Christianity' and traces the birth of Christianity not out of the 'spirit' *per se* but out of a particular kind of spirit, namely, *ressentiment*; the Second Essay provides a 'psychology of the conscience', where it is conceived not as the voice of God in man but as the instinct of cruelty that has been internalized after it can no longer discharge itself externally; the Third Essay inquires into the meaning of ascetic ideals, examines the perversion of the human will, and explores the possibility of a counter-ideal. Nietzsche says that he provides an answer to the question where the power of the ascetic ideal, 'the *harmful* ideal *par excellence*', comes from, and he argues that this is simply because to date it has been the *only* ideal; no counter-ideal has been made available '*until the advent of Zarathustra*'.

The *Genealogy* is a subversive book that needs to be read with great care. It contains provocative imagery of 'blond beasts of prey' and of the Jewish 'slave revolt in morality' which can easily mislead the unwary reader about the nature of Nietzsche's immoralism. In the preface, Nietzsche mentions the importance of readers familiarizing themselves with his previous books – throughout the book he refers to various sections and aphorisms from them, and occasionally he makes partial citations from them. The critique of morality Nietzsche carries out in the book is a complex one; its nuances are lost if one extracts isolated images and concepts from the argument of the book as a whole. His contribution to the study of 'morality' has three essential aspects: first, a criticism of moral genealogists for bungling the object of their study through the lack of a genuine historical sense; second, a criticism of modern evolutionary theory as a basis for the study of morality; and third, a critique of moral values that demands a thorough revaluation of them. Nietzsche's polemical contribution is intended to question the so-called self-evident 'facts' about morality and it has lost none of its force today.

Reading Nietzsche

Nietzsche is often referred to as an 'aphoristic' writer, but this falls short of capturing the sheer variety of forms and styles he adopted. In fact, the number of genuine aphorisms in his works is relatively small; instead, most of what are called Nietzsche's 'aphorisms' are more substantial paragraphs which exhibit a unified train of thought (frequently encapsulated in a paragraph heading indicating the subject matter), and it is from these building blocks that the other, larger structures are built in more or less extended sequences. Nietzsche's style, then, is very different from standard academic writing, from that of the 'philosophical workers' he describes so condescendingly in *Beyond Good and Evil* (*BGE*, 211). His aim is always to energize and enliven philosophical style through an admixture of aphoristic and, broadly speaking, 'literary' forms. His stylistic ideal, as he puts it on the title page of *The Case of Wagner* (parodying Horace), is the paradoxical one of 'ridendo dicere severum' ('saying what is sombre through what is laughable'), and these two modes, the sombre and the sunny, are mischievously intertwined in his philosophy, without the reader necessarily being sure which is uppermost at any one time.

Nietzsche lays down a challenge to his readers, and sets them a pedagogical, hermeneutic task, that of learning to read him well. He acknowledges that the aphoristic form of his writing causes difficulty, and emphasizes that an aphorism has not been 'deciphered' simply when it has been read out; rather, for full understanding to take place, an 'art of interpretation' or exegesis is required (the German word is *Auslegung*, literally a laying out). He gives the attentive reader a hint of what kind of exegesis he thinks is needed when he claims that the Third Essay of the book 'is a commentary on the aphorism that precedes it' (he intends the opening section of the essay, not the epigraph from *Zarathustra*).

Genealogy and morality

For Nietzsche, morality represents a system of errors that we have incorporated into our basic ways of thinking, feeling and living; it is the great symbol of our profound ignorance of ourselves and the world. In *The Gay Science* 115, it is noted how humankind has been educated by 'the four errors': we see ourselves only incompletely; we endow ourselves with fictitious attributes; we place ourselves in a 'false rank' in relation to animals and nature – that is, we see ourselves as being inherently superior to them; and, finally, we invent ever new tables of what is good and then accept them as eternal and unconditional. However, Nietzsche does not propose we should make ourselves feel guilty about our incorporated errors (they have provided us with new drives); and neither does he want us simply to accuse or blame the past. We need to strive to be more just in our evaluations of life and the living by, for example, thinking 'beyond good and evil'. For Nietzsche, it is largely the prejudices of morality that stand in the way of this; morality assumes knowledge of things it does not have.

The criticism Nietzsche levels at morality – what we moderns take it to be and to represent – is that it is a menacing and dangerous system that makes the present live at the expense of the future (*GM*, Preface, 6). Nietzsche's concern is that the human species may never attain its '*highest potential and splendour*' (ibid.). The task of culture is to produce sovereign individuals, but what we really find in history is a series of deformations and perversions of that cultural task. Thus, in the modern world the aim and meaning of culture is taken to be 'to breed a tame and civilized animal, a *household pet*, out of the beast of prey "man"' (*GM*, I, 11), so that now man strives to become 'better' all the time, meaning 'more comfortable, more mediocre, more indifferent, more Chinese, more Christian . . .' (*GM*, I, 12). This, then, is the great danger of modern culture: it will produce an animal that takes taming to be an end in itself, to the point where the free-thinker will announce that the end of history has been attained (for Nietzsche's criticism of the 'free-thinker' see *GM*, I, 9). Nietzsche argues that we moderns are in danger of being tempted by a new European type of Buddhism, united in our belief in the supreme value of a morality of communal compassion, 'as if it were morality itself, the summit, the *conquered* summit of humankind, the only hope for the future, comfort in the present, the great redemption from all past guilt . . .' (*BGE*, 202).

Nietzsche argues that in their attempts to account for morality philosophers have not developed the suspicion that morality might be 'something problematic'; in effect what they have done is to articulate 'an erudite form of true belief in the prevailing morality', and, as a result, their inquiries remain 'a part of the state of affairs within a particular morality' (*BGE*, 186). Modern European morality is 'herd animal morality' which considers itself to be the definition of morality and the only morality possible or desirable (*BGE*, 202); at work in modern thinking is the assumption that there is a single morality valid for all (*BGE*, 228). Nietzsche seeks to develop a genuinely critical approach to morality, in which all kinds of novel, surprising and daring questions are posed. Nietzsche does not so much inquire into a 'moral sense' or a moral faculty as attempt to uncover *the different senses* of morality, that is the different 'meanings' morality can be credited with in the history of human development: morality as symptom, as mask, as sickness, as stimulant, as poison, and so on. Morality, Nietzsche holds, is a surface phenomenon that requires meta-level interpretation in accordance with a different, superior set of extra-moral values 'beyond good and evil'.

On several occasions in the *Genealogy*, Nietzsche makes it clear that certain psychologists and moralists have been doing something we can call 'genealogy' (see, for example, *GM*, I, 2 and II, 4, 12). He finds all these attempts insufficiently critical. In particular, Nietzsche has in mind the books of his former friend, Paul Rée (1849–1901), to whom he refers in the book's preface. In section 4 he admits that it was Rée's book on the origin of moral sensations, published in 1877, that initially stimulated him to develop his own hypotheses on the origin of morality. Moreover, it was in this book that he 'first directly encountered the back-to-front and perverse kind of genealogical hypotheses', which he calls 'the English kind'. In section 7 Nietzsche states that he wishes to develop the sharp, unbiased eye of the critic of morality in a better direction than we find in Rée's speculations. He wants, he tells us, to think in the direction 'of a real *history of morality*' (*die wirkliche* Historie der Moral); in contrast to the 'English hypothesis-mongering *into the blue*' – that is, looking vainly into the distance as in the blue yonder – he will have recourse to the colour 'grey' to aid his genealogical inquiries, for this denotes, 'that which can be documented, which can actually be confirmed and has actually existed . . . the whole, long, hard-to-decipher hieroglyphic script of man's moral past!' (*GM*, Preface, 7). Because the moral genealogists are so caught up in 'merely "modern" experience' they are altogether lacking in knowledge; they have 'no will to know the past, still less an instinct for history . . .' (*GM*, II, 4). An examination of the books of moral genealogists would show, ultimately, that they all take it to be something given and place it beyond questioning. Although he detects a few preliminary attempts to explore the history of moral feelings and valuations, Nietzsche maintains that even among more refined researchers no attempt at critique has been made. Instead, the popular superstition of Christian Europe that selflessness and compassion are what is characteristic of morality is maintained and endorsed.

Nietzsche begins the *Genealogy* proper by paying homage to 'English psychologists', a group of researchers who have held a microscope to the soul and, in the process, pioneered the search for a new set of truths: 'plain, bitter, ugly, foul, unchristian, immoral . . .' (*GM*, I, 1). The work of these psychologists has its basis in the empiricism of John Locke, and in David Hume's new approach to the mind that seeks to show that so-called complex, intellectual activity emerges out of processes that are, in truth, 'stupid', such as the *vis inertiae* of habit and the random coupling and mechanical association of ideas. In the attempt of 'English psychologists' to show the real mechanisms of the mind Nietzsche sees at work not a malicious and mean instinct, and not simply a pessimistic suspicion about the human animal, but the research of proud and generous spirits who have sacrificed much to the cause of truth. He admires the honest craftsmanship of their intellectual labours. He criticizes them, however, for their lack of a real historical sense and for bungling their moral genealogies as a result, and for failing to raise questions of value and future legislation. This is why he describes empiricism as being limited by a 'plebeian ambition' (*BGE*, 213). What the 'English' essentially lack, according to Nietzsche, is 'spiritual vision of real *depth* – in short, philosophy' (*BGE*, 252).

In section 12 of the Second Essay Nietzsche attempts to expose what he takes to be the fundamental naïveté of the moral genealogists. This consists in highlighting some purpose that a contemporary institution or practice purportedly has, and then placing this purpose at the start of the historical process which led to the modern phenomenon in question. In *GM*, II, 13 he says that only that which has no history can be defined, and draws attention to the 'synthesis of meanings' that accrues to any given phenomenon. His fundamental claim, one that needs, he says, to inform all kinds of historical research, is that the origin of the development of a thing and its 'ultimate usefulness' are altogether separate. This is because what exists is 'continually interpreted anew . . . transformed and redirected to a new purpose' by a superior power. Nietzsche is challenging the assumption that the manifest purpose of a thing ('its utility, form and shape') constitutes the reason for its existence, such as the view that the eye is made to see and the hand to grasp. He argues against the view that we can consider the development of a thing in terms of a 'logical *progressus*' towards a goal. This naïvely teleological conception of development ignores the random and contingent factors within evolution, be it the evolution of a tradition or an organ. However, he also claims that 'every purpose and use is just a *sign* that the will to power' is in operation in historical change. This further claim has not found favour among theorists impressed by Nietzsche's ideas on evolution because they see it as relying upon an extravagant metaphysics. It is clear from his published presentations of the theory of the will to power that Nietzsche did not intend it to be such.

Nietzsche knows that he will shock his readers with the claims he makes on behalf of the will to power, for example, that it is the '*primordial fact* of all history' (*BGE*, 259). To say that the will to power is a 'fact' is not, for Nietzsche, to be committed to any simple-minded form of philosophical empiricism. Rather, Nietzsche's training as a philologist inclined him to the view that no fact exists apart from an interpretation, just as no text speaks for itself, but always requires an interpreting reader. When those of a modern democratic disposition consider nature and regard everything in it as equally subject to a fixed set of 'laws of nature', are they not projecting on to nature their own aspirations for human society, by construing nature as a realm that exhibits the rational, well-ordered egalitarianism which they wish to impose on all the various forms of human sociability? Might they be, as Nietzsche insinuates, masking their 'plebeian enmity towards everything privileged and autocratic, as well as a new and more subtle atheism'? But if even these purported facts about nature are really a matter of interpretation and not text, would it not be possible for a thinker to deploy the opposite intention and look, with his interpretive skill, at the same nature and the same phenomena, reading 'out of it the ruthlessly tyrannical and unrelenting assertion of power claims'? Nietzsche presents his readers with a contest of interpretations. His critical claim is that, whereas the modern 'democratic' interpretation suffers from being moralistic, his does not; his interpretation of the 'text' of nature as will to power allows for a much richer appreciation of the economy of life, including its active emotions. In the *Genealogy*, Nietzsche wants the seminal role played by the active affects to be appreciated (*GM*, II, 11). We suffer from the 'democratic idiosyncrasy' that opposes in principle everything that dominates and wants to dominate (*GM*, II, 12). Against Darwinism, he argues that it is insufficient to account for life solely in terms of adaptation to external circumstances. Such a conception deprives life of its most important dimension, which he names '*Aktivität*' (activity). It does this, he contends, by overlooking the primacy of the 'spontaneous, expansive, aggressive . . . formative forces' that provide life with new directions and new interpretations, and from which adaptation takes place only once these forces have had their effect. He tells us that he lays 'stress on this major point of historical method because it runs counter to the prevailing instinct and fashion which would much rather come to terms with absolute randomness, and even the mechanistic senselessness of all events, than the theory that a *power-will* is acted out in all that happens' (*GM*, II, 12).

Nietzsche's polemic challenges the assumptions of standard genealogies, for example, that there is a line of descent that can be continuously traced from a common ancestor, and that would enable us to trace moral notions and legal practices back to a natural single and fixed origin. His emphasis is rather on fundamental transformations, on disruptions, and on psychological innovations and moral inventions that emerge in specific material and cultural contexts.

Undue emphasis should not be placed, however, on the role Nietzsche accords to contingency and discontinuity within history, as this would be to make a fetish of them as principles. Contrary to Michel Foucault's influential reading of genealogy, Nietzsche does not simply oppose himself to the search for origins, and neither is he opposed to the attempt to show that the past actively exists in the present, secretly continuing to animate it.[2] Much of what Nietzsche is doing in the book is only intelligible if we take him to be working with the idea that it does. Nietzsche opposes himself to the search for origins only where this involves what we might call a genealogical narcissism. Where it involves the discovery of difference at the origin, of the kind that surprises and disturbs us, Nietzsche is in favour of such a search. This is very much the case with his analysis of the bad conscience. For Nietzsche, this is an 'origin' (*Ursprung*) that is to be treated as a fate and as one that still lives on in human beings today.

---

[2] Michel Foucault, 'Nietzsche, Genealogy, and History' (1971), in *The Essential Works of Foucault*, volume II: 1954–84, ed. James Faubion, trans. Robert Hurley and others (London: Penguin Books, 2000), pp. 369–93.

'Good, bad and evil'

In the first of the three essays of which the *Genealogy* is composed, Nietzsche invites us to imagine a society which is split into two distinct groups: a militarily and politically dominant group of 'masters' exercises absolute control over a completely subordinate group of 'slaves'. The 'masters' in this model are construed as powerful, active, relatively unreflective agents who live a life of immediate physical self-affirmation: they drink, they brawl, they wench, they hunt, whenever the fancy takes them, and they are powerful enough, by and large, to succeed in most of these endeavours, and uninhibited enough to enjoy living in this way. They use the term 'good' to refer in an approving way to this life and to themselves as people who are capable of leading it. As an afterthought, they also sometimes employ the term 'bad' to refer to those people – most notably, the 'slaves' – who by virtue of their weakness are not capable of living the life of self-affirming physical exuberance. The terms 'good' and 'bad' then form the basis of a variety of different 'masters' moralities'. One of the most important events in Western history occurs when the *slaves* revolt against the masters' form of valuation. The slaves are, after all, not only physically weak and oppressed, they are also by virtue of their very weakness debarred from spontaneously seeing themselves and their lives in an affirmative way. They develop a reactive and negative sentiment against the oppressive masters which Nietzsche calls '*ressentiment*', and this *ressentiment* eventually turns creative, allowing the slaves to take revenge in the imagination on the masters whom they are too weak to harm physically. The form this revenge takes is the invention of a new concept and an associated new form of valuation: 'evil'. 'Evil' is used to refer to the life the masters lead (which *they* call 'good') but it is used to refer to it in a *disapproving* way. In a 'slave' morality this negative term 'evil' is central, and slaves can come to a pale semblance of self-affirmation only by observing that they are *not* like the 'evil' masters. In the mouths of the slaves, 'good' comes to refer not to a life of robust vitality, but to one that is 'not-evil', i.e. not in any way like the life that the masters live. Through a variety of further conceptual inventions (notably, 'free will'), the slaves stylize their own natural weakness into the result of a choice for which they can claim moral credit. Western morality has historically been a struggle between elements that derive from a basic form of valuation derived from 'masters' and one derived from 'slaves'.

The fate of bad conscience

In the Second Essay, Nietzsche develops a quite extraordinary story about the origins and emergence of feelings of responsibility and debt (personal obligation). He is concerned with nothing less than the evolution of the human mind and how its basic ways of thinking have come into being, such as inferring, calculating, weighing and anticipating. Indeed, he points out that our word 'man' (*manas*) denotes a being that values, measures and weighs. Nietzsche is keen to draw the reader's attention to what he regards as an important historical insight: the principal moral concept of 'guilt' (*Schuld*) descends from the material concept of 'debts' (*Schulden*). In this sphere of legal obligations, he stresses, we find the breeding-ground of the 'moral conceptual world' of guilt, conscience and duty (*GM*, II, 6).

Nietzsche opens the Second Essay by drawing attention to a paradoxical task of nature, namely, that of breeding an animal that is sanctioned to promise and so exist as a creature of time, a creature that can remember the past and anticipate the future, a creature that can in the present bind its own will relative to the future in the certain knowledge that it will in the future effectively remember that its will has been bound. For this cultivation of effective memory and imagination to be successful, culture needs to work against the active force of forgetting, which serves an important physiological function. The exercise of a memory of the will supposes that the human animal can make a distinction between what happens by accident and what happens by design or intention, and it also presupposes an ability to think causally about an anticipated future. In section 2, Nietzsche makes explicit that what he is addressing is the 'long history of the origins of *responsibility*'. The successful cultivation of an animal sanctioned to promise requires a labour by which man is made into something 'regular, reliable, and uniform'. This has been achieved by what Nietzsche calls the 'morality of custom' (*Sittlichkeit der Sitte*) and the 'social straitjacket' which it imposes. The disciplining of the human animal into an agent that has a sense of responsibility (*Verantwortlichkeit*) for its words and deeds has not taken place through gentle methods, but through the harsh and cruel measures of coercion and punishment. As Nietzsche makes clear at one point in the text: 'Each step on earth, even the smallest, was in the past a struggle that was won with spiritual and physical torment . . .' (III, 9). The problem for culture is that it has to deal with an animal that is partly dull, that has an inattentive mind and a strong propensity to active forgetfulness. In most societies and ages, this problem has not been solved by gentle methods: 'A thing must be burnt in so that it stays in the memory' (II, 3). Nietzsche's insight is that without blood, torture and sacrifice, including 'disgusting mutilations', what we know as 'modern psychology' would never have arisen. All religions are at bottom systems of cruelty, Nietzsche contends; blood and horror lies at the basis of all 'good things'. In a certain sense it is possible to locate the whole of asceticism in this sphere of torment: 'a few ideas have to be made ineradicable . . . unforgettable and fixed in order to hypnotize the whole nervous and intellectual system through these "fixed ideas" . . .' (ibid.).

The fruit of this labour of *Cultur* performed on man in the pre-historical period is the sovereign individual who is master of a strong and durable will, a will that can make and keep promises. On this account freedom of the will is an achievement of culture and operates in the context of specific material practices and social relations. Nietzsche calls this individual autonomous and supra-ethical (*übersittlich*): it is supra-ethical simply in the sense that it has gone beyond the level of custom. For Nietzsche the period of 'the morality of custom' pre-dates what we call 'world history' and is to be regarded as the 'decisive historical period' which has determined the character of man (*GM*, III, 9). The sublime work of morality can be explained as the 'natural' and necessary work of culture (of tradition and custom). The sovereign individual is the kind of self-regulating animal that is required for the essential functions of culture (for example, well-functioning creditor–debtor relations). It cannot be taken to be his ideal in any simple or straightforward sense.[3]

In *GM*, II, 16 Nietzsche advances, albeit in a preliminary fashion, his own theory on the 'origin' of the bad conscience. He looks upon it 'as a serious illness to which man was forced to succumb by the pressure of the most fundamental of all changes which he experienced'. This change refers to the establishment of society and peace and their confining spaces, which brings with it a suspension and devaluation of the instincts. Nietzsche writes of the basic instinct of freedom – the will to power – being forced back and repressed (II, 17–18). Human beings now walk as if a 'terrible heaviness' bears down on them. In this new scenario the old animal instincts, such as animosity, cruelty, the pleasure of changing and destroying, do not cease to make their demands, but have to find new and

---

[3] Nietzsche criticizes the ideal of 'a single, rigid and unchanging *individuum*' in *Human, All Too Human* 618.

underground satisfactions. Through internalization, in which no longer dischargeable instincts turn inward, comes the invention of what is popularly called the human 'soul': 'The whole inner world, originally stretched thinly as though between two layers of skin, was expanded and extended itself and granted depth, breadth, and height in proportion to the degree that the external discharge of man's instincts was *obstructed*.' Nietzsche insists that *this* is 'the origin of "bad conscience"'. He uses striking imagery in his portrait of this momentous development.

On the one hand, Nietzsche approaches the bad conscience as the most insidious illness that has come into being and from which man has yet to recover, his sickness of himself. On the other hand, he maintains that the 'prospect of an animal soul turning against itself' is an event and a spectacle too interesting 'to be played senselessly unobserved on some ridiculous planet'. Furthermore, as a development that was prior to all *ressentiment*, and that *cannot* be said to represent any organic assimilation into new circumstances, the bad conscience contributes to the appearance of an animal on earth that 'arouses interest, tension, hope', as if through it 'something . . . were being prepared, as though man were not an end but just a path, an episode, a bridge, a great promise' (*GM*, II, 16). Nietzsche observes that although it represents a painful and ugly growth, the bad conscience is not simply to be looked upon in disparaging terms; indeed, he speaks of the '*active* bad conscience'. It can be regarded as the 'true womb of ideal and imaginative events'; through it an abundance of 'disconcerting beauty and affirmation' has been brought to light.

In the course of history, the illness of bad conscience reached a terrible and sublime peak. In prehistory, argues Nietzsche, the basic creditor–debtor relationship that informs human social and economic activity also finds expression in religious rites and worship, for example, the way a tribal community expresses thanks to earlier generations. Over time the ancestor is turned into a god and associated with the feeling of fear (the birth of superstition). Christianity cultivates further the moral or religious sentiment of debt, and does so in terms of a truly monstrous level of sublime feeling: God is cast as the ultimate ancestor who cannot be repaid (*GM*, II, 20).

Sin and the ascetic ideal

The sense of 'guilt' has evolved through several momentous and fateful events in history. In its initial expression it is to be viewed 'as a piece of animal psychology, no more . . .' (*GM*, III, 20). In the earliest societies, a person is held answerable for his deeds and obliged to honour his debts. In the course of history this material sense of obligation is increasingly subject to moralization, reaching its summit with guilt before the Christian God. In the Third Essay, the ascetic priest comes into his own. Nietzsche had introduced the 'priests' into his account in the First Essay as a faction of the ruling class of 'masters', who distinguish themselves from the other masters by an extreme concern for purity (*GM*, I, 6–7). Originally, this concern is no more than a variant of the superiority of the master-caste as a whole over the slaves: the priests are masters and thus can afford to wash, wear clean clothes, avoid certain malodorous or unhealthy foods, etc. Slaves have no such luxury. Priestly purity, however, has a dangerous tendency to develop into more and more extreme and more and more internalized forms. Priests become expert in asceticism, and in dealing with all forms of human suffering. It is in the hands of the priest, an artist in feelings of guilt, Nietzsche says, that guilt assumes form and shape: ' "Sin" – for that is the name for the priestly reinterpretation of the animal "bad conscience" . . . – has been the greatest event in the history of the sick soul up till now: with sin we have the most dangerous and disastrous trick of religious interpretation' (*GM*, III, 20). The value of the priestly type of existence, says Nietzsche, lies in the fact that it succeeds in changing the direction of *ressentiment* (*GM*, III, 15).

In the First Essay, we saw the slaves in the grip of a creative *ressentiment* directed against the masters which could be expressed in the following terms: they – the masters – are 'evil', whereas we are not-evil (therefore, good). Important as the invention of the concept of 'evil' is historically, in itself it does not yet solve the slaves' problem. In fact, in some ways it makes it more acute: If we are good, why do we suffer? The correct answer to this question, Nietzsche believes, is that the slaves suffer because they are inherently weak, and it is simply a biological fact that some humans are much weaker than others, either by nature or as a result of unfortunate circumstances. This answer, however, is one no slave can be expected to tolerate because it seems to make his situation hopeless and irremediable, which, in fact, Nietzsche thinks it is. Humans can bear suffering; what they cannot bear is seemingly senseless suffering, and this is what the slaves' suffering is. It has no meaning, it is a mere brute fact. The priests' intervention consists in giving the slaves a way of interpreting their suffering which at least allows them to make some sense of it. 'You slaves are suffering', so runs the priestly account, '*because* **you** are evil'. The *ressentiment* that was directed at the masters is now turned by the slaves on themselves. The sick, suffering slave becomes a 'sinner'. In addition to this diagnosis of the cause of suffering, the priests also have a proposed therapy. Since 'evil' designates the kind of intense vitality the masters exhibit in their lives, the way to escape it is to engage in a progressive spiral of forms of life-abnegation and self-denial. In the long run, this therapy makes the original 'disease' – the suffering that results from human weakness – worse, but in the short run of 2,000 years or so, it has mobilized what energy the slaves command in the service of creating what we know as Western culture.

The 'healing instinct of life' operates through the priest, in which ideas of guilt, sin, damnation, and so on, serve 'to make the sick *harmless* to a degree', and the instincts of the sufferer are exploited 'for the purpose of self-discipline, self-surveillance, and self-overcoming' (*GM*, III, 16). The priests' remedy for human suffering is the ascetic ideal, the ideal of a human will turned utterly against itself, or self-abnegation *for its own sake*. Such an ideal seems to express a self-contradiction in as much as we seem to encounter with it life operating against life. Nietzsche argues, however, that viewed from physiological and psychological angles this amounts to nonsense. In section 13 of the Third Essay he suggests that, on closer examination, the self-contradiction turns out to be only apparent, it is 'a psychological misunderstanding of something, the real nature of which was far from being understood . . .'. His argument is that the ascetic ideal has its source or origins in what he calls 'the protective and healing instincts of a degenerating life'. The ideal indicates a partial physiological exhaustion, in the face of which 'the deepest instincts of life, which have remained intact, continually struggle with new methods and inventions'. The ascetic ideal amounts, in effect, to a trick or artifice (*Kunstgriff*) for the preservation of life. The interpretation of suffering developed by the ascetic ideal for a long time now has succeeded in shutting the door on a suicidal nihilism by giving humanity a goal: morality. The ideal has added new dimensions and layers to suffering by making it deeper and more internal, creating a suffering that gnaws more intensely at life and bringing it within the perspective of metaphysical-moral guilt. But this saving of the will has been won at the expense of the future and fostered a hatred of the conditions of human existence. It expresses a 'fear of happiness and beauty' and 'a longing to get away from appearance, transience, growth, death'.

The real problem, according to Nietzsche, is not the past, not even Christianity, but present-day Christian-moral Europe. 'After such vistas and with such a burning hunger in our conscience and science', he writes in an aphorism on the great health, 'how could we still be satisfied with *present-day man?*' (*GS*, 382). We live in an age in which the desire for man and his future – a future beyond mere self-preservation, security and comfort – seems to be disappearing from the face of the earth. Modern atheists who have emancipated themselves from the affliction of past errors – the error of God, of the world conceived as a unity, of free will, and so on – have only freed themselves from something and not for something. They either believe in nothing at all or have a blind commitment to science and uphold the unconditional nature of the will to truth. By contrast, Nietzsche commits himself to the *'supreme affirmation'* that is born out of fullness, and this is 'an affirmation without reservation even of suffering, even of guilt, even of all that is strange and questionable in existence'. Nietzsche stresses that this 'Yes to life' is both the highest and deepest insight that is 'confirmed and maintained by truth and knowledge' (*EH* 'BT', 2). It is not, then, a simple-minded, pre-cognitive 'Yes' to life that he wants us to practise, but one, as he stresses, secured by 'truth and knowledge'. The 'free spirit' knows what kind of 'you shall' he has obeyed, Nietzsche writes; and in so doing, 'he also knows what he now *can*, what only now he – *may* do . . .' (*HH*, Preface).

Nietzsche and political thought

Nietzsche's political thinking remains a source of difficulty, even embarrassment, because it fails to accord with the standard liberal ways of thinking about politics which have prevailed in the last 200 and more years. As in liberalism, Nietzsche's conception of politics is an instrumental one, but he differs radically from the liberal view in his valuation of life. For liberalism, politics is a means to the peaceful coexistence of individual agents; for Nietzsche, by contrast, it is a means to the production of human greatness. Nietzsche challenges what we might call the ontological assumptions that inform the positing of the liberal subject, chiefly that its identity is largely imaginary because it is posited only at the expense of neglecting the cultural and historical formation of the subject. The liberal formulation of the subject assumes individual identity and liberty to be a given, in which the individual exists independently of the mediations of culture and history and outside the medium of ethical contest and spiritual labour. Nietzsche is committed to the enhancement of man and this enhancement does not consist in improving the conditions of existence for the majority of human beings, but in the generation of a few, striking and superlatively vital 'highest exemplars' of the species. Nietzsche looks forward to new philosophers who will be strong and original enough to revalue and reverse so-called 'eternal values' and, in teaching human beings that the future depends on their will, 'will prepare the way for great risk-taking and joint experiments in discipline and breeding', and in this way, 'put an end to that terrible reign of nonsense and coincidence that until now has been known as "history"' (*BGE*, 203).

In the two early essays from 1871–2 included in this volume, 'The Greek State' and 'Homer's Contest', we see at work the stress Nietzsche places on political life not as an end in itself but as a means to the production of great human beings and an aristocratic culture. Nietzsche presents a stark choice between 'culture' and 'politics' (or the claims of justice). He argues that if we wish to promote greatness and serve the ends of culture, then it is necessary to recognize that an essential aspect of society is economic servitude for the majority of individuals. We must not let the 'urge for justice . . . swamp all other ideas'; or, as Nietzsche memorably puts it, the 'cry of compassion' must not be allowed to tear down the 'walls of culture'.

When Nietzsche took up his teaching appointment at Basel University, he sought to make a contribution to the so-called 'Homeric question' which was centred on issues about the authenticity, authorship and significance of the works ascribed to 'Homer'. He addressed the topic in his inaugural lecture given in 1869, which was entitled 'Homer and Classical Philology' (originally conceived as an essay on 'Homer's Personality'). He comments upon the significance of the Greek *agon* (contest) in research he had done on a neglected (and maligned) Florentine manuscript on an imaginary contest between Homer and Hesiod (the first part of this research was published in 1870 and a second part in 1873).[4] An exploration of what constitutes the kernel of the Hellenic idea of the contest (*agon, certamen*) becomes the major concern of Nietzsche's speculations on the 'event' of Homer in the unpublished essay 'Homer's Contest' that we publish here. Two points are worth noting about this research work by the young Nietzsche: first, that it is an early exercise in genealogy in the sense that it focuses on what it means to reclaim something from the past – in

---

[4] See Nietzsche, *Kritische Gesamtausgabe Werke*, ed. Giorgio Colli and Mazzino Montinari (Berlin and New York: Walter de Gruyter, 1967 ff.), 2.1, pp. 271–339.

this case antiquity – for the present, and, second, that the motif of the contest is one that persists in Nietzsche and runs throughout his writings.

Nietzsche's positions on ethics and politics may not ultimately compel us but they are more instructive than is commonly supposed, and certainly not as horrific as many of his critics would have us believe.[5] He is out to disturb our satisfaction with ourselves as moderns and as knowers. Although we may find it difficult to stomach some of his specific proposals for the overcoming of man and morality, his conception of genealogy has become a constitutive feature of our efforts at self-knowledge.

[5] See the fine study by John Richardson, *Nietzsche's New Darwinism* (Oxford and New York: Oxford University Press, 2004).

Chronology

1871	January: Unsuccessfully applies for the Chair of Philosophy at University of Basel.
1872	January: Publication of first book, *The Birth of Tragedy Out of the Spirit of Music* (originally entitled 'On Greek Cheerfulness').
	22 May: Nietzsche accompanies Wagner on the occasion of the latter's fifty-ninth birthday to the laying of the foundation-stone of the Bayreuth theatre.
1873–5	Publication of *Untimely Meditations*.
1876	August: First Bayreuth festival. Beginnings of estrangement from Wagner.
	September: Leaves Bayreuth in the company of Paul Rée.
1878	First part of *Human, All Too Human* (dedicated to Voltaire).
	3 January: Wagner sends Nietzsche a copy of the recently published text of *Parsifal*.
	May: Nietzsche writes his last letter to Wagner and encloses a copy of *Human, All Too Human: A Book for Free Spirits*. End of friendship with Wagner.
1879	Volume 2, part 1 of *Human, All Too Human: Assorted Opinions and Maxims*.
	Nietzsche is forced to resign from his Chair at Basel due to ill health. For the next ten years he leads the life of a solitary wanderer living in hotel rooms and lodgings.
1880	Volume 2, part 2 of *Human, All Too Human – The Wanderer and his Shadow*.
1881	*Daybreak. Thoughts on the Prejudices of Morality*.
	First Summer in Sils-Maria in the Upper Engadine, where he experiences the abysmal thought of the eternal recurrence of the same.
1882	*The Gay Science*. In aphorism 125, a madman announces the 'death of God'.
	March: Paul Rée leaves Nietzsche in Genoa and travels to Rome, where he meets and falls in love with Lou Salomé.
	April: In Rome, Nietzsche proposes marriage, first via Rée and then in person. Although he is turned down, he is content with the promise of an intellectual *ménage à trois* made up of himself, Rée and Salomé.
	By the end of the year, Nietzsche has broken with both Rée and Salomé, and feels betrayed by both.

1883	Writes first and second parts of *Thus Spoke Zarathustra: A Book for all and None*.
	13 February: Death of Wagner.
1884–5	Third and fourth parts of *Zarathustra*.
1886	*Beyond Good and Evil. A Prelude to a Philosophy of the Future*.
1887	10 November: *On the Genealogy of Morality: A Polemic*.
1888	May–August: *The Case of Wagner*, finishes *Dithyrambs of Dionysus* (published 1891).
	September: Writes *The Anti-Christ* (published 1894).
	October–November: Writes *Ecce Homo* (publication delayed by Elisabeth Förster-Nietzsche until 1908).
	December: Writes *Nietzsche contra Wagner* (published 1895).
1889	*Twilight of the Idols* (original title 'The Idleness of a Psychologist').
	3 January: Nietzsche breaks down in the Piazza Carlo Alberto in Turin and throws his arms round an old carthorse that is being beaten by its owner.
	18 January: Admitted as a mental patient to the psychiatric clinic of the University of Jena. Doctors diagnose 'progressive paralysis'.
1890–1900	Nietzsche in the care of his mother and then of his sister in Naumburg and Weimar.
1900	25 August: Nietzsche dies in Weimar. Buried in Röcken next to his father.

Further reading

Biographies

Hayman, Ronald, *Nietzsche: A Critical Life* (London: Weidenfeld and Nicolson; New York: Oxford University Press, 1980)

Hollingdale, R. J., *Nietzsche: The Man and his Philosophy*, 2nd edn (Cambridge and New York: Cambridge University Press, 1999)

Safranski, Rüdiger, *Nietzsche: A Philosophical Biography*, trans. Shelley Frisch (New York: Norton; London: Granta, 2002)

Small, Robin, *Nietzsche and Rée: A Star Friendship* (Oxford: Clarendon Press; New York: Oxford University Press, 2005)

Introductions

Gilman, Sander L., *Nietzschean Parody: An Introduction to Reading Nietzsche* (Bonn: Bouvier Verlag Herbert Grundmann, 1976)

Jaspers, Karl, *Nietzsche: An Introduction to his Philosophical Activity*, trans. C. F. Walraff and F. J. Schmitz (Baltimore: Johns Hopkins University Press, 1997)

Kaufmann, Walter, *Nietzsche: Philosopher, Psychologist, Anti-Christ*, 4th edn (Princeton, NJ and London: Princeton University Press, 1974)

Salomé, Lou, *Nietzsche*, trans. Siegfried Mandel (Redding Ridge, CT: Black Swan Books, 1988; reprinted Urbana and Chicago: University of Illinois Press, 2001)

Stern, J. P., *A Study of Nietzsche* (Cambridge and New York: Cambridge University Press, 1979)

Edited collections

Acampora, Christa Davis and Ralph R., *A Nietzschean Bestiary: Becoming Animal Beyond Docile and Brutal* (New York: Rowman and Littlefield, 2004)

Ansell Pearson, Keith (ed.), *A Companion to Nietzsche* (Malden, MA and Oxford: Basil Blackwell, 2006)

Gillespie, Michael Allen, and Tracy B. Strong (eds.), *Nietzsche's New Seas: Explorations in Philosophy, Aesthetics, and Politics* (Chicago and London: University of Chicago Press, 1988)

Janaway, Christopher (ed.), *Willing and Nothingness: Schopenhauer as Nietzsche's Educator* (Oxford: Clarendon Press; New York: Oxford University Press, 1988)

Magnus, Bernd, and Kathleen M. Higgins (eds.), *The Cambridge Companion to Nietzsche* (Cambridge and New York: Cambridge University Press, 1996)

Richardson, John, and Brian Leiter (eds.), *Nietzsche* (Oxford and New York: Oxford University Press, 2001)

Monographs and critical studies

Assoun, Paul-Laurent, *Freud and Nietzsche*, trans. Richard L. Collier, Jr (London and New Brunswick, NJ: Athlone Press, 2000)

Deleuze, Gilles, *Nietzsche and Philosophy*, trans. Hugh Tomlinson (London: Athlone Press; New York: Columbia University Press, 1983)

Heidegger, Martin, *Nietzsche*, ed. David Farrell Krell, trans. David Farrell Krell et al., four volumes (San Francisco and London: Harper & Row, 1979–87)

Kofman, Sarah, *Nietzsche and Metaphor*, trans. Duncan Large (London: Athlone Press; Stanford, CA: Stanford University Press, 1993)

Löwith, Karl, *From Hegel to Nietzsche: The Revolution in Nineteenth-Century Thought*, trans. David E. Green (New York: Holt, Rinehart and Winston, 1964)

Nehamas, Alexander, *Nietzsche: Life as Literature* (Cambridge, MA and London: Harvard University Press, 1985)

Richardson, John, *Nietzsche's System* (New York and Oxford: Oxford University Press, 1996)
  Nietzsche's New Darwinism (New York and Oxford: Oxford University Press, 2004)

Schrift, Alan D., *Nietzsche and the Question of Interpretation: Between Hermeneutics and Deconstruction* (New York and London: Routledge, 1990)

Simmel, Georg, *Schopenhauer and Nietzsche*, trans. Helmut Loiskandl, Deena Weinstein and Michael Weinstein (Amherst: University of Massachusetts Press, 1986; reprinted Urbana and Chicago: University of Illinois Press, 1991)

Staten, Henry, *Nietzsche's Voice* (Ithaca, NY and London: Cornell University Press, 1990)

'On the Genealogy of Morality'

Acampora, Christa Davis (ed.), *Critical Essays on the Classics: Nietzsche's* On the Genealogy of Morals (Lanham, MD and Oxford: Rowman and Littlefield, 2006)

Foucault, Michel, 'Nietzsche, Genealogy, and History', in *The Essential Works of Foucault*, volume II: 1954–84, ed. James Faubion, trans. Robert Hurley and others (London: Penguin Books, 2000), pp. 369–93

Havas, Randall, *Nietzsche's Genealogy: Nihilism and the Will to Knowledge* (Ithaca, NY and London: Cornell University Press, 1995)

Leiter, Brian, *Nietzsche on Morality* (London and New York: Routledge, 2002)

Ridley, Aaron, *Nietzsche's Conscience: Six Character Studies from the 'Genealogy'* (Ithaca, NY and London: Cornell University Press, 1998)

Schacht, Richard (ed.), *Nietzsche, Genealogy, Morality: Essays on Nietzsche's 'Genealogy of Morals'* (Berkeley, Los Angeles and London: University of California Press, 1994)

Scheler, Max, *Ressentiment*, ed. Lewis A. Coser, trans. William W. Holdheim (New York: Free Press of Glencoe, 1961)

Ethics

Berkowitz, Peter, *Nietzsche: The Ethics of an Immoralist* (Cambridge, MA and London: Harvard University Press, 1995)

Hunt, Lester H., *Nietzsche and the Origin of Virtue* (London and New York: Routledge, 1991)

May, Simon, *Nietzsche's Ethics and his War on 'Morality'* (Oxford: Clarendon Press; New York: Oxford University Press, 1999)

Politics

Conway, Daniel C., *Nietzsche and the Political* (London and New York: Routledge, 1997)

Detwiler, Bruce, *Nietzsche and the Politics of Aristocratic Radicalism* (Chicago and London: University of Chicago Press, 1990)

Hatab, Lawrence J., *A Nietzschean Defense of Democracy: An Experiment in Postmodern Politics* (Chicago and La Salle, IL: Open Court, 1995)

Owen, David, *Nietzsche, Politics and Modernity: A Critique of Liberal Reason* (London, Thousand Oaks, CA and New Delhi: Sage, 1995)

Strong, Tracy B., *Friedrich Nietzsche and the Politics of Transfiguration*, 3rd edn (Urbana and Chicago: University of Illinois Press, 2000)

Warren, Mark, *Nietzsche and Political Thought* (Cambridge, MA and London: MIT Press, 1988)

Biographical synopses

Anacreon (*c*.582 BC–*c*.485 BC), Greek lyric poet born on the island of Teos.

Bahnsen, Julius (1830–1881), German philosopher influenced by Schopenhauer and author of books on characterology and the philosophy of history.

Buckle, Henry Thomas (1821–1862), Victorian historian of civilization. His reading of history rests on the view that the causes of social growth, and of divergent forms of social organization which characterize different historical cultures, are 'material' (factors such as climate, food, soil, etc.) as opposed to racial.

Deussen, Paul (1845–1919), German philologist and philosopher, like Nietzsche the son of a Protestant clergyman. Developed a close friendship with Nietzsche, published his 'Reminiscences' in 1901. Deussen was the first Western philosopher to include Eastern thought in a general history of philosophy in any scientific way. Published *The System of Vedanta* in 1881. An enthusiastic interpreter of Schopenhauer and founder of the Schopenhauer Society.

Doudan, Ximénès (1800–1872), French critic, author of several posthumously published volumes, including *Mixed Writings and Letters* (1876–7) and *Thoughts and Fragments, and the Revolutions of Taste* (1881).

Dühring, Eugen (1833–1921), German philosopher and political economist. Wrote virulent attacks on religion, militarism, Marxism, Judaism and the Bismarckian state. He held that the feeling of sympathy is the foundation of morality, which led him to advocate harmony between capitalists and proletarians.

Epicurus (342 BC–270 BC), Greek philosopher best known for his hedonism and atomism.

Feuerbach, Ludwig (1804–1872), German philosopher best known for his *Essence of Christianity* (1841) and his *Principles of the Philosophy of the Future* (1843), which greatly influenced the young Marx.

Fischer, Kuno (1824–1907), German historian of philosophy whose major work on the *History of Modern Philosophy* (1852–77) was extensively consulted by Nietzsche.

Geulincx, Arnold (1624–1669), Flemish metaphysician and moralist, heavily influenced by Descartes, and best known for his 'occasionalist' theory of causation.

Hartmann, Eduard von (1842–1906), German philosopher who espoused a pessimistic philosophy based on a synthesis of German Idealism (Hegel, Schelling) and Schopenhauer. Only pessimism, he held, can serve as a foundation for a viable ethical system and provide a teleological perspective from which religion, including contemporary Christianity, can be assessed. Author of *Philosophy of the Unconscious* (1864) and *Phenomenology of Ethical Consciousness* (1879).

Heraclitus (*c*.540 BC–*c*.480 BC), Greek philosopher who believed that the world was best understood as a unity of opposites.

Herwegh, Georg (1817–1875), German poet whose best-known collection is *Poems of the Living One* (1841).

Huxley, Thomas Henry (1825–1895), educational reformer and biologist. A champion of Darwin's theory of evolution. His view of nature as an unending struggle for existence led him to posit a conflict between the ends of nature and those of morality. Man is a product of evolution but he has an obligation to subjugate the amoral or immoral aspects of evolution to moral ends.

Janssen, Johannes (1829–1891), Roman Catholic German historian best known for his *History of the German People from the Close of the Middle Ages* (8 vols., 1876–91), which was received with enthusiasm by German Catholics but sharply criticized by Protestant historians for its partisan approach.

La Rochefoucauld, Francois VI, duc de (1613–1680), French classical author, cynic and leading exponent of the *maxime*, a literary form of epigram designed to express an unpalatable or paradoxical truth with brevity. Published *Reflexions ou sentences et maximes morales* in 1665.

Mainländer, Philipp (1841–1876), German philosopher influenced by Schopenhauer. Author of *Philosophy of Redemption* (1876).

Mirabeau, Comte de (1749–1791), prominent figure in the early stages of the French Revolution.

Moore, Thomas (1779–1852), Irish poet, satirist, composer and musician, and friend of Byron and Shelley.

Ranke, Leopold (1795–1886), leading German historian who defined the task of the historian as the quest for 'objectivity'. Nietzsche's early untimely meditation of 1874 on the uses and abuses of history for life can be read as a polemic against what he saw as the stultifying influence of Ranke's historicism on German intellectual life.

Rée, Paul (1849–1901), German (Jewish) psychologist, philosopher and atheist who became a close associate of Nietzsche's, introducing him to Lou Salomé and exerting a powerful influence on the writings of his 'middle period' (1878–82). Author of *Psychological Observations* (1875) and *The Origin of the Moral Sensations* (1877).

Renan, Ernest (1823–1892), influential French historian who abandoned a priestly calling in order to devote himself to secular teaching and writing. Author of a life of Jesus in six volumes (1863–81), including volumes on the *Origins of Christianity* (1863) and the *Antichrist* (1876).

Spencer, Herbert (1820–1903), English philosopher who attempted to unify the biological and the social sciences by means of a generalized philosophical notion of evolution.

Taine, Hippolyte (1828–1893), French critic and historian. One of the leading exponents of positivism in France in the nineteenth century, he attempted to apply the scientific method to the study of the humanities.

Tertullian (*c*.AD155–220), important early Christian theologian, polemicist and moralist from North Africa.

Theognis (late 6th–early 5th century BC), Greek elegiac poet of Megara, his poems are important for their depiction of aristocratic society in a changing world. Nietzsche wrote his dissertation on Theognis in 1864, which became his first publication in the field of philology in 1867.

Virchow, Rudolf (1821–1902), German pathologist and statesman, and one of the most prominent physicians in the nineteenth century.

Von Gwinner, Wilhelm (1825–1917), German jurist and civil servant, of importance to Nietzsche as the executor of Schopenhauer's literary estate who destroyed his autobiographical papers, only to write three volumes of biography himself (1862–78).

Whitefield, George (1714–1770), methodist revivalist.

ON THE GENEALOGY
OF MORALITY

A Polemic

Preface

I

We are unknown to ourselves, we knowers: and with good reason. We have never looked for ourselves, – so how are we ever supposed to *find* ourselves? How right is the saying: 'Where your treasure is, there will your heart be also';[1] *our* treasure is where the hives of our knowledge are. As born winged-insects and intellectual honey-gatherers we are constantly making for them, concerned at heart with only one thing – to 'bring something home'. As far as the rest of life is concerned, the so-called 'experiences', – who of us ever has enough seriousness for them? or enough time? I fear we have never really been 'with it' in such matters: our heart is simply not in it – and not even our ear! On the contrary, like somebody divinely absent-minded and sunk in his own thoughts who, the twelve strokes of midday having just boomed into his ears, wakes with a start and wonders 'What hour struck?', sometimes we, too, *afterwards* rub our ears and ask, astonished, taken aback, 'What did we actually experience then?' or even, 'Who *are* we, in fact?' and afterwards, as I said, we count all twelve reverberating strokes of our experience, of our life, of our *being* – oh! and lose count . . . We remain strange to ourselves out of necessity, we do not understand ourselves, we *must* confusedly mistake who we are, the motto[2] 'everyone is furthest from himself' applies to us for ever, – we are not 'knowers' when it comes to ourselves . . .

[1] Gospel according to Matthew 6.21.
[2] 'Jeder ist sich selbst der Fernste' is a reversal of the common German saying, 'Jeder ist sich selbst der Nächste' 'Everyone is closest to himself' i.e. 'Charity begins at home', cf. also Terence, *Andria* IV. 1.12.

2

– My thoughts on the *descent* of our moral prejudices – for that is what this polemic is about – were first set out in a sketchy and provisional way in the collection of aphorisms entitled *Human, All Too Human. A Book for Free Spirits*,[3] which I began to write in Sorrento during a winter that enabled me to pause, like a wanderer pauses, to take in the vast and dangerous land through which my mind had hitherto travelled. This was in the winter of 1876–7; the thoughts themselves go back further. They were mainly the same thoughts which I shall be taking up again in the present essays – let us hope that the long interval has done them good, that they have become riper, brighter, stronger and more perfect! The fact *that* I still stick to them today, and that they themselves in the meantime have stuck together increasingly firmly, even growing into one another and growing into one, makes me all the more blithely confident that from the first, they did not arise in me individually, randomly or sporadically but as stemming from a single root, from a *fundamental will* to knowledge deep inside me which took control, speaking more and more clearly and making ever clearer demands. And this is the only thing proper for a philosopher. We have no right to stand out *individually*: we must not either make mistakes or hit on the truth individually. Instead, our thoughts, values, every 'yes', 'no', 'if' and 'but' grow from us with the same inevitability as fruits borne on the tree – all related and referring to one another and a testimonial to one will, one health, one earth, one sun. – Do *you* like the taste of our fruit? – But of what concern is that to the trees? And of what concern is it to *us* philosophers? . . .

3

With a characteristic scepticism to which I confess only reluctantly – it relates to *morality* and to all that hitherto on earth has been celebrated as morality –, a scepticism which sprang up in my life so early, so unbidden, so unstoppably, and which was in such conflict with my surroundings, age, precedents and lineage that I would almost be justified in calling it my '*a priori*', – eventually my curiosity and suspicion were bound to fix on the question of *what origin* our terms good and evil actually have. Indeed, as a thirteen-year-old boy, I was preoccupied with the problem of the origin of evil: at an age when one's heart was 'half-filled with childish

[3] *Human, All Too Human*, trans. R. J. Hollingdale (Cambridge University Press, 1986).

games, half-filled with God',[4] I dedicated my first literary childish game, my first philosophical essay, to this problem – and as regards my 'solution' to the problem at that time, I quite properly gave God credit for it and made him the *father* of evil. Did my '*a priori*' want *this* of me? That new, immoral, or at least immoralistic '*a priori*': and the oh-so-anti-Kantian, so enigmatic 'categorical imperative'[5] which spoke from it and to which I have, in the meantime, increasingly lent an ear, and not just an ear? . . . Fortunately I learnt, in time, to separate theological from moral prejudice and I no longer searched for the origin of evil *beyond* the world. Some training in history and philology, together with my innate fastidiousness with regard to all psychological problems, soon transformed my problem into another: under what conditions did man invent the value judgments good and evil? *and what value do they themselves have?* Have they up to now obstructed or promoted human flourishing? Are they a sign of distress, poverty and the degeneration of life? Or, on the contrary, do they reveal the fullness, strength and will of life, its courage, its confidence, its future? To these questions I found and ventured all kinds of answers of my own, I distinguished between epochs, peoples, grades of rank between individuals, I focused my inquiry, and out of the answers there developed new questions, investigations, conjectures, probabilities until I had my own territory, my own soil, a whole silently growing and blossoming world, secret gardens, as it were, the existence of which nobody must be allowed to suspect . . . Oh! how *happy* we are, we knowers, provided we can keep quiet for long enough! . . .

4

I was given the initial stimulation to publish something about my hypotheses on the origin of morality by a clear, honest and clever, even too-clever little book, in which I first directly encountered the back-to-front and perverse kind of genealogical hypotheses, actually the *English* kind, which drew me to it – with that power of attraction which everything contradictory and antithetical has. The title of the little book was

---

[4] Goethe, *Faust* I. 3781f.
[5] Immanuel Kant gives a number of different formulations of what he takes to be the basic principle of morality in his two major works on ethics, *The Groundwork of the Metaphysics of Morals* (1785) and the *Critique of Practical Reason* (1788). The first formulation of the 'categorical imperative' in *The Groundwork of the Metaphysics of Morals* reads: 'Act only on that maxim through which you can at the same time will that it become a universal law' (*Groundwork*, section 1).

The Origin of the Moral Sensations; its author was Dr Paul Rée; the year of its publication 1877. I have, perhaps, never read anything to which I said 'no', sentence by sentence and deduction by deduction, as I did to this book: but completely without annoyance and impatience. In the work already mentioned which I was working on at the time, I referred to passages from this book more or less at random, not in order to refute them – what business is it of mine to refute! – but, as befits a positive mind, to replace the improbable with the more probable and in some circumstances to replace one error with another. As I said, I was, at the time, bringing to the light of day those hypotheses on descent to which these essays are devoted, clumsily, as I am the first to admit, and still inhibited because I still lacked my own vocabulary for these special topics, and with a good deal of relapse and vacillation. In particular, compare what I say about the dual prehistory of good and evil in *Human, All Too Human*, section 45 (namely in the sphere of nobles and slaves); likewise section 136 on the value and descent of ascetic morality; likewise sections 96 and 99 and volume II, section 89 on the 'Morality of Custom', that much older and more primitive kind of morality which is *toto coelo*⁶ removed from altruistic evaluation (which Dr Rée, like all English genealogists, sees as the moral method of valuation *as such*); likewise section 92, *The Wanderer*, section 26, and *Daybreak*, section 112, on the descent of justice as a balance between two roughly equal powers (equilibrium as the precondition for all contracts and consequently for all law); likewise *The Wanderer*, sections 22 and 33 on the descent of punishment, the deterrent [*terroristisch*] purpose of which is neither essential nor inherent (as Dr Rée thinks: – instead it is introduced in particular circumstances and is always incidental and added on).⁷

5

Actually, just then I was preoccupied with something much more important than the nature of hypotheses, mine or anybody else's, on the origin of morality (or, to be more exact: the latter concerned me only for one end, to which it is one of many means). For me it was a question of the *value* of morality, – and here I had to confront my great teacher Schopenhauer, to whom that book of mine spoke as though he were still

---

⁶ 'completely, utterly'.
⁷ All the passages Nietzsche mentions here are to be found below in the supplementary material of this edition.

present, with its passion and its hidden contradiction (– it, too, being a 'polemic'). I dealt especially with the value of the 'unegoistic', the instincts of compassion, self-denial, self-sacrifice which Schopenhauer[8] had for so long gilded, deified and transcendentalized until he was finally left with them as those 'values as such' on the basis of which he *said 'no'* to life and to himself as well. But against *these* very instincts I gave vent to an increasingly deep mistrust, a scepticism which dug deeper and deeper! Precisely here I saw the *great* danger to mankind, its most sublime temptation and seduction – temptation to what? to nothingness? – precisely here I saw the beginning of the end, standstill, mankind looking back wearily, turning its will *against* life, and the onset of the final sickness becoming gently, sadly manifest: I understood the morality of compassion, casting around ever wider to catch even philosophers and make them ill, as the most uncanny symptom of our European culture which has itself become uncanny, as its detour to a new Buddhism? to a new Euro-Buddhism? to – *nihilism?* . . . This predilection for and overvaluation of compassion that modern philosophers show is, in fact, something new: up till now, philosophers were agreed as to the *worthlessness* of compassion. I need only mention Plato, Spinoza, La Rochefoucauld and Kant, four minds as different from one another as it is possible to be, but united on one point: their low opinion of compassion. –

6

This problem of the *value* of compassion and of the morality of compassion (– I am opposed to the disgraceful modern softness of feeling –) seems at first to be only an isolated phenomenon, a lone question mark; but whoever pauses over the question and *learns* to ask, will find what I found: – that a vast new panorama opens up for him, a possibility makes him giddy, mistrust, suspicion and fear of every kind spring up, belief in morality, all morality, wavers, – finally, a new demand becomes articulate. So let us give voice to this *new demand*: we need a *critique* of moral values, *the value of these values should itself, for once, be examined* – and so we need to know about the conditions and circumstances under which the values grew up, developed and changed (morality as result, as symptom, as mask, as tartuffery, as sickness, as misunderstanding; but also morality as cause,

---

[8] In his 'Über die Grundlagen der Moral' (1840) Schopenhauer claimed that compassion was the basis of morality.

remedy, stimulant, inhibition, poison), since we have neither had this knowledge up till now nor even desired it. People have taken the *value* of these 'values' as given, as factual, as beyond all questioning; up till now, nobody has had the remotest doubt or hesitation in placing higher value on 'the good man' than on 'the evil', higher value in the sense of advancement, benefit and prosperity for man in general (and this includes man's future). What if the opposite were true? What if a regressive trait lurked in 'the good man', likewise a danger, an enticement, a poison, a narcotic, so that the present *lived at the expense of the future?* Perhaps in more comfort and less danger, but also in a smaller-minded, meaner manner? . . . So that morality itself were to blame if man, as species, never reached his *highest potential power and splendour?* So that morality itself was the danger of dangers? . . .

7

Suffice it to say that since this revelation, I had reason to look around for scholarly, bold, hardworking colleagues (I am still looking). The vast, distant and hidden land of morality – of morality as it really existed and was really lived – has to be journeyed through with quite new questions and as it were with new eyes: and surely that means virtually *discovering* this land for the first time? . . . If, on my travels, I thought about the above-mentioned Dr Rée, amongst others, this was because I was certain that, judging from the questions he raised, he himself would have to adopt a more sensible method if he wanted to find the answers. Was I mistaken? At any rate, I wanted to focus this sharp, unbiased eye in a better direction, the direction of a real *history of morality*, and to warn him, while there was still time, against such English hypothesis-mongering *into the blue*. It is quite clear which colour is a hundred times more important for a genealogist than blue: namely *grey*, which is to say, that which can be documented, which can actually be confirmed and has actually existed, in short, the whole, long, hard-to-decipher hieroglyphic script of man's moral past! *This* was unknown to Dr Rée; but he had read Darwin: – and so, in his hypotheses, the Darwinian beast and the ultra-modern, humble moral weakling who 'no longer bites' politely shake hands in a way that is at least entertaining, the latter with an expression of a certain good-humoured and cultivated indolence on his face, in which even a grain of pessimism and fatigue mingle: as if it were really not worth taking all these things – the problems of morality – so seriously. Now I, on the contrary, think there is nothing which more *rewards* being taken seriously; the reward being, for example, the possibility of one day being allowed to take them cheerfully. That cheerfulness, in fact, or to put it into my parlance, that *gay science* – is a reward: a reward for a long, brave, diligent, subterranean seriousness for which, admittedly, not everyone is suited. The day we can say, with conviction: 'Forwards! even our old morality would make a *comedy*!' we shall have discovered a new twist and possible outcome for the Dionysian drama of the 'fate of the soul' –: and he'll make good use of it, we can bet, he, the grand old eternal writer of the comedy of our existence! . . .

<h1 style="text-align:center">8</h1>

– If anyone finds this script incomprehensible and hard on the ears, I do not think the fault necessarily lies with me. It is clear enough, assuming, as I do, that people have first read my earlier works without sparing themselves some effort: because they really are not easy to approach. With regard to my *Zarathustra*, for example, I do not acknowledge anyone as an expert on it if he has not, at some time, been both profoundly wounded and profoundly delighted by it, for only then may he enjoy the privilege of sharing, with due reverence, the halcyon element from which the book was born and its sunny brightness, spaciousness, breadth and certainty. In other cases, the aphoristic form causes difficulty: this is because this form is *not taken seriously enough these days*. An aphorism, properly stamped and moulded, has not been 'deciphered' just because it has been read out; on the contrary, this is just the beginning of its proper *interpretation*, and for this, an art of interpretation is needed. In the third essay of this book I have given an example of what I mean by 'interpretation' in such a case: – this treatise is a commentary on the aphorism that precedes it. I admit that you need one thing above all in order to practise the requisite *art* of reading, a thing which today people have been so good at forgetting – and so it will be some time before my writings are 'readable' –, you almost need to be a cow for this one thing and certainly *not* a 'modern man': it is *rumination* . . .

Sils-Maria, Upper Engadine
July 1887.

First essay: 'Good and Evil', 'Good and Bad'

– These English psychologists, who have to be thanked for having made the only attempts so far to write a history of the emergence of morality, – provide us with a small riddle in the form of themselves; in fact, I admit that as living riddles they have a significant advantage over their books – *they are actually interesting!* These English psychologists – just what do they want? You always find them at the same task, whether they want to or not, pushing the *partie honteuse* of our inner world to the foreground, and looking for what is really effective, guiding and decisive for our development where man's intellectual pride would least wish to find it (for example, in the *vis inertiae* of habit, or in forgetfulness, or in a blind and random coupling and mechanism of ideas, or in something purely passive, automatic, reflexive, molecular and thoroughly stupid) – what is it that actually drives these psychologists in precisely *this* direction all the time? Is it a secret, malicious, mean instinct to belittle humans, which it might well not admit to itself? Or perhaps a pessimistic suspicion, the mistrust of disillusioned, surly idealists who have turned poisonous and green? Or a certain subterranean animosity and *rancune* towards Christianity (and Plato), which has perhaps not even passed the threshold of consciousness? Or even a lewd taste for the strange, for the painful paradox, for the dubious and nonsensical in life? Or finally – a bit of everything, a bit of meanness, a bit of gloominess, a bit of anti-Christianity, a bit of a thrill and need for pepper? . . . But people tell me that they are just old, cold, boring frogs crawling round men and hopping into them as if they were in their element, namely a *swamp*. I am resistant to hearing this and, indeed, I do not believe it; and if it is permissible to wish where it is impossible to know, I sincerely hope that the reverse is true, – that these analysts holding a microscope to the soul are actually brave, generous and proud animals, who know how to control their own pleasure and pain and have been taught to sacrifice desirability to truth, *every* truth, even a plain, bitter, ugly, foul, unchristian, immoral truth . . . Because there are such truths. –

2

So you have to respect the good spirits which preside in these historians of morality! But it is unfortunately a fact that *historical spirit* itself is lacking in them, they have been left in the lurch by all the good spirits of history itself! As is now established philosophical practice, they all think in a way that is *essentially* unhistorical; this can't be doubted. The idiocy of their moral genealogy is revealed at the outset when it is a question of conveying the descent of the concept and judgment of 'good'. 'Originally' – they decree – 'unegoistic acts were praised and called good by their recipients, in other words, by the people to whom they were *useful*; later, everyone *forgot* the origin of the praise and because such acts had always been *habitually* praised as good, people also began to experience them as good – as if they were something good *as such*'. We can see at once: this first deduction contains all the typical traits of idiosyncratic English psychologists, – we have 'usefulness', 'forgetting', 'habit' and finally 'error', all as the basis of a respect for values of which the higher man has hitherto been proud, as though it were a sort of general privilege of mankind. This pride *must be* humbled, this valuation devalued: has that been achieved? . . . Now for me, it is obvious that the real breeding-ground for the concept 'good' has been sought and located in the wrong place by this theory: the judgment 'good' does *not* emanate from those to whom goodness is shown! Instead it has been 'the good' themselves, meaning the noble, the mighty, the high-placed and the high-minded, who saw and judged themselves and their actions as good, I mean first-rate, in contrast to everything lowly, low-minded, common and plebeian. It was from this *pathos of distance* that they first claimed the right to create values and give these values names: usefulness was none of their concern! The standpoint of usefulness is as alien and inappropriate as it can be to such a heated eruption of the highest rank-ordering and rank-defining value judgments: this is the point where feeling reaches the opposite of the low temperatures needed for any calculation of prudence or reckoning of usefulness, – and not just for once, for one exceptional moment, but permanently. The pathos of nobility and distance, as I said, the continuing and predominant feeling of complete and fundamental superiority of a higher ruling kind in relation to a lower kind, to those 'below' – *that* is the origin of the antithesis 'good' and 'bad'. (The seigneurial privilege of giving names even allows us to conceive of the origin of language itself as a manifestation of the power of the rulers: they say 'this *is* so and so', they set their seal on everything and every occurrence with a sound and thereby take possession of it, as it were). It is because of this origin that from the outset, the word 'good' is absolutely *not* necessarily attached to 'unegoistic' actions: as the superstition of these moral genealogists would have it. On the contrary, it is only with a *decline* of aristocratic value judgments that this whole antithesis between 'egoistic' and 'unegoistic' forces itself more and more on man's conscience, – it is, to use my language, the *herd instinct* which, with that, finally gets its word in (and makes *words*). And even then it takes long enough for this instinct to become sufficiently dominant for the valuation of moral values to become enmeshed and embedded in the antithesis (as is the case in contemporary Europe, for example: the prejudice which takes 'moral', 'unegoistic' and '*désintéressé*' as equivalent terms already rules with the power of a 'fixed idea' and mental illness).

3

But secondly: quite apart from the fact that that hypothesis about the descent of the value judgment 'good' is historically untenable, it also suffers from an inner psychological contradiction. The usefulness of unegoistic behaviour is supposed to be the origin of the esteem in which it is held, and this origin is supposed to have been *forgotten*: – but how was such forgetting *possible*? Did the usefulness of such behaviour suddenly cease at some point? The opposite is the case: it is that this usefulness has been a permanent part of our everyday experience, something, then, that has been constantly stressed anew; consequently, instead of fading from consciousness, instead of becoming forgettable, it must have impressed itself on consciousness with ever greater clarity. How much more sensible is the opposite theory (that doesn't make it any more true –), which is held, for example, by Herbert Spencer: he judges the concept 'good' as essentially the same as 'useful', 'practical', so that in their judgments 'good' and 'bad', people sum up and sanction their *unforgotten, unforgettable* experiences of what is useful-practical, harmful-impractical. According to this theory, good is what has always shown itself to be useful: so it can claim validity as 'valuable in the highest degree', as 'valuable as such'. This route towards an explanation is wrong, as I said, but at least the explanation in itself is rational and psychologically tenable.

4

– I was given a pointer in the *right* direction by the question as to what the terms for 'good', as used in different languages, mean from the etymological point of view: then I found that they all led me back to the *same conceptual transformation*, – that everywhere, 'noble', 'aristocratic' in social terms[9] is the basic concept from which, necessarily, 'good' in the sense of 'spiritually noble', 'aristocratic', of 'spiritually highminded', 'spiritually privileged' developed: a development that always runs parallel with that other one which ultimately transfers 'common', 'plebeian', 'low' into the concept 'bad'. The best example for the latter is the German word '*schlecht*' (bad) itself: which is identical with '*schlicht*' (plain, simple) – compare '*schlechtweg*' (plainly), '*schlechterdings*' (simply) – and originally referred to the simple, the common man with no derogatory implication, but simply in contrast to the nobility. Round about the time of the Thirty Years War, late enough, then, this meaning shifted into its current usage. – To me, this seems an *essential* insight into moral genealogy; that it has been discovered so late is due to the obstructing influence which the democratic bias within the modern world exercises over all questions of descent. And this is the case in the apparently most objective of fields, natural science and physiology, as I shall just mention here. The havoc this prejudice can wreak, once it is unbridled to the point of hatred, particularly for morality and history, can be seen in the famous case of Buckle; the *plebeianism* of the modern spirit, which began in England, broke out there once again on its native soil as violently as a volcano of mud, and with that salted, overloud, vulgar loquacity with which all volcanoes have spoken up till now. –

5

With regard to *our* problem, which can justifiably be called a *quiet* problem and fastidiously addresses itself to only a few ears, it is of no little

9 Nietzsche here uses a derivative of the word '*Stand*' ('estate').

13

interest to discover that, in these words and roots which denote 'good', we can often detect the main nuance which made the noble feel they were men of higher rank. True, in most cases they might give themselves names which simply show superiority of power (such as 'the mighty', 'the masters', 'the commanders') or the most visible sign of this superiority, such as 'the rich', 'the propertied' (that is the meaning of *arya*; and the equivalent in Iranian and Slavic). But the names also show a *typical character trait*: and this is what concerns us here. For example, they call themselves 'the truthful': led by the Greek aristocracy, whose mouthpiece is the Megarian poet Theognis.[10] The word used specifically for this purpose, ἐσθλός,[11] means, according to its root, one who *is*, who has reality, who really exists and is true; then, with a subjective transformation, it becomes the slogan and catch-phrase of the aristocracy and is completely assimilated with the sense of 'aristocratic', in contrast to the *deceitful* common man, as taken and shown by Theognis, – until, finally, with the decline of the aristocracy, the word remains as a term for spiritual *noblesse*, and, as it were, ripens and sweetens. Cowardice is underlined in the word χαχός,[12] as in δειλός[13] (the plebeian in contrast to the ἀγαθός): perhaps this gives a clue as to where we should look for the etymological derivation of the ambiguous term ἀγαθός.[14] In the Latin word *malus*[15] (to which I juxtapose μέλας)[16] the common man could be characterized as the dark-skinned and especially the dark-haired man ('*hic niger est –*'),[17] as the pre-Aryan occupant of Italian soil who could most easily be distinguished from the blond race which had become dominant, namely the Aryan conquering race, by its colour; at any rate, I have found exactly the same with Gaelic peoples, – fin (for example in Fin-gal), the word designating the aristocracy and finally the good, noble, pure, was originally a blond person in contrast to the dark-skinned, dark-haired native inhabitants. By the way, the Celts were a completely blond race; it is wrong to connect those traces of an essentially dark-haired population, which can be seen on carefully prepared ethnological maps in Germany,

---

[10] Cf. esp. 1. 53–68 (ed. Diehl).
[11] This word seems originally to have meant 'genuine, real', it later becomes one of the most commonly used words for 'noble'.
[12] (Greek) 'weak, ugly, cowardly, worthless'.
[13] (Greek) 'cowardly (and thus despicable)'.
[14] (Greek) 'capable, useful, good'.
[15] 'bad, evil'.
[16] (Greek) 'dark, black'.
[17] 'That man is a dangerous character', literally 'He is black' (Horace, *Satires* I. 85).

with any Celtic descent and mixing of blood in such a connection, as Virchow does: it is more a case of the *pre-Aryan* population of Germany emerging at these points. (The same holds good for virtually the whole of Europe: to all intents and purposes the subject race has ended up by regaining the upper hand in skin colour, shortness of forehead and perhaps even in intellectual and social instincts: who can give any guarantee that modern democracy, the even more modern anarchism, and indeed that predilection for the 'commune', the most primitive form of social structure which is common to all Europe's socialists, are not in essence a huge *throw-back* – and that the conquering *master race*, that of the Aryans, is not physiologically being defeated as well? . . .) I think I can interpret the Latin *bonus*[18] as 'the "warrior"': providing I am correct in tracing *bonus* back to an older *duonus* (compare *bellum*[19] = *duellum* = *duenlum*, which seems to me to contain that *duonus*). Therefore *bonus* as a man of war, of division (*duo*), as warrior: one can see what made up a man's 'goodness' in ancient Rome. Take our German '*gut*': does it not mean 'the godlike man', the man 'of godlike race'? And is it not identical with the popular (originally noble), name of the Goths? The grounds for this supposition will not be gone into here. –

6

If the highest caste is at the same time the *clerical* caste and therefore chooses a title for its overall description which calls its priestly function to mind, this does not yet constitute an exception to the rule that the concept of political superiority always resolves itself into the concept of psychological superiority (although this may be the occasion giving rise to exceptions). This is an example of the first juxtaposition of 'pure' and 'impure' as signs of different estates; and later 'good' and 'bad' develop in a direction which no longer refers to social standing. In addition, people should be wary of taking these terms 'pure' and 'impure' too seriously, too far or even symbolically: all ancient man's concepts were originally understood – to a degree we can scarcely imagine – as crude, coarse, detached, narrow, direct and in particular *unsymbolic*. From the outset the 'pure man' was just a man who washed, avoided certain foods which cause skin complaints, did not sleep with the filthy women from

---

[18] 'good'.
[19] Both 'bellum' and 'duellum' mean 'war' (Latin).

the lower orders and had a horror of blood, – nothing more, not much more! And yet the very nature of an essentially priestly aristocracy shows how contradictory valuations could become dangerously internalized and sharpened, precisely in such an aristocracy at an early stage; and in fact clefts were finally driven between man and man which even an Achilles of free-thinking would shudder to cross. From the very beginning there has been something *unhealthy* about these priestly aristocracies and in the customs dominant there, which are turned away from action and are partly brooding and partly emotionally explosive, resulting in the almost inevitable bowel complaints and neurasthenia which have plagued the clergy down the ages; but as for the remedy they themselves found for their sickness, – surely one must say that its after-effects have shown it to be a hundred times more dangerous than the disease it was meant to cure? People are still ill from the after-effects of these priestly quack-cures! For example, think of certain diets (avoidance of meat), of fasting, sexual abstinence, the flight 'into the desert' (Weir-Mitchell's bed-rest, admittedly without the subsequent overfeeding and weight-gain that constitute the most effective antidote to all hysteria brought on by the ascetic ideal): think, too, of the whole metaphysics of the clergy, which is antagonistic towards the senses, making men lazy and refined, think, too, of their Fakir-like and Brahmin-like self-hypnotizing – Brahminism as crystal ball and fixed idea – and the final, all-too-comprehensible general disenchantment with its radical cure, *nothingness* (or God: – the yearning for a *unio mystica* with God is the Buddhist yearning for nothingness, Nirvâna – and no more!) Priests make *everything* more dangerous, not just medicaments and healing arts but pride, revenge, acumen, debauchery, love, lust for power, virtue, sickness; – in any case, with some justification one could add that man first became an *interesting animal* on the foundation of this *essentially dangerous* form of human existence, the priest, and that the human soul became *deep* in the higher sense and turned *evil* for the first time – and of course, these are the two basic forms of man's superiority, hitherto, over other animals! . . .

7

– You will have already guessed how easy it was for the priestly method of valuation to split off from the chivalric-aristocratic method and then to develop further into the opposite of the latter; this receives a special impetus when the priestly caste and warrior caste confront one another in jealousy and cannot agree on the prize of war. The chivalric-aristocratic value judgments are based on a powerful physicality, a blossoming, rich, even effervescent good health that includes the things needed to maintain it, war, adventure, hunting, dancing, jousting and everything else that contains strong, free, happy action. The priestly-aristocratic method of valuation – as we have seen – has different criteria: woe betide it when it comes to war! As we know, priests make the most *evil enemies* – but why? Because they are the most powerless. Out of this powerlessness, their hate swells into something huge and uncanny to a most intellectual and poisonous level. The greatest haters in world history, and the most intelligent [*die geistreichsten Hasser*], have always been priests: – nobody else's intelligence [*Geist*] stands a chance against the intelligence [*Geist*] of priestly revenge.[20] The history of mankind would be far too stupid a thing if it had not had the intellect [*Geist*] of the powerless injected into it: – let us take the best example straight away. Nothing that has been done on earth against 'the noble', 'the mighty', 'the masters' and 'the rulers', is worth mentioning compared with what *the Jews* have done against them: the Jews, that priestly people, which in the last resort was able to gain satisfaction from its enemies and conquerors only through a radical revaluation of their values, that is, through an act of *the most deliberate revenge [durch einen Akt der geistigsten Rache]*. Only this was fitting for a priestly people with the most entrenched priestly vengefulness. It was the Jews who, rejecting the aristocratic value equation (good = noble = powerful = beautiful = happy = blessed) ventured, with awe-inspiring consistency, to bring about a reversal and held it in the teeth of the most unfathomable hatred (the hatred of the powerless), saying: 'Only those who suffer are good, only the poor, the powerless, the lowly are good; the suffering, the deprived, the sick, the ugly, are the only pious people, the only ones saved, salvation is for them alone, whereas you rich, the noble and powerful, you are eternally wicked, cruel, lustful, insatiate, godless, you will also be eternally wretched, cursed and damned!' . . . We know *who* became heir to this Jewish revaluation . . . With regard to the huge and incalculably disastrous initiative taken by the Jews with this most fundamental of all declarations of war, I recall the words I wrote on another occasion (*Beyond Good and Evil*, section 195)[21] – namely,

---

[20] The German term *Geist* and its derivatives, are generally rendered by 'spirit' and its derivatives, but can also, as in this sentence, be translated as 'intelligence' and, as elsewhere, 'mind', 'intellectual', etc.

[21] See below, Supplementary material, p. 145.

that *the slaves' revolt in morality* begins with the Jews: a revolt which has two thousand years of history behind it and which has only been lost sight of because – it was victorious . . .

8

– But you don't understand that? You don't have eyes for something that needed two millennia to achieve victory? . . . There is nothing surprising about that: all *long* things are difficult to see, to see round. But *that* is what happened: from the trunk of the tree of revenge and hatred, Jewish hatred – the deepest and most sublime, indeed a hatred which created ideals and changed values, the like of which has never been seen on earth – there grew something just as incomparable, a *new love*, the deepest and most sublime kind of love: – and what other trunk could it have grown out of? . . . But don't make the mistake of thinking that it had grown forth as a denial of the thirst for revenge, as the opposite of Jewish hatred! No, the reverse is true! This love grew out of the hatred, as its crown, as the triumphant crown expanding ever wider in the purest brightness and radiance of the sun, the crown which, as it were, in the realm of light and height, was pursuing the aims of that hatred, victory, spoils, seduction with the same urgency with which the roots of that hatred were burrowing ever more thoroughly and greedily into everything that was deep and evil. This Jesus of Nazareth, as the embodiment of the gospel of love, this 'redeemer' bringing salvation and victory to the poor, the sick, to sinners – was he not seduction in its most sinister and irresistible form, seduction and the circuitous route to just those very *Jewish* values and innovative ideals? Did Israel not reach the pinnacle of her sublime vengefulness via this very 'redeemer', this apparent opponent of and disperser of Israel? Is it not part of a secret black art of a truly *grand* politics of revenge, a far-sighted, subterranean revenge, slow to grip and calculating, that Israel had to denounce her actual instrument of revenge before all the world as a mortal enemy and nail him to the cross so that 'all the world', namely all Israel's enemies, could safely nibble at this bait? And could anyone, on the other hand, using all the ingenuity of his intellect, think up a more *dangerous* bait? Something to equal the enticing, intoxicating, benumbing, corrupting power of that symbol of the 'holy cross', to equal that horrible paradox of a 'God on the Cross', to equal that mystery of an unthinkable final act of extreme cruelty and self-crucifixion of God for the *salvation of mankind?* . . . At least it is certain that *sub hoc signo*[22] Israel, with its revenge and revaluation of all former values, has triumphed repeatedly over all other ideals, all *nobler* ideals. – –

9

– 'But why do you talk about *nobler* ideals! Let's bow to the facts: the people have won – or "the slaves", the "plebeians", "the herd", or whatever you want to call them – if the Jews made this come about, good for them! No people ever had a more world-historic mission. "The Masters" are deposed; the morality of the common people has triumphed. You might take this victory for blood-poisoning (it did mix the races up) – I do not deny it; but undoubtedly this intoxication has *succeeded*. The "salvation" of the human race (I mean, from "the Masters") is well on course; everything is being made appreciably Jewish, Christian or plebeian (never mind the words!). The passage of this poison through the whole body of mankind seems unstoppable, even though its tempo and pace, from now on, might tend to be slower, softer, quieter, calmer – there is no hurry . . . With this in view, does the Church still have a *necessary* role, indeed, does it have a right to exist? Or could one do without it? *Quaeritur.*[23] It seems that the Church rather slows down and blocks the passage of poison instead of accelerating it? Well, that might be what makes it useful . . . Certainly it is by now something crude and boorish, resistant to a more tender intelligence, to a truly modern taste. Should not the Church at least try to be more refined? . . . Nowadays it alienates, more than it seduces . . . Who amongst us would be a free-thinker if it were not for the Church? We loathe the Church, *not* its poison . . . Apart from the Church, we too love the poison . . .' – This is the epilogue by a 'free-thinker' to my speech, an honest animal as he clearly shows himself to be, and moreover a democrat; he had listened to me up to that point, and could not stand listening to my silence. As a matter of fact, there is much for me to keep silent about at this point. –

---

[22] Eusebius of Caesarea reports that Constantine (later called 'the Great') once had a vision of a cross with the attached legend: 'By this, conquer' ('τούτῳ νίχα') (*De vita Constantini* I.28). This phrase was eventually transformed into the Latin: 'In hoc signo vinces' ('In this sign you will conquer'). 'Sub hoc signo' ('Under this sign') is presumably to be understood as a variant of 'In hoc signo'. In AD 312 Constantine defeated Maxentius at the Battle of the Milvian Bridge, becoming the first Christian Emperor.

[23] 'That is the question'.

10

The beginning of the slaves' revolt in morality occurs when *ressentiment* itself turns creative and gives birth to values: the *ressentiment* of those beings who, denied the proper response of action, compensate for it only with imaginary revenge. Whereas all noble morality grows out of a triumphant saying 'yes' to itself, slave morality says 'no' on principle to everything that is 'outside', 'other', 'non-self': and *this* 'no' is its creative deed. This reversal of the evaluating glance – this *essential* orientation to the outside instead of back onto itself – is a feature of *ressentiment*: in order to come about, slave morality first has to have an opposing, external world, it needs, physiologically speaking, external stimuli in order to act at all, – its action is basically a reaction. The opposite is the case with the noble method of valuation: this acts and grows spontaneously, seeking out its opposite only so that it can say 'yes' to itself even more thankfully and exultantly, – its negative concept 'low', 'common', 'bad' is only a pale contrast created after the event compared to its positive basic concept, saturated with life and passion, 'we the noble, the good, the beautiful and the happy!' When the noble method of valuation makes a mistake and sins against reality, this happens in relation to the sphere with which it is *not* sufficiently familiar, a true knowledge of which, indeed, it rigidly resists: in some circumstances, it misjudges the sphere it despises, that of the common man, the rabble; on the other hand, we should bear in mind that the distortion which results from the feeling of contempt, disdain and superciliousness, always assuming that the image of the despised person is *distorted*, remains far behind the distortion with which the entrenched hatred and revenge of the powerless man attacks his opponent – in effigy of course. Indeed, contempt has too much negligence, nonchalance, complacency and impatience, even too much personal cheerfulness mixed into it, for it to be in a position to transform its object into a real caricature and monster. Nor should one fail to hear the almost kindly nuances which the Greek nobility, for example, places in all words that it uses to distinguish itself from the rabble; a sort of sympathy, consideration and indulgence incessantly permeates and sugars them, with the result that nearly all words referring to the common man remain as expressions for 'unhappy', 'pitiable' (compare δειλός, δείλαιος, πονηρός, μοχθηρός, the last two actually designating the common man as slave worker and beast of burden) – and on the other hand, 'bad', 'low' and 'unhappy' have never ceased to reverberate in the Greek ear in a tone in which 'unhappy' predominates: this is a legacy of the old, nobler, aristocratic method of valuation that does not deny itself even in contempt (– philologists will remember the sense in which οἴζυρος,[24] ἄνολβος,[25] τλήμων,[26] δυϲτυχεῖν,[27] ξυμφορά[28] are used). The 'well-born' *felt* they were 'the happy'; they did not need first of all to construct their happiness artificially by looking at their enemies, or in some cases by talking themselves into it, *lying themselves into it* (as all men of *ressentiment* are wont to do); and also, as complete men bursting with strength and therefore *necessarily* active, they knew they must not separate happiness from action, – being active is by necessity counted as part of happiness (this is the etymological derivation of εὐπράττειν)[29] – all very much the opposite of 'happiness' at the level of the powerless, the oppressed, and those rankled with poisonous and hostile feelings, for whom it manifests itself as essentially a narcotic, an anaesthetic, rest, peace, 'sabbath', relaxation of the mind and stretching of the limbs, in short as something *passive*. While the noble man is confident and frank with himself (γενναῖος, 'of noble birth', underlines the nuance 'upright' and probably 'naïve' as well), the man of *ressentiment* is neither upright nor naïve, nor honest and straight with himself. His soul *squints*; his mind loves dark corners, secret paths and back-doors, everything secretive appeals to him as being *his* world, *his* security, *his* comfort; he knows all about keeping quiet, not forgetting, waiting, temporarily humbling and abasing himself. A race of such men of *ressentiment* will inevitably end up *cleverer* than any noble race, and will respect cleverness to a quite different degree as well: namely, as a condition of existence of the first rank, whilst the cleverness of noble men can easily have a subtle aftertaste of luxury and refinement about it: – precisely because in this area, it is nowhere near as important as the complete certainty of function of the governing *unconscious* instincts, nor indeed as important as a certain lack of cleverness, such as a daring charge at danger or at the enemy, or those frenzied sudden fits of anger, love, reverence, gratitude and revenge by which noble souls down the ages have

---

[24] 'Oi' is an interjection expressive of pain. A person whose life gives ample occasion for the use of this interjection is 'oizuros'.

[25] 'not prosperous, unfortunate'.

[26] 'tlēnai' = to bear, endure, suffer. A person who must endure things is 'tlemon'.

[27] 'to have bad luck'.

[28] 'accident, misfortune'.

[29] This expression (*eu prattein*) has something like the ambiguity of the English 'do well' = 'engage in some activity successfully' or 'fare well'. There is no expression in common use in German with a parallel ambiguity.

recognized one another. When *ressentiment* does occur in the noble man himself, it is consumed and exhausted in an immediate reaction, and therefore it does not *poison*, on the other hand, it does not occur at all in countless cases where it is unavoidable for all who are weak and power-less. To be unable to take his enemies, his misfortunes and even his *mis-deeds* seriously for long – that is the sign of strong, rounded natures with a superabundance of a power which is flexible, formative, healing and can make one forget (a good example from the modern world is Mirabeau, who had no recall for the insults and slights directed at him and who could not forgive, simply because he – forgot.) A man like this shakes from him, with one shrug, many worms which would have burrowed into another man; actual '*love* of your enemies' is also possible here and here alone – assuming it is possible at all on earth.[30] How much respect a noble man has for his enemies! – and a respect of that sort is a bridge to love . . . For he insists on having his enemy to himself, as a mark of distinction, indeed he will tolerate as enemies none other than such as have nothing to be despised and a *great deal* to be honoured! Against this, imagine 'the enemy' as conceived of by the man of *ressentiment* – and here we have his deed, his creation: he has conceived of the 'evil enemy', '*the evil one*' as a basic idea to which he now thinks up a copy and counterpart, the 'good one' – himself! . . .

I I

Exactly the opposite is true of the noble one who conceives of the basic idea 'good' by himself, in advance and spontaneously, and only then creates a notion of 'bad'! This 'bad' of noble origin and that 'evil' from the cauldron of unassuaged hatred – the first is an afterthought, an aside, a complementary colour, whilst the other is the original, the beginning, the actual *deed* in the conception of slave morality – how different are the two words 'bad' and 'evil', although both seem to be the opposite for the same concept, 'good'! But it is *not* the same concept 'good'; on the contrary, one should ask *who* is actually evil in the sense of the morality of *ressentiment*. The stern reply is: *precisely* the 'good' person of the other morality, the noble, powerful, dominating one, but re-touched, re-interpreted and reviewed through the poisonous eye of *ressentiment*. Here there is one point we would be the last to deny: anyone who came to know these 'good

---

[30] Gospel according to Matthew 5.43–4.

men' as enemies came to know nothing but '*evil enemies*', and the same people who are so strongly held in check by custom, respect, habit, gratitude and even more through spying on one another and through peer-group jealousy, who, on the other hand, behave towards one another by showing such resourcefulness in consideration, self-control, delicacy, loyalty, pride and friendship, – they are not much better than uncaged beasts of prey in the world outside where the strange, the foreign, begin. There they enjoy freedom from every social constraint, in the wilderness they compensate for the tension which is caused by being closed in and fenced in by the peace of the community for so long, they *return* to the innocent conscience of the wild beast, as exultant monsters, who perhaps go away having committed a hideous succession of murder, arson, rape and torture, in a mood of bravado and spiritual equilibrium as though they had simply played a student's prank, convinced that poets will now have something to sing about and celebrate for quite some time. At the centre of all these noble races we cannot fail to see the beast of prey, the magnificent *blond beast* avidly prowling round for spoil and victory; this hidden centre needs release from time to time, the beast must out again, must return to the wild: – Roman, Arabian, Germanic, Japanese nobility, Homeric heroes, Scandinavian Vikings – in this requirement they are all alike. It was the noble races which left the concept of 'barbarian' in their traces wherever they went; even their highest culture betrays the fact that they were conscious of this and indeed proud of it (for example, when Pericles, in that famous funeral oration, tells his Athenians: 'Our daring has forced a path to every land and sea, erecting timeless memorials to itself everywhere for good *and ill*').[31] This 'daring' of the noble races, mad, absurd and sudden in the way it manifests itself, the unpredictability and even the improbability of their undertakings – Pericles singles out the ῥαθυμία of the Athenians for praise – their unconcern and scorn for safety, body, life, comfort, their shocking cheerfulness and depth of delight in all destruction, in all the debauches of victory and cruelty – all this, for those who suffered under it, was summed up in the image of the 'barbarian', the 'evil enemy', perhaps the 'Goth' or the 'Vandal'. The deep and icy mistrust that the German arouses as soon as he comes to power, which we see again even today – is still the aftermath of that inextinguishable horror with which Europe viewed the raging of the blond Germanic beast for centuries (although between the old Germanic peoples and us Germans there is

---

[31] Thucydides II. 39ff.

scarcely an idea in common, let alone a blood relationship). I once remarked on Hesiod's dilemma[32] when he thought up the series of cultural eras and tried to express them in gold, silver and iron: he could find no other solution to the contradiction presented to him by the magnificent but at the same time so shockingly violent world of Homer than to make two eras out of one, which he now placed one behind the other – first the era of heroes and demigods from Troy and Thebes, as that world retained in the memory of the noble races, who had their own ancestry in it; then the iron era, as that same world appeared to the descendants of the down-trodden, robbed, ill-treated, and those carried off and sold: as an era of iron, hard, as I said, cold, cruel, lacking feeling and conscience, crushing everything and coating it with blood. Assuming that what is at any rate believed as 'truth' were indeed true, that it is the *meaning of all culture* to breed a tame and civilized animal, a *household pet*, out of the beast of prey 'man', then one would undoubtedly have to view all instinctive reaction and instinctive *ressentiment*, by means of which the noble races and their ideals were finally wrecked and overpowered, as the actual *instruments of culture*; which, however, is not to say that the *bearers* of these instincts were themselves representatives of the culture. Instead, the opposite would be not only probable – no! it is *visible* today! These bearers of oppressive, vindictive instincts, the descendants of all European and non-European slavery, in particular of all pre-Aryan population – represent the *decline* of mankind! These 'instruments of culture' are a disgrace to man, more a grounds for suspicion of, or an argument against, 'culture' in general! We may be quite justified in retaining our fear of the blond beast at the centre of every noble race and remain on our guard: but who would not, a hundred times over, prefer to fear if he can admire at the same time, rather than *not* fear, but thereby permanently retain the disgusting spectacle of the failed, the stunted, the wasted away and the poisoned? And is that not *our* fate? What constitutes *our* aversion to 'man' today? – for we *suffer* from man, no doubt about that. – *Not* fear; rather, the fact that we have nothing to fear from man; that 'man' is first and foremost a teeming mass of worms; that the 'tame man', who is incurably mediocre and unedifying, has already learnt to view himself as the aim and pinnacle, the meaning of history, the 'higher man'; – yes, the fact that he has a certain right to feel like that in so far as he feels distanced from the superabundance of failed,

---

[32] Hesiod, *Works & Days* 143ff.; cf. also *Daybreak*, section 189, and 'Homer's Contest' (see below, Supplementary material, pp. 174–81).

sickly, tired and exhausted people of whom today's Europe is beginning to reek, and in so far as he is at least relatively successful, at least still capable of living, at least saying 'yes' to life . . .

12

– At this juncture I cannot suppress a sigh and one last hope. What do I find absolutely intolerable? Something which I just cannot cope alone with and which suffocates me and makes me feel faint? Bad air! Bad air! That something failed comes near me, that I have to smell the bowels of a failed soul! . . . Apart from that, what cannot be borne in the way of need, deprivation, bad weather, disease, toil, solitude? Basically we can cope with everything else, born as we are to an underground and battling existence; again and again we keep coming up to the light, again and again we experience our golden hour of victory, – and then there we stand, the way we were born, unbreakable, tense, ready for new, more difficult and distant things, like a bow that is merely stretched tauter by affliction. – But from time to time grant me – assuming that there are divine benefactresses beyond good and evil – a glimpse, grant me just one glimpse of something perfect, completely finished, happy, powerful, triumphant, that still leaves something to fear! A glimpse of a man who justifies man *himself*, a stroke of luck, an instance of a man who makes up for and redeems man, and enables us to retain our *faith in mankind!* . . . For the matter stands like so: the stunting and levelling of European man conceals *our* greatest danger, because the sight of this makes us tired . . . Today we see nothing that wants to expand, we suspect that things will just continue to decline, getting thinner, better-natured, cleverer, more comfortable, more mediocre, more indifferent, more Chinese, more Christian – no doubt about it, man is getting 'better' all the time . . . Right here is where the destiny of Europe lies – in losing our fear of man we have also lost our love for him, our respect for him, our hope in him and even our will to be man. The sight of man now makes us tired – what is nihilism today if it is not *that?* . . . We are tired of *man* . . .

13

– But let us return: the problem of the *other* origin of 'good', of good as thought up by the man of *ressentiment*, demands its solution. – There is nothing strange about the fact that lambs bear a grudge towards large birds of prey: but that is no reason to blame the large birds of prey for carrying off the little lambs. And if the lambs say to each other, 'These birds of prey are evil; and whoever is least like a bird of prey and most like its opposite, a lamb, – is good, isn't he?', then there is no reason to raise objections to this setting-up of an ideal beyond the fact that the birds of prey will view it somewhat derisively, and will perhaps say: 'We don't bear any grudge at all towards these good lambs, in fact we love them, nothing is tastier than a tender lamb.' – It is just as absurd to ask strength *not* to express itself as strength, *not* to be a desire to overthrow, crush, become master, to be a thirst for enemies, resistance and triumphs, as it is to ask weakness to express itself as strength. A quantum of force is just such a quantum of drive, will, action, in fact it is nothing but this driving, willing and acting, and only the seduction of language (and the fundamental errors of reason petrified within it), which construes and misconstrues all actions as conditional upon an agency, a 'subject', can make it appear otherwise. And just as the common people separates lightning from its flash and takes the latter to be a *deed*, something performed by a subject, which is called lightning, popular morality separates strength from the manifestations of strength, as though there were an indifferent substratum behind the strong person which had the *freedom* to manifest strength or not. But there is no such substratum; there is no 'being' behind the deed, its effect and what becomes of it; 'the doer' is invented as an after-thought, – the doing is everything. Basically, the common people double a deed; when they see lightning, they make a doing-a-deed out of it: they posit the same event, first as cause and then as its effect. The scientists do no better when they say 'force moves, force causes' and such like, – all our science, in spite of its coolness and freedom from emotion, still stands exposed to the seduction of language and has not rid itself of the changelings foisted upon it, the 'subjects' (the atom is, for example, just such a changeling, likewise the Kantian 'thing-in-itself'): no wonder, then, if the entrenched, secretly smouldering emotions of revenge and hatred put this belief to their own use and, in fact, do not defend any belief more passionately than that *the strong are free* to be weak, and the birds of prey are free to be lambs: – in this way, they gain the right to make the birds of prey *responsible* for being birds of prey . . . When the oppressed, the downtrodden, the violated say to each other with the vindictive cunning of powerlessness: 'Let us be different from evil people, let us be good! And a good person is anyone who does not rape, does not harm anyone, who does not attack, does not retaliate, who leaves the taking of revenge to God, who keeps hidden as we do, avoids all evil and asks little from life in general, like us who are patient, humble and upright' – this means, if heard coolly and impartially, nothing more than: 'We weak people are just weak; it is good to do nothing *for which we are not strong enough*' – but this grim state of affairs, this cleverness of the lowest rank which even insects possess (which play dead, in order not to 'do too much' when in great danger), has, thanks to the counterfeiting and self-deception of powerlessness, clothed itself in the finery of self-denying, quiet, patient virtue, as though the weakness of the weak were itself – I mean its *essence*, its effect, its whole unique, unavoidable, irredeemable reality – a voluntary achievement, something wanted, chosen, a *deed*, an *accomplishment*. This type of man *needs* to believe in an unbiased 'subject' with freedom of choice, because he has an instinct of self-preservation and self-affirmation in which every lie is sanctified. The reason the subject (or, as we more colloquially say, *the soul*) has been, until now, the best doctrine on earth, is perhaps because it facilitated that sublime self-deception whereby the majority of the dying, the weak and the oppressed of every kind could construe weakness itself as freedom, and their particular mode of existence as an *accomplishment*.

<h1 style="text-align:center">14</h1>

– Would anyone like to have a little look down into the secret of how *ideals are fabricated* on this earth? Who has enough pluck? . . . Come on! Here we have a clear glimpse into this dark workshop. Just wait one moment, Mr Nosy Daredevil: your eyes will have to become used to this false, shimmering light . . . There! That's enough! Now you can speak! What's happening down there? Tell me what you see, you with your most dangerous curiosity – now *I* am the one who's listening. –

– 'I cannot see anything but I can hear all the better. There is a guarded, malicious little rumour-mongering and whispering from every nook and cranny. I think people are telling lies; a sugary mildness clings to every sound. Lies are turning weakness into an *accomplishment*, no doubt about it – it's just as you said.' –

– Go on!

– 'and impotence which doesn't retaliate is being turned into "goodness"; timid baseness is being turned into "humility"; submission to people one hates is being turned into "obedience" (actually towards someone who, they say, orders this submission – they call him God). The inoffensiveness of the weakling, the very cowardice with which he is richly endowed, his standing-by-the-door, his inevitable position of having to wait, are all given good names such as "patience", also known as *the* virtue; not-being-able-to-take-revenge is called not-wanting-to-take-revenge, it might even be forgiveness ("for *they* know not what they do – but we know what *they* are doing!").[33] They are also talking about "loving your enemies" – and sweating while they do it.'

– Go on!

– 'They are miserable, without a doubt, all these rumour-mongers and clandestine forgers, even if they do crouch close together for warmth – but they tell me that their misery means they are God's chosen and select, after all, people beat the dogs they love best; perhaps this misery is just a preparation, a test, a training, it might be even more than that – something that will one day be balanced up and paid back with enormous interest in gold, no! in happiness. They call that "bliss".'

– Go on!

– 'They are now informing me that not only are they better than the powerful, the masters of the world whose spittle they have to lick (*not* from fear, not at all from fear! but because God orders them to honour those in authority)[34] – not only are they better, but they have a "better time", or at least will have a better time one day. But enough! enough! I can't bear it any longer. Bad air! Bad air! This workshop where *ideals are fabricated* – it seems to me just to stink of lies.'

– No! Wait a moment! You haven't said anything yet about the masterpieces of those black magicians who can turn anything black into whiteness, milk and innocence: – haven't you noticed their perfect *raffinement*, their boldest, subtlest, most ingenious and mendacious stunt? Pay attention! These cellar rats full of revenge and hatred – what do they turn revenge and hatred into? Have you ever heard these words? Would you suspect, if you just went by what they said, that the men around you were nothing but men of *ressentiment*? . . .

– 'I understand, I'll open my ears once more (oh! oh! oh! and *hold* my nose). Now, at last, I can hear what they have been saying so often: "We good people – *we are the just*" – what they are demanding is not called retribution, but "the triumph of *justice*"; what they hate is not their enemy, oh no! they hate "*injustice*", "godlessness"; what they believe and hope for

---

[33] Gospel according to Luke 23.34.
[34] Romans 13.1.

is not the prospect of revenge, the delirium of sweet revenge (– Homer early on dubbed it "sweeter than honey"),[35] but the victory of God, the *just* God, over the Godless; all that remains for them to love on earth are not their brothers in hate but their "brothers in love",[36] as they say, all good and just people on earth.'

– And what do they call that which serves as a consolation for all the sufferings of the world – their phantasmagoria of anticipated future bliss?

– 'What? Do I hear correctly? They call it "the last judgment", the coming of *their* kingdom, the "kingdom of God" – but *in the meantime* they live "in faith", "in love", "in hope".'[37]

– Enough! Enough!

15

Faith in what? Love of what? Hope for what? – These weaklings – in fact *they*, too, want to be the powerful one day, this is beyond doubt, one day *their* 'kingdom' will come too – 'the kingdom of God' *simpliciter* is their name for it, as I said: they are so humble about everything! Just to experience *that*, you need to live long, well beyond death, – yes, you need eternal life in order to be able to gain eternal recompense in 'the kingdom of God' for that life on earth 'in faith', 'in love', 'in hope'. Recompense for what? Recompense through what? . . . It seems to me that Dante made a gross error when, with awe-inspiring naïvety he placed the inscription over the gateway to his hell: 'Eternal love created me as well':[38] – at any rate, this inscription would have a better claim to stand over the gateway to Christian Paradise and its 'eternal bliss': 'Eternal *hate* created me as well' – assuming that a true statement can be placed above the gateway to a lie! For *what* is the bliss of this Paradise? . . . We might have guessed already; but it is better to be expressly shown it by no less an authority in such matters than Thomas Aquinas, the great teacher and saint. 'Beati in regno coelesti', he says as meekly as a lamb, 'videbunt poenas damnatorum, *ut beatitudo illis magis complaceat.*'[39] Or, if you want

---

35 *Iliad* XVIII, 107ff.
36 First Thessalonians 1.3.
37 First Corinthians 13.13; First Thessalonians 1.3.
38 Dante, *Inferno* III. 5–6.
39 The blessed in the heavenly kingdom will see the torment of the damned *so that they may even more thoroughly enjoy their blessedness.* Thomas Aquinas, *Summa Theologiae* Supplement to the *Third Part*, question XCVII, article i, 'conclusio'. Some modern editions do not contain this 'conclusio'.

it even more forcefully, for example from the mouth of a triumphant Church Father[40] who advised his Christians against the cruel voluptuousness of the public spectacles – but why? 'Faith offers us much more' – he says, *De Spectaculis.* Chs. 29ff[41] – 'something *much stronger*; thanks to salvation, quite other joys are at our command; instead of athletes we have our martyrs; we want blood, well then, we have the blood of Christ . . . But think what awaits us on the day of his second coming, of his triumph!' – and then the enraptured visionary goes on: 'At enim supersunt alia spectacula, ille ultimus et perpetuus judicii dies, ille nationibus insperatus, ille derisus, cum tanta saeculi vetustas et tot ejus nativitates uno igne haurientur. Quae tunc spectaculi latitudo! *Quid admirer! Quid rideam! Ubi gaudeam! Ubi exultem*, spectans tot et tantos *reges*, qui in coelum recepti nuntiabantur, cum ipso Jove et ipsis suis testibus in imis tenebris congemescentes! Item praesides (the Provincial Governors) persecutores dominici nominis saevioribus quam ipsi flammis saevierunt insultantibus contra Christianos liquescentes! Quos praeterea sapientes illos philosophos coram discipulis suis una conflagrantibus erubescentes, quibus nihil ad deum pertinere suadebant, quibus animas aut nullas aut non in pristina corpora redituras affirmabant! Etiam poëtàs non ad Rhadamanti nec ad Minois, sed ad inopinati Christi tribunal palpitantes! Tunc magis tragoedi audiendi, magis scilicet vocales (in better voice, screaming even louder) in sua propria calamitate; tunc histriones cognoscendi, solutiores multo per ignem; tunc spectandus auriga in flammea rota totus rubens, tunc xystici contemplandi non in gymnasiis, sed in igne jaculati, nisi quod ne tunc quidem illos velim vivos, ut qui malim ad eos potius conspectum insatiabilem conferre, qui in dominum desaevierunt. "Hic est ille, dicam, fabri aut quaestuariae filius (Tertullian refers to the Jews from now on, as is shown by what follows and in particular by this well-known description of the mother of Jesus from the Talmud), sabbati destructor, Samarites et daemonium habens. Hic est, quem a Juda redemistis, hic est ille arundine et colaphis diverberatus, sputamentis dedecoratus, felle et aceto potatus. Hic est, quem clam discentes subripuerunt, ut resurrexisse dicatur vel hortulanus detraxit, ne lactucae suae frequentia commeantium laederentur." Ut talia spectes, *ut*

---

[40] Tertullian.

[41] In chapter XV of *The Decline and Fall of the Roman Empire*, Gibbon cites this same passage and comments: 'the Christians, who, in this world, found themselves oppressed by the power of the pagans, were sometimes seduced by resentment and spiritual pride to delight in the prospect of their future triumph'.

talibus exultes, quis tibi praetor aut consul aut quaestor aut sacerdos de sua liberalitate praestabit? Et tamen haec jam habemus quodammodo *per fidem* spiritu imaginante repraesentata. Ceterum qualia illa sunt, quae nec oculus vidit nec auris audivit nec in cor hominis ascenderunt? (1. Cor. 2, 9) Credo circo et utraque cavea (first and fourth rank or, according to others, the comic and tragic stages) et omni stadio gratiora.'[42]

(*Per fidem:*[43] that is what is written.)

16

Let us draw to a close. The two *opposing* values 'good and bad', 'good and evil' have fought a terrible battle for thousands of years on earth; and

---

[42] But there are yet other spectacles: that final and everlasting day of judgement, that day that was not expected and was even laughed at by the nations, when the whole old world and all it gave birth to are consumed in one fire. What an ample breadth of sights there will be then! *At which one shall I gaze in wonder? At which shall I laugh? At which rejoice? At which exult*, when I see so many great *kings* who were proclaimed to have been taken up into heaven, groaning in the deepest darkness together with those who claimed to have witnessed their apotheosis and with Jove himself. And when I see those [provincial] governors, persecutors of the Lord's name, melting in flames more savage than those with which they insolently raged against Christians! When I see those wise philosophers who persuaded their disciples that nothing was of any concern to God and who affirmed to them either that we have no souls or that our souls will not return to their original bodies! Now they are ashamed before those disciples, as they are burned together with them. Also the poets trembling before the tribunal not of Minos or of Radamanthus, but of the unexpected Christ! Then the tragic actors will be easier to hear because they will be in better voice [i.e. screaming even louder] in their own tragedy. Then the actors of pantomime will be easy to recognize, being much more nimble than usual because of the fire. Then the charioteer will be on view, all red in a wheel of flame and the athletes, thrown not in the gymnasia but into the fire. Unless even then I don't want to see them [alive +], preferring to cast an *insatiable* gaze on those who raged against the Lord. 'This is he', I will say, 'that son of a carpenter or prostitute [– Tertullian refers to the Jews from now on, as is shown by what follows and in particular by this well-known description of the mother of Jesus from the Talmud –] that destroyer of the Sabbath, that Samaritan, that man who had a devil. He it is whom you bought from Judas, who was beaten with a reed and with fists, who was defiled with spit and had gall and vinegar to drink. He it is whom his disciples secretly took away so that it might be said that he had risen again, or whom the gardener removed so that his lettuces would not be harmed by the crowd of visitors.' What praetor or consul or quaestor or priest will grant you from his largesse the chance of seeing and *exulting in such things?* And yet to some extent we have such things already *through faith*, made present in the imagining spirit. Furthermore what sorts of things are those which the eye has not seen nor the ear heard, and which have not come into the human heart? (1. Cor. 2, 9) I believe that they are more pleasing than the circus or both of the enclosures [first and fourth rank of seats, or, according to others, the comic and the tragic stages] or than any race-track.'

The material above in square brackets is Nietzsche's addition to Tertullian's text. At '[alive +]' Nietzsche incorrectly reads 'vivos' ('alive') for 'visos' ('seen').

[43] 'By my faith'.

although the latter has been dominant for a long time, there is still no lack of places where the battle remains undecided. You could even say that, in the meantime, it has reached ever greater heights but at the same time has become ever deeper and more intellectual: so that there is, today, perhaps no more distinguishing feature of the *'higher nature'*, the intellectual nature, than to be divided in this sense and really and truly a battle ground for these opposites. The symbol of this fight, written in a script which has hitherto remained legible throughout human history, is 'Rome against Judea, Judea against Rome': – up to now there has been no greater event than *this* battle, *this* question, *this* contradiction of mortal enemies. Rome saw the Jew as something contrary to nature, as though he were its antipodean monster (*Monstrum*); in Rome, the Jew was looked upon as *convicted* of hatred against the whole of mankind:[44] rightly, if one is right in linking the well being and future of the human race with the unconditional rule of aristocratic values, Roman values. What, on the other hand, did the Jews feel about Rome? We can guess from a thousand indicators; but it is enough to call once more to mind the Apocalypse of John, the wildest of all outbursts ever written which revenge has on its conscience. (By the way, we must not underestimate the profound consistency of Christian instinct in inscribing this book of hate to the disciple of love, the very same to whom it attributed that passionately ecstatic gospel –: there is some truth in this, however much literary counterfeiting might have been necessary to the purpose.) So the Romans were the strong and noble, stronger and nobler than anybody hitherto who had lived or been dreamt of on earth; their every relic and inscription brings delight, provided one can guess *what* it is that is doing the writing there. By contrast, the Jews were a priestly nation of *ressentiment par excellence*, possessing an unparalleled genius for popular morality: compare peoples with similar talents, such as the Chinese or the Germans, with the Jews, and you will realize who are first rate and who are fifth. Which of them has *prevailed* for the time being, Rome or Judea? But there is no trace of doubt: just consider to whom you bow down in Rome itself, today, as though to the embodiment of the highest values – and not just in Rome, but over nearly half the earth, everywhere where man has become tame or wants to become tame, to *three Jews*, as we know, and *one Jewess* (to Jesus of Nazareth, Peter the Fisherman, Paul the Carpet-Weaver and the mother of Jesus mentioned first, whose

---

[44] At *Annals* XV. 44 Tacitus describes 'those popularly called "Christians"' as 'convicted of hatred against the whole human species'; at *Histories* V.5 he claims that the Jews show benevolence to one another, but exhibit hatred of all the rest of the world.

name was Mary). This is very remarkable: without a doubt Rome has been defeated. However, in the Renaissance there was a brilliant, uncanny reawakening of the classical ideal, of the noble method of valuing everything: Rome itself woke up, as though from suspended animation, under the pressure of the new, Judaic Rome built over it, which looked like an ecumenical synagogue and was called 'Church': but Judea triumphed again at once, thanks to that basically proletarian (German and English) *ressentiment*-movement which people called the Reformation, including its inevitable consequence, the restoration of the church, – as well as the restoration of the ancient, tomb-like silence of classical Rome. In an even more decisive and profound sense than then, Judea once again triumphed over the classical ideal with the French Revolution: the last political nobility in Europe, that of the *French* seventeenth and eighteenth centuries, collapsed under the *ressentiment*-instincts of the rabble, – the world had never heard greater rejoicing and more uproarious enthusiasm! True, the most dreadful and unexpected thing happened in the middle: the ancient ideal itself appeared *bodily* and with unheard-of splendour before the eye and conscience of mankind, and once again, stronger, simpler and more penetrating than ever, in answer to the old, mendacious *ressentiment* slogan of *priority for the majority*, of man's will to baseness, abasement, levelling, decline and decay, there rang out the terrible and enchanting counterslogan: *priority for the few*! Like a last signpost to the *other* path, Napoleon appeared as a man more unique and late-born for his times than ever a man had been before, and in him, the problem of the *noble ideal itself* was made flesh – just think *what* a problem that is: Napoleon, this synthesis of *Unmensch* (brute) and *Übermensch* (overman) . . .

17

– Was it over after that? Was that greatest among all conflicts of ideals placed *ad acta* for ever? Or just postponed, postponed indefinitely? . . . Won't there have to be an even more terrible flaring up of the old flame, one prepared much longer in advance? And more: shouldn't one desire *that* with all one's strength? or will it, even? or even promote it? . . . Whoever, like my readers, now starts to ponder these points and reflect further, will have difficulty coming to a speedy conclusion, – reason enough, then, for me to come to a conclusion myself, assuming that it has been sufficiently clear for some time what I *want*, what I actually want with that dangerous slogan which is written on the spine of my last book, *Beyond Good and Evil* . . . at least this does *not* mean 'Beyond Good and Bad.' – –

Note. I take the opportunity presented to me by this essay, of publicly and formally expressing a wish that I have only expressed in occasional conversations with scholars up till now: that is, that some Faculty of Philosophy should do the great service of promoting the study of *the history of morality* by means of a series of academic prize essays: – perhaps this book might serve to give a powerful impetus in such a direction. With regard to such a possibility, I raise the following question for consideration: it merits the attention of philologists and historians as well as those who are actually philosophers by profession:

> '*What signposts does linguistics, especially the study of etymology, give to the history of the evolution of moral concepts?*'

– On the other hand, it is just as essential to win the support of physiologists and doctors for these problems (on the *value* of all previous valuations): we can leave it to the professional philosophers to act as advocates and mediators in this, once they have completely succeeded in transforming the originally so reserved and suspicious relationship between philosophy, physiology and medicine into the most cordial and fruitful exchange. Indeed, every table of values, every 'thou shalt' known to history or the study of ethnology, needs first and foremost a *physiological* elucidation and interpretation, rather than a psychological one; and all of them await critical study from medical science. The question: what is this or that table of values and 'morals' *worth*? needs to be asked from different angles; in particular, the question 'value for *what*?' cannot be examined too finely. Something, for example, which obviously had value with regard to the longest possible life-span of a race (or to the improvement of its abilities to adapt to a particular climate, or to maintaining the greatest number) would not have anything like the same value if it was a question of developing a stronger type. The good of the majority and the good of the minority are conflicting moral standpoints: we leave it to the naïvety of English biologists to view the first as higher in value as *such* . . . *All* sciences must, from now on, prepare the way for the future work of the philosopher: this work being understood to mean that the philosopher has to solve the *problem of values* and that he has to decide on the *rank order of values*. –

Second essay: 'Guilt', 'bad conscience' and related matters

I

To breed an animal with the prerogative to *promise* – is that not precisely the paradoxical task which nature has set herself with regard to humankind? is it not the real problem *of* humankind? . . . The fact that this problem has been solved to a large degree must seem all the more surprising to the person who can fully appreciate the opposing force, *forgetfulness.* Forgetfulness is not just a *vis inertiae,* as superficial people believe, but is rather an active ability to suppress, positive in the strongest sense of the word, to which we owe the fact that what we simply live through, experience, take in, no more enters our consciousness during digestion (one could call it spiritual ingestion) than does the thousand-fold process which takes place with our physical consumption of food, our so-called ingestion. To shut the doors and windows of consciousness for a while; not to be bothered by the noise and battle with which our underworld of serviceable organs work with and against each other; a little peace, a little *tabula rasa* of consciousness to make room for something new, above all for the nobler functions and functionaries, for ruling, predicting, predetermining (our organism runs along oligarchic lines, you see) – that, as I said, is the benefit of active forgetfulness, like a doorkeeper or guardian of mental order, rest and etiquette: from which we can immediately see how there could be no happiness, cheerfulness, hope, pride, *immediacy,* without forgetfulness. The person in whom this apparatus of suppression is damaged, so that it stops working, can be compared (and not just compared –) to a dyspeptic; he cannot 'cope' with anything . . . And precisely

35

this necessarily forgetful animal, in whom forgetting is a strength, representing a form of *robust* health, has bred for himself a counter-device,
memory, with the help of which forgetfulness can be suspended in certain
cases, – namely in those cases where a promise is to be made: consequently, it is by no means merely a passive inability to be rid of an impression once it has made its impact, nor is it just indigestion caused by giving
your word on some occasion and finding you cannot cope, instead it is an
active *desire* not to let go, a desire to keep on desiring what has been, on
some occasion, desired, really it is the *will's memory*: so that a world of
strange new things, circumstances and even acts of will may be placed
quite safely in between the original 'I will', 'I shall do' and the actual discharge of the will, its *act*, without breaking this long chain of the will. But
what a lot of preconditions there are for this! In order to have that degree
of control over the future, man must first have learnt to distinguish
between what happens by accident and what by design, to think causally,
to view the future as the present and anticipate it, to grasp with certainty
what is end and what is means, in all, to be able to calculate, compute –
and before he can do this, man himself will really have to become *reliable,*
regular, necessary, even in his own self-image, so that he, as someone
making a promise is, is answerable for his own *future!*

2

That is precisely what constitutes the long history of the origins of
responsibility. That particular task of breeding an animal with the prerogative to promise includes, as we have already understood, as precondition
and preparation, the more immediate task of first *making* man to a certain
degree necessary, uniform, a peer amongst peers, orderly and consequently predictable. The immense amount of labour involved in what I
have called the 'morality of custom' [see *Daybreak*, I, 9; 14; 16][45], the actual
labour of man on himself during the longest epoch of the human race, his
whole *prehistoric* labour, is explained and justified on a grand scale, in spite
of the hardness, tyranny, stupidity and idiocy it also contained, by this fact:
with the help of the morality of custom and the social straitjacket, man was
made truly predictable. Let us place ourselves, on the other hand, at the
end of this immense process where the tree actually bears fruit, where
society and its morality of custom finally reveal what they were simply *the*

---

[45] See below, supplementary material, pp. 133–7.

means to: we then find the *sovereign individual* as the ripest fruit on its tree, like only to itself, having freed itself from the morality of custom, an autonomous, supra-ethical individual (because 'autonomous' and 'ethical' are mutually exclusive), in short, we find a man with his own, independent, enduring will, whose *prerogative it is to promise* – and in him a proud consciousness quivering in every muscle of *what* he has finally achieved and incorporated, an actual awareness of power and freedom, a feeling that man in general has reached completion. This man who is now free, who actually *has* the *prerogative* to promise, this master of the *free* will, this sovereign – how could he remain ignorant of his superiority over everybody who does not have the prerogative to promise or answer to himself, how much trust, fear and respect he arouses – he '*merits*' all three – and how could he, with his self-mastery, not realise that he has necessarily been given mastery over circumstances, over nature and over all creatures with a less enduring and reliable will? The 'free' man, the possessor of an enduring, unbreakable will, thus has his own *standard of value*: in the possession of such a will: viewing others from his own standpoint, he respects or despises; and just as he will necessarily respect his peers, the strong and the reliable (those with the prerogative to promise), – that is everyone who promises like a sovereign, ponderously, seldom, slowly, and is sparing with his trust, who *confers an honour* when he places his trust, who gives his word as something that can be relied on, because he is strong enough to remain upright in the face of mishap or even 'in the face of fate' –: so he will necessarily be ready to kick the febrile whippets who promise without that prerogative, and will save the rod for the liar who breaks his word in the very moment it passes his lips. The proud knowledge of the extraordinary privilege of *responsibility*, the consciousness of this rare freedom and power over himself and his destiny, has penetrated him to his lowest depths and become an instinct, his dominant instinct: – what will he call his dominant instinct, assuming that he needs a word for it? No doubt about the answer: this sovereign human being calls it his *conscience* . . .

3

His conscience? . . . We can presume, in advance, that the concept 'conscience', which we meet here in its highest, almost disconcerting form, already has a long history and metamorphosis behind it. To be answerable to oneself, and proudly, too, and therefore *to have the prerogative to say 'yes'* to oneself – is, as I said, a ripe fruit, but also a *late* fruit: –

how long must this fruit have hung, bitter and sour, on the tree! And for even longer there was nothing to see of this fruit, – nobody could have promised it would be there, although it is certain that everything about the tree was ready and growing towards it! – 'How do you give a memory to the animal, man? How do you impress something upon this partly dull, partly idiotic, inattentive mind, this personification of forgetfulness, so that it will stick?' . . . This age-old question was not resolved with gentle solutions and methods, as can be imagined; perhaps there is nothing more terrible and strange in man's prehistory than his *technique of mnemonics*. 'A thing must be burnt in so that it stays in the memory: only something that continues *to hurt* stays in the memory' – that is a proposition from the oldest (and unfortunately the longest-lived) psychology on earth. You almost want to add that wherever on earth you still find ceremonial, solemnity, mystery, gloomy shades in the lives of men and peoples, some-thing of the dread with which everyone, everywhere, used to make promises, give pledges and commendation, is *still working*: the past, the most prolonged, deepest, hardest past, breathes on us and rises up in us when we become 'solemn'. When man decided he had to make a memory for himself, it never happened without blood, torments and sacrifices: the most horrifying sacrifices and forfeits (the sacrifice of the first-born belongs here), the most disgusting mutilations (for example, castration), the cruellest rituals of all religious cults (and all religions are, at their most fundamental, systems of cruelty) – all this has its origin in that particular instinct which discovered that pain was the most powerful aid to mnemonics. In a certain sense, the whole of asceticism belongs here: a few ideas have to be made ineradicable, ubiquitous, unforgettable, 'fixed', in order to hypnotize the whole nervous and intellectual system through these 'fixed ideas' – and ascetic procedures and lifestyles are a method of freeing those ideas from competition with all other ideas, of making them 'unforgettable'. The worse man's memory has been, the more dreadful his customs have appeared; in particular, the harshness of the penal law gives a measure of how much trouble it had in conquering forgetfulness, and *preserving* a few primitive requirements of social life in the minds of these slaves of the mood and desire of the moment. We Germans certainly do not regard ourselves as a particularly cruel or hard-hearted people, still less as particularly irresponsible and happy-go-lucky; but you only have to look at our old penal code in order to see how difficult it was on this earth to breed a 'nation of thinkers' (by which I mean: *the* nation in Europe that still contains the maximum of reliability, solemnity, tastelessness and sobriety, qualities which give it the right to breed all sorts of European mandarin). These Germans made a memory for themselves with dreadful methods, in order to master their basic plebeian instincts and the brutal crudeness of the same: think of old German punishments such as stoning (– even the legend drops the millstone on the guilty person's head), breaking on the wheel (a unique invention and speciality of German genius in the field of punishment!), impaling, ripping apart and trampling to death by horses ('quartering'), boiling of the criminal in oil or wine (still in the fourteenth and fifteenth centuries), the popular flaying ('cutting strips'), cutting out flesh from the breast; and, of course, coating the wrong-doer with honey and leaving him to the flies in the scorching sun. With the aid of such images and procedures, man was eventually able to retain five or six 'I-don't-want-to's' in his memory, in connection with which a *promise* had been given, in order to enjoy the advantages of society – and there you are! With the aid of this sort of memory, people finally came to 'reason'! – Ah, reason, solemnity, mastering of emotions, this really dismal thing called reflection, all these privileges and splendours man has: what a price had to be paid for them! how much blood and horror lies at the basis of all 'good things'! . . .

4

How, then, did that other 'dismal thing', the consciousness of guilt, the whole 'bad conscience', come into the world? – And with this we return to our genealogists of morality. I'll say it again – or maybe I haven't said it yet? – they are no good. No more than five spans of their own, merely 'modern' experience; no knowledge and no will to know the past; still less an instinct for history, a 'second sight' so necessary at this point – and yet they go in for the history of morality: of course, this must logically end in results that have a more than brittle relationship to the truth. Have these genealogists of morality up to now ever remotely dreamt that, for example, the main moral concept '*Schuld*' ('guilt') descends from the very material concept of '*Schulden*' ('debts')? Or that punishment, as *retribution*, evolved quite independently of any assumption about freedom or lack of freedom of the will? – and this to the point where a *high* degree of humanization had first to be achieved, so that the animal 'man' could begin to differentiate between those much more primitive nuances 'intentional', 'negligent', 'accidental', 'of sound mind' and their opposites, and take them into account when dealing out punishment. That inescapable thought, which is now so cheap and apparently natural, and which has had to serve as an explanation of how the sense of justice came about at all on earth, 'the criminal deserves to be punished *because* he could have acted otherwise', is actually an extremely late and refined form of human judgment and inference; whoever thinks it dates back to the beginning is laying his coarse hands on the psychology of primitive man in the wrong way. Throughout most of human history, punishment has *not* been meted out *because* the miscreant was held responsible for his act, therefore it was *not* assumed that the guilty party alone should be punished: – but rather, as parents still punish their children, it was out of anger over some wrong that had been suffered, directed at the perpetrator, – but this anger was held in check and modified by the idea that every injury has its *equivalent* which can be paid in compensation, if only through the *pain* of the person who injures. And where did this primeval, deeply-rooted and perhaps now ineradicable idea gain its power, this idea of an equivalence between injury and pain? I have already let it out: in the contractual relationship between *creditor* and *debtor*, which is as old as the very conception of a 'legal subject' and itself refers back to the basic forms of buying, selling, bartering, trade and traffic.

5

To be sure, thinking about these contractual relationships, as can be expected from what has gone before, arouses all kinds of suspicion and hostility towards the primitive men who created them or permitted them. Precisely here, *promises are made*; precisely here, the person making the promise has to have a memory *made* for him: precisely here, we may suppose, is a repository of hard, cruel, painful things. The debtor, in order to inspire confidence that the promise of repayment will be honoured, in order to give a guarantee of the solemnity and sanctity of his promise, and in order to etch the duty and obligation of repayment into his conscience, pawns something to the creditor by means of the contract in case he does not pay, something that he still 'possesses' and controls, for example, his body, or his wife, or his freedom, or his life (or, in certain religious circumstances, even his after-life, the salvation of his soul, finally, even his peace in the grave: as in Egypt, where the corpse of a debtor found no peace from the creditor even in the grave – and this peace meant a lot precisely to the Egyptians). But in particular, the creditor could inflict all kinds of dishonour and torture on the body of the debtor, for example, cutting as much flesh off as seemed appropriate for the debt: – from this standpoint there were everywhere, early on, estimates which went into horrifyingly minute and fastidious detail, *legally* drawn up estimates for individual limbs and parts of the body. I regard it as definite progress and proof of a freer, more open-handed calculation, of *a more Roman* pricing of justice, when Rome's code of the Twelve Tables decreed that it did not matter how much or how little a creditor cut off in such a circumstance, '*si plus minusve secuerunt, ne fraude esto*'.[46] Let's be quite clear about the logic of this whole matter of compensation: it is strange enough. The equivalence is provided by the fact that instead of an advantage directly making up for the wrong (so, instead of compensation in money, land or possessions of any kind), a sort of *pleasure* is given to the creditor as repayment and compensation, – the pleasure of having the right to exercise power over the powerless without a thought, the pleasure '*de faire le mal pour le plaisir de le faire*',[47] the enjoyment of violating: an enjoyment that is prized all the higher, the lower and baser the position of the creditor in the social scale, and which can easily seem a delicious titbit to him, even a foretaste of higher rank. Through punishment of the debtor, the creditor takes part in the *rights of the masters*: at last he, too, shares the elevated feeling of being in a position to despise and maltreat someone as an 'inferior' – or at least, when the actual power of punishment, of exacting punishment, is already transferred to the 'authorities', of *seeing* the debtor despised and maltreated. So, then, compensation is made up of a warrant for and entitlement to cruelty. –

6

In *this* sphere of legal obligations, then, the moral conceptual world of 'debt', 'conscience', 'duty', 'sacred duty', has its breeding ground – all began with a thorough and prolonged bloodletting, like the beginning of all great things on earth. And may we not add that this world has really never quite lost a certain odour of blood and torture? (not even with old Kant: the categorical imperative smells of cruelty . . .). In the same way, it was here that the uncanny and perhaps inextricable link-up between the

[46] 'If they have cut off more or less, let that not be considered a crime.' This is from the Third Table, section 6. Modern editions read a slightly different text here with 'se' (= sine) for 'ne': 'If they have cut off more or less, let it be honestly done.'
[47] P. Mérimée, *Lettres à une inconnue* (Paris, 1874), I. 8: 'To do evil for the pleasure of doing it'.

ideas of 'debt and suffering' was first crocheted together. I ask again: to what extent can suffering be a compensation for 'debts'? To the degree that *to make* someone suffer is pleasure in its highest form, and to the degree that the injured party received an extraordinary counter-pleasure in exchange for the injury and distress caused by the injury: to *make* someone suffer, – a true *feast*, something that, as I mentioned, rose in price the more it contrasted with the rank and social position of the creditor. I say all this in speculation: because such subterranean things are difficult to fathom out, besides being embarrassing; and anyone who clumsily tries to interject the concept 'revenge' has merely obscured and darkened his own insight, rather than clarified it (– revenge itself just leads us back to the same problem: 'how can it be gratifying to make someone suffer?'). It seems to me that the delicacy and even more the tartuffery of tame house-pets (meaning modern man, meaning us) revolts against a truly forceful realization of the degree to which *cruelty* is part of the festive joy of the ancients and, indeed, is an ingredient in nearly every pleasure they have; on the other hand, how naïve and innocent their need for cruelty appears, and how fundamental is that 'disinterested malice' (or, to use Spinoza's words, the *sympathia malevolens*) they assume is a *normal* human attribute –: making it something to which conscience says a hearty '*yes*'! A more piercing eye would perhaps be able to detect, even now, plenty of these most primitive and basic festive joys of man; in *Beyond Good and Evil*, VII, section 229[48] (earlier in *Daybreak*, I, sections 18, 77, 113)[49] I pointed a wary finger at the ever-growing intellectualization and 'deification' of cruelty, which runs though the whole history of higher culture (and indeed, constitutes it in an important sense). At all events, not so long ago it was unthinkable to hold a royal wedding or full-scale festival for the people without executions, tortures or perhaps an *auto-da-fé*, similarly, no noble household was without creatures on whom people could discharge their malice and cruel taunts with impunity (– remember Don Quixote, for example, at the court of the Duchess:[50] today we read the whole of Don Quixote with a bitter taste in the mouth, it is almost an ordeal, which would make us seem very strange and incomprehensible to the author and his contemporaries, – they read it with a clear conscience as the funniest of books, it made them nearly laugh themselves to death). To see suffering does you good, to make suffer, better still – that

---

[48] See below, Supplementary material, pp. 153–4.
[49] See below, Supplementary material, pp. 137–9, pp. 140–1, pp. 143–4.
[50] *Don Quixote*, Book II, chs 31–7.

is a hard proposition, but an ancient, powerful, human-all-too-human proposition to which, by the way, even the apes might subscribe: as people say, in thinking up bizarre cruelties they anticipate and, as it were, act out a 'demonstration' of what man will do. No cruelty, no feast: that is what the oldest and longest period in human history teaches us – and punishment, too, has such very strong *festive* aspects! –

7

– By the way, these ideas certainly don't make me wish to help provide our pessimists with new grist for their discordant and creaking mills of disgust with life; on the contrary, I expressly want to place on record that at the time when mankind felt no shame towards its cruelty, life on earth was more cheerful than it is today, with its pessimists. The heavens darkened over man in direct proportion to the increase in his feeling shame *at being man.* The tired, pessimistic outlook, mistrust of life's riddle, the icy 'no' of nausea at life – these are not signs of the *wickedest* epoch of the human race: on the contrary, they come to light as the bog-plants they are only in their natural habitat, the bog, – I mean the sickly mollycoddling and sermonizing, by means of which the animal 'man' is finally taught to be ashamed of all his instincts. On the way to becoming an 'angel' (not to use a stronger word here), man has upset his stomach and developed a furry tongue so that he finds not only that the joy and innocence of animals is disgusting, but that life itself is distasteful: – so that every now and again, he is so repelled by himself that he holds his nose and disapprovingly recites a catalogue of his offensive features, with Pope Innocent the Third ('conception in filth, loathsome method of feeding in the womb, sinfulness of the raw material of man, terrible stench, secretion of saliva, urine and excrement').[51] Now, when suffering is always the first of the arguments marshalled *against* life, as its most questionable feature, it is salutary to remember the times when people made the opposite assessment because they could not do without *making* people suffer and saw first-rate magic in it, a veritable seductive lure *to* life. Perhaps

---

[51] This is not a quotation, but rather Nietzsche's own summary of the topics discussed in the first few sections of *De miseria humanae conditionis* (also known as *De contemptu mundi* and by various other titles). This short treatise, written in 1195 by Cardinal Lotario dei Segni (who in 1198 acceded to the Papacy as Innocent III) was extremely popular in the late Middle Ages, sizable chunks of it turning up, for instance, in *The Canterbury Tales* (particularly in the Man of Law's 'Prologue' and 'Tale').

pain – I say this to comfort the squeamish – did not hurt as much then as it does now; at least, a doctor would be justified in assuming this, if he had treated a Negro (taken as a representative for primeval man) for serious internal inflammations which would drive the European with the stoutest constitution to distraction; – they do *not* do that to Negroes. (The curve of human capacity for pain actually does seem to sink dramatically and almost precipitously beyond the first ten thousand or ten million of the cultural élite; and for myself, I do not doubt that in comparison with one night of pain endured by a single, hysterical blue stocking, the total suffering of all the animals who have been interrogated by the knife in scientific research is as nothing.) Perhaps I can even be allowed to admit the possibility that pleasure in cruelty does not really need to have died out: perhaps, just as pain today hurts more, it needed, in this connection, some kind of sublimation and subtilization, it had to be transformed into the imaginative and spiritual, and adorned with such inoffensive names that they do not arouse the suspicion of even the most delicate hypocritical conscience ('tragic pity' is one such name, another is *'les nostalgies de la croix'*). What actually arouses indignation over suffering is not the suffering itself, but the senselessness of suffering: but neither for the Christian, who saw in suffering a whole, hidden machinery of salvation, nor for naïve man in ancient times, who saw all suffering in relation to spectators or to instigators of suffering, was there any such *senseless* suffering. In order to rid the world of concealed, undiscovered, unseen suffering and deny it in all honesty, people were then practically obliged to invent gods and intermediate beings at every level, in short, something that also roamed round in obscurity, which could see in the dark and which would not miss out on an interesting spectacle of pain so easily. With the aid of such inventions, life then played the trick it has always known how to play, of justifying itself, justifying its 'evil'; nowadays it might need rather different inventions to help it (for example, life as a riddle, life as a problem of knowledge). 'All evil is justified if a god takes pleasure in it': so ran the primitive logic of feeling – and was this logic really restricted to primitive times? The gods viewed as the friends of *cruel* spectacles – how deeply this primeval concept still penetrates into our European civilization! Maybe we should consult Calvin and Luther on the matter. At all events, the *Greeks* could certainly think of offering their gods no more acceptable a side-dish to their happiness than the joys of cruelty. So how do you think Homer made his gods look down on the fortunes of men? What final, fundamental meaning did the Trojan War and similar tragic atrocities have? We can be in no doubt: they were intended to be *festivals* for the gods: and, to the extent that the poet has a more 'god-like' nature in these matters, probably festivals for the poets, too . . . It was no different when later Greek moral philosophers thought that the eyes of the gods still looked down on moral struggles, on the heroism and self-inflicted torture of the virtuous: the 'Heracles of duty' was on stage and knew it; unwitnessed virtue was something inconceivable for this nation of actors. Might it not be the case that that extremely foolhardy and fateful philosophical invention, first devised for Europe, of the 'free will', of man's absolute freedom [*Spontaneität*] to do good or evil, was chiefly thought up to justify the idea that the interest of the gods in man, in man's virtue, *could never be exhausted*? On the stage of this earth there would never be any lack of real novelty, real unheard-of suspense, intrigues, catastrophes: a world planned on completely deterministic lines would have been predictable and therefore soon boring for the gods, – sufficient reason for these *friends of the gods*, the philosophers, not to impute a deterministic world of that sort to their gods! Everybody in antiquity is full of tender consideration for 'the spectator', people in antiquity form an essentially public, essentially visible world, incapable of conceiving of happiness without spectacles and feasts. – And, as already stated, severe *punishment*, too, has very strong festive features! . . .

8

The feeling of guilt, of personal obligation, to pursue our train of inquiry again, originated, as we saw, in the oldest and most primitive personal relationship there is, in the relationship of buyer and seller, creditor and debtor: here person met person for the first time, and *measured himself* person against person. No form of civilization has been discovered which is so low that it did not display something of this relationship. Fixing prices, setting values, working out equivalents, exchanging – this preoccupied man's first thoughts to such a degree that in a certain sense it *constitutes* thought: the most primitive kind of cunning was bred here, as was also, presumably, the first appearance of human pride, man's sense of superiority over other animals. Perhaps our word 'man' (*manas*) expresses something of *this* first sensation of self-confidence: man designated himself as the being who measures values, who values and measures, as the 'calculating animal as such'. Buying and selling, with their psychological trappings, are older even than the beginnings of any social form of organization or association: it is much more the case that the germinating sensation of barter, contract, debt, right, duty, compensation was simply *transferred* from the most rudimentary form of the legal rights of persons to the most crude and elementary social units (in their relations with similar units), together with the habit of comparing power with power, of measuring, of calculating. Now the eye was focused in this direction in any case: and with the ponderous consistency characteristic of the ancients' way of thinking, which, though difficult to get started, never deviated once it was moving, man soon arrived at the great generalization: 'Every thing has its price: *everything* can be compensated for' – the oldest, most naïve canon of morals relating to *justice*, the beginning of all 'good naturedness', 'equity', all 'good will', all 'objectivity' on earth. Justice at this first level is the good will, between those who are roughly equal, to come to terms with each other, to 'come to an understanding' again by means of a settlement – and, in connection with those who are less powerful, to *force* them to reach a settlement amongst themselves. –

9

Still measuring with the standard of prehistoric times (a prehistory which, by the way, exists at all times or could possibly re-occur): the community has the same basic relationship to its members as the creditor to the debtor. You live in a community, you enjoy the benefits of a community (oh, what benefits! sometimes we underestimate them today), you live a sheltered, protected life in peace and trust, without any worry of suffering certain kinds of harm and hostility to which the man *outside*, the 'man without peace', is exposed – a German understands what 'misery', *élend*,[52] originally means –, you make pledges and take on obligations to the community with just that harm and hostility in mind. What happens *if you do not?* The community, the cheated creditor, will make you pay up as best it can, you can be sure of that. The immediate damage done by the offender is what we are talking about least: quite apart from this, the lawbreaker is a 'breaker', somebody who has broken his contract and his word *to the whole*, in connection with all the valued features and amenities of communal life that he has shared up till now. The lawbreaker is a debtor who not only fails to repay the benefits and advances granted to him, but also actually assaults the creditor: so, from now on, as is fair, he is not only

---

[52] literally 'other country' i.e. banishment, exile.

deprived of all these valued benefits, – he is now also reminded *how important these benefits are*. The anger of the injured creditor, the community, makes him return to the savage and outlawed state from which he was sheltered hitherto: he is cast out – and now any kind of hostile act can be perpetrated on him. 'Punishment' at this level of civilization is simply a copy, a *mimus*, of normal behaviour towards a hated, disarmed enemy who has been defeated, and who has not only forfeited all rights and safeguards, but all mercy as well; in fact, the rules of war and the victory celebration of *vae victis!*[53] in all their mercilessness and cruelty: – which explains the fact that war itself (including the warlike cult of the sacrificial victim) has given us all *forms* in which punishment manifests itself in history.

10

As a community grows in power, it ceases to take the offence of the individual quite so seriously, because these do not seem to be as dangerous and destabilizing for the survival of the whole as they did earlier: the wrongdoer is no longer 'deprived of peace' and cast out, nor can the general public vent their anger on him with the same lack of constraint, – instead the wrongdoer is carefully shielded by the community from this anger, especially from that of the immediate injured party, and given protection. A compromise with the anger of those immediately affected by the wrongdoing; and therefore an attempt to localize the matter and head off further or more widespread participation and unrest; attempts to work out equivalents and settle the matter (the *compositio*); above all, the will, manifesting itself ever more distinctly, to treat every offence as being something that *can be paid off*, so that, at least to a certain degree, the wrongdoer is *isolated* from his deed – these are the characteristics imprinted more and more clearly into penal law in its further development. As the power and self-confidence of a community grows, its penal law becomes more lenient; if the former is weakened or endangered, harsher forms of the latter will re-emerge. The 'creditor' always becomes more humane as his wealth increases; finally, the *amount* of his wealth determines how much injury he can sustain without suffering from it. It is not impossible to imagine society *so conscious of its power* that it could allow itself the noblest luxury available to it, – that of letting its

---

[53] 'Woe to the vanquished' (Livy v. 48).

malefactors go *unpunished*. 'What do I care about my parasites', it could say, 'let them live and flourish: I am strong enough for all that!' . . . Justice, which began by saying 'Everything can be paid off, everything must be paid off', ends by turning a blind eye and letting off those unable to pay, – it ends, like every good thing on earth, by *sublimating itself*. The self-sublimation of justice: we know what a nice name it gives itself – *mercy*; it remains, of course, the prerogative of the most powerful man, better still, his way of being beyond the law.

II

– Now a derogatory mention of recent attempts to seek the origin of justice elsewhere, – namely in *ressentiment*. A word in the ear of the psychologists, assuming they are inclined to study *ressentiment* close up for once: this plant thrives best amongst anarchists and anti-Semites today, so it flowers like it always has done, in secret, like a violet but with a different scent. And just as like always gives rise to like, it will come as no surprise to find attempts coming once more from these circles, as so often before – see section 14 [Essay I] above, – to sanctify *revenge* with the term *justice* – as though justice were fundamentally simply a further development of the feeling of having been wronged – and belatedly to legitimize with revenge emotional *reactions* in general, one and all. The latter is something with which I least take issue: with regard to the whole biological problem (where the value of these emotions has been underestimated up till now), I even view it as *a merit*. All I want to point out is the fact that this new nuance of scientific balance (which favours hatred, envy, resentment, suspicion, *rancune* and revenge) stems from the spirit of *ressentiment* itself. This 'scientific fairness' immediately halts and takes on aspects of a deadly animosity and prejudice the minute it has to deal with a different set of emotions, which, to my mind, are of much greater biological value than those of reaction and therefore truly deserve to be *scientifically* valued, highly valued: namely the actual *active* emotions such as lust for mastery, greed and the like. (E. Dühring, *The Value of Life. A Course in Philosophy*; basically, all of it.) So much for my general objections to this tendency; but concerning Dühring's specific proposition that the seat of justice is found in the territory of reactive sentiment, for the sake of accuracy we must unceremoniously replace this with another proposition: the *last* territory to be conquered by the spirit of justice is that of reactive sentiment! If it actually happens that the just man remains just even towards someone who has wronged him (and not just cold, moderate, remote and indifferent: to be just is always a *positive* attitude), if the just and *judging* eye, gazing with a lofty, clear objectivity both penetrating and merciful, is not dimmed even in the face of personal injury, of scorn and suspicion, well, that is a piece of perfection, the highest form of mastery to be had on earth, – and even something that we would be wise not to expect and should certainly find difficult to *believe*. Certainly, on average, even a small dose of aggression, malice or insinuation is enough to make the most upright man see red and drive moderation *out of* his sight. The active, aggressive, over-reaching man is still a hundred paces nearer to justice then the man who reacts; he simply does not need to place a false and prejudiced interpretation on the object of his attention, like the man who reacts does, has to do. In fact, this explains why the aggressive person, as the stronger, more courageous, nobler man, has always had a *clearer* eye, a *better* conscience on his side: on the other hand it is easy to guess who has the invention of 'bad conscience' on his conscience, – the man of *ressentiment*! Finally, just cast your eye around in history: in what sphere, up till now, has the whole treatment of justice, and the actual need for justice, resided? With men who react, perhaps? Not in the least: but with the active, the strong, the spontaneous and the aggressive. Historically speaking, justice on earth represents – I say this to the annoyance of the above-mentioned agitator (who himself once confessed: 'The doctrine of revenge has woven its way though all my work and activities as the red thread of justice')[54] – the battle, then, *against* reactive sentiment, the war waged against the same on the part of active and aggressive forces, which have partly expended their strength in trying to put a stop to the spread of reactive pathos, to keep it in check and within bounds, and to force a compromise with it. Everywhere that justice is practised and maintained, the stronger power can be seen looking for means of putting an end to the senseless ravages of *ressentiment* amongst those inferior to it (whether groups or individuals), partly by lifting the object of *ressentiment* out of the hands of revenge, partly by substituting, for revenge, a struggle against the enemies of peace and order, partly by working out compensation, suggesting, sometimes enforcing it, and partly by promoting certain equivalences for wrongs into a norm which *ressentiment*, from now on, has to take into account. The most decisive thing, however, that the higher authorities can invent and enforce against

---

[54] E. Dühring, *Sache, Leben, und Feinde* (Karlsruhe, Leipzig, 1882), p. 293.

the even stronger power of hostile and spiteful feelings – and they do it as soon as they are strong enough – is the setting up of a *legal system*, the imperative declaration of what counts as permissible in their eyes, as just, and what counts as forbidden, unjust: once the legal code is in place, by treating offence and arbitrary actions against the individual or groups as a crime, as violation of the law, as insurrection against the higher authorities themselves, they distract attention from the damage done by such violations, and ultimately achieve the opposite of what revenge sets out to do, which just sees and regards as valid the injured party's point of view –: from then on the eye is trained for an evermore *impersonal* interpretation of the action, even the eye of the injured party (although, as stated, this happens last). – Therefore 'just' and 'unjust' only start from the moment when a legal system is set up (and *not*, as Dühring says, from the moment when the injury is done.) To talk of 'just' and 'unjust' *as such* is meaningless, an act of injury, violence, exploitation or destruction cannot be 'unjust' *as such*, because life functions *essentially* in an injurious, violent, exploitative and destructive manner, or at least these are its fundamental processes and it cannot be thought of without these characteristics. One has to admit to oneself something even more unpalatable: that viewed from the highest biological standpoint, states of legality can never be anything but *exceptional states*, as partial restrictions of the true will to life, which seeks power and to whose overall purpose they subordinate themselves as individual measures, that is to say, as a means of creating greater units of power. A system of law conceived as sovereign and general, not as a means for use in the fight between units of power but as a means *against* fighting in general, rather like Dühring's communistic slogan that every will should regard every other will as its equal, this would be a principle *hostile to life*, an attempt to assassinate the future of man, a sign of fatigue and a secret path to nothingness. –

12

Now another word on the origin and purpose of punishment – two problems which are separate, or ought to be: unfortunately people usually throw them together. How have the moral genealogists reacted so far in this matter? Naively, as is their wont –: they highlight some 'purpose' in punishment, for example, revenge or deterrence, then innocently place the purpose at the start, as *causa fiendi* of punishment, and – have finished. But 'purpose in law' is the last thing we should apply to the history of the emergence of law: on the contrary, there is no more important proposition for every sort of history than that which we arrive at only with great effort but which we really *should* reach, – namely that the origin of the emergence of a thing and its ultimate usefulness, its practical application and incorporation into a system of ends, are *toto coelo* separate; that anything in existence, having somehow come about, is continually interpreted anew, requisitioned anew, transformed and redirected to a new purpose by a power superior to it; that everything that occurs in the organic world consists of *overpowering*, *dominating*, and in their turn, overpowering and dominating consist of re-interpretation, adjustment, in the process of which their former 'meaning' [*Sinn*] and 'purpose' must necessarily be obscured or completely obliterated. No matter how perfectly you have understood the *usefulness* of any physiological organ (or legal institution, social custom, political usage, art form or religious rite), you have not yet thereby grasped how it emerged: uncomfortable and unpleasant as this may sound to more elderly ears,– for people down the ages have believed that the obvious purpose of a thing, its utility, form and shape, are its reason for existence, the eye is made to see, the hand to grasp. So people think punishment has evolved for the purpose of punishing. But every purpose and use is just a *sign* that the will to power has achieved mastery over something less powerful, and has impressed upon it its own idea [*Sinn*] of a use function; and the whole history of a 'thing', an organ, a tradition can to this extent be a continuous chain of signs, continually revealing new interpretations and adaptations, the causes of which need not be connected even amongst themselves, but rather sometimes just follow and replace one another at random. The 'development' of a thing, a tradition, an organ is therefore certainly not its *progressus* towards a goal, still less is it a logical *progressus*, taking the shortest route with least expenditure of energy and cost, – instead it is a succession of more or less profound, more or less mutually independent processes of subjugation exacted on the thing, added to this the resistances encountered every time, the attempted transformations for the purpose of defence and reaction, and the results, too, of successful countermeasures. The form is fluid, the 'meaning' [*Sinn*] even more so . . . It is no different inside any individual organism: every time the whole grows appreciably, the 'meaning' [*Sinn*] of the individual organs shifts, – sometimes the partial destruction of organs, the reduction in their number (for example, by the destruction of intermediary parts) can be a sign of increasing vigour and perfection. To speak plainly: even the partial *reduction in usefulness*, decay and degeneration, loss of meaning [*Sinn*] and functional purpose, in short death, make up the conditions of true *progressus:* always appearing, as it does, in the form of the will and way to *greater power* and always emerging victorious at the cost of countless smaller forces. The amount of 'progress' can actually be *measured* according to how much has had to be sacrificed to it; man's sacrifice *en bloc* to the prosperity of one single *stronger* species of man – that *would be* progress . . . – I lay stress on this major point of historical method, especially as it runs counter to just that prevailing instinct and fashion which would much rather come to terms with absolute randomness, and even the mechanistic senselessness of all events, than the theory that a *power-will* is acted out in all that happens. The democratic idiosyncrasy of being against everything that dominates and wants to dominate, the modern *misarchism* (to coin a bad word for a bad thing) has gradually shaped and dressed itself up as intellectual, most intellectual, so much so that it already, today, little by little penetrates the strictest, seemingly most objective sciences, and is *allowed* to do so; indeed, I think it has already become master of the whole of physiology and biology, to their detriment, naturally, by spiriting away their basic concept, that of actual *activity*. On the other hand, the pressure of this idiosyncrasy forces 'adaptation' into the foreground, which is a second-rate activity, just a reactivity, indeed life itself has been defined as an increasingly efficient inner adaptation to external circumstances (Herbert Spencer). But this is to misunderstand the essence of life, its *will to power*, we overlook the prime importance that the spontaneous, aggressive, expansive, re-interpreting, re-directing and formative forces have, which 'adaptation' follows only when they have had their effect; in the organism itself, the dominant role of these highest functionaries, in whom the life-will is active and manifests itself, is denied. One recalls what Huxley reproached Spencer with, – his 'administrative nihilism': but we are dealing with *more* than 'administration' . . .

13

– To return to our topic, namely *punishment*, we have to distinguish between two of its aspects: one is its relative *permanence*, the custom, the act, the 'drama', a certain strict sequence of procedures, the other is its *fluidity*, its meaning [*Sinn*], purpose and expectation, which is linked to the carrying out of such procedures. And here, without further ado, I assume, *per analogiam*, according to the major point of historical method

just developed, that the procedure itself will be something older, pre-
dating its use as punishment, that the latter was only *inserted* and interpreted into the procedure (which had existed for a long time though it
was thought of in a different way), in short, that the matter is *not* to be
understood in the way our naïve moral and legal genealogists assumed up
till now, who all thought the procedure had been *invented* for the purpose
of punishment, just as people used to think that the hand had been
invented for the purpose of grasping. With regard to the other element in
punishment, the fluid one, its 'meaning', the concept 'punishment' presents, at a very late stage of culture (for example, in Europe today), not
just one meaning but a whole synthesis of 'meanings' [*Sinnen*]: the
history of punishment up to now in general, the history of its use for a
variety of purposes, finally crystallizes[55] in a kind of unity which is difficult to dissolve back into its elements, difficult to analyse and, this has to
be stressed, is absolutely *undefinable*. (Today it is impossible to say precisely *why* people are actually punished: all concepts in which an entire
process is semiotically concentrated defy definition; only something
which has no history can be defined.) At an earlier stage, however, the
synthesis of 'meanings' appeared much easier to undo and shift; we can
still make out how, in every single case, the elements of the synthesis
change valence and alter the order in which they occur so that now this,
then that element stands out and dominates, to the detriment of the
others, indeed, in some circumstances one element (for example, the
purpose of deterrence) seems to overcome all the rest. To at least give an
impression of how uncertain, belated and haphazard the 'meaning' of
punishment is, and how one and the same procedure can be used, interpreted and adapted for fundamentally different projects: you have here a
formula that suggested itself to me on the basis of relatively restricted and
random material. Punishment as a means of rendering harmless, of pre-
venting further harm. Punishment as payment of a debt to the creditor in
any form (even one of emotional compensation). Punishment as a means
of isolating a disturbance of balance, to prevent further spread of the disturbance. Punishment as a means of inspiring the fear of those who determine and execute punishment. Punishment as a sort of counter-balance
to the privileges which the criminal has enjoyed up till now (for example,
by using him as a slave in the mines). Punishment as a rooting-out of
degenerate elements (sometimes a whole branch, as in Chinese law:

[55] Cf. Stendhal, *De l'amour*, chs 11ff.

whereby it becomes a means of keeping the race pure or maintaining a social type). Punishment as a festival, in the form of violating and mocking an enemy, once he is finally conquered. Punishment as an *aide memoire*, either for the person suffering the punishment – so called 'reform', or for those who see it carried out. Punishment as payment of a fee stipulated by the power which protects the wrongdoer from the excesses of revenge. Punishment as a compromise with the natural state of revenge, in so far as the latter is still nurtured and claimed as a privilege by more powerful clans. Punishment as a declaration of war and a war measure against an enemy of peace, law, order, authority, who is fought as dangerous to the life of the community, in breach of the contract on which the community is founded, as a rebel, a traitor and breaker of the peace, with all the means war can provide. –

14

The list is certainly not complete; punishment can clearly be seen to be richly laden with benefits of all kinds. This provides all the more justification for us to deduct one *supposed* benefit that counts as its most characteristic in popular perception, – faith in punishment, which is shaky today for several reasons, has its strongest support in precisely this. Punishment is supposed to have the value of arousing the *feeling of guilt* in the guilty party; in it, people look for the actual *instrumentum* of the mental reflex which we call 'bad conscience' or 'pang of conscience'. But by doing this, people are violating reality and psychology even as it is today: and much more so for the longest period in the history of mankind, its prehistory! The real pang of conscience, precisely amongst criminals and convicts, is something extremely rare, prisons and gaols are *not* nurseries where this type of gnawing pang chooses to thrive: – on this, all conscientious observers are agreed, in many cases reaching such a conclusion reluctantly and against their personal inclinations. On the whole, punishment makes men harder and colder, it concentrates, it sharpens the feeling of alienation; it strengthens the power to resist. If it does happen that a man's vigour is broken, resulting in his wretched prostration and self-abasement, a result of this sort is certainly less edifying than the average effect of punishment: as characterised by a dry, morose solemnity. If we just think about those centuries *before* the history of mankind, we can safely conclude that the evolution of a feeling of guilt was most strongly *impeded* through punishment, – at any rate, with regard to the victims on whom the primitive measures were carried out. Nor must we underestimate the degree to which the mere sight of the judicial executive procedures inhibits the criminal himself from experiencing his act, his mode of conduct, as reprehensible *as such*: because he sees the same kind of action practised in the service of justice and given approval, practised with a good conscience: like spying, duping, bribing, setting traps, the whole intricate and wily skills of the policeman and prosecutor, as well as the most thorough robbery, violence, slander, imprisonment, torture and murder, carried out without even having emotion as an excuse, all practices that are manifest in the various kinds of punishment, – none of which is seen by his judges as a depraved and condemned act *as such*, but only in certain respects and applications. 'Bad conscience', the most uncanny and most interesting plant of our earthly vegetation, did *not* grow in this soil, – in fact, for most of the time it did *not* enter the consciousness of those who judged and punished that they were dealing with a 'guilty party'. Instead, it was a question of someone who had caused harm, an irresponsible piece of fate. He himself, the recipient of punishment, which again descended like a piece of fate, felt no 'inner pain' beyond what he would feel if something unforeseen suddenly happened, a terrible natural disaster, a boulder falling on him and crushing him, where resistance is futile.

15

Spinoza became aware of this in a way that made him show his true colours (to the annoyance of his critics, who systematically *attempt* to misunderstand him on this point, Kuno Fischer,[56] for example), when, one afternoon, rummaging around among who knows what memories, he turned his attention to the question of what actually remained for him, himself, of that famous *morsus conscientiae*[57] – he who had relegated good and evil to man's imagination and angrily defended the honour of his 'free' God against the blasphemers who asserted that God operates everything *sub ratione boni*[58] ('but that would mean that God is subject to fate and would really be the greatest of all absurdities' –).[59] For Spinoza, the world had returned to that state of innocence in which it had lain before the invention of bad conscience: what had then become of *morsus*

---

[56] Cf. his *Geschichte der neueren Philosophie* (Heidelberg, 1865), 1.2.
[57] 'bite of conscience'. Cf. Spinoza, *Ethics* III, Definitions XVI, XVII, XXVI.
[58] 'to attain some good'.
[59] Spinoza, *Ethics* Proposition II scholium 2.

conscientiae? 'The opposite of *gaudium*',[60] he finally said to himself, '– a sadness accompanied by the notion of a past event which turned out contrary to expectation.' *Eth iii, Propos. xviii Schol. i ii.* For millennia, wrongdoers overtaken by punishment have felt *no different than Spinoza* with regard to their 'offence': 'something has gone unexpectedly wrong here', *not* 'I ought not to have done that' –, they submitted to punishment as you submit to illness or misfortune or death, with that brave, unrebellious fatalism that still gives the Russians, for example, an advantage over us Westerners in the way they handle life. If, in those days, there was any criticism of the deed, it came from intelligence, which practised criticism: we must certainly seek the actual *effect* of punishment primarily in the sharpening of intelligence, in a lengthening of the memory, in a will to be more cautious, less trusting, to go about things more circumspectly from now on, in the recognition that one was, once and for all, too weak for many things, in a sort of improvement of self-assessment. What can largely be achieved by punishment, in man or beast, is the increase of fear, the intensification of intelligence, the mastering of desires: punishment *tames* man in this way but does not make him 'better', – we would be more justified in asserting the opposite. ('You can learn from your mistakes' as the saying goes, but what you learn also makes you bad. Fortunately it often enough makes you stupid.)

16

At this point I can no longer avoid giving a first, preliminary expression to my own theory on the origin of 'bad conscience': it is not easy to get a hearing for this hypothesis and it needs to be pondered, watched and slept on. I look on bad conscience as a serious illness to which man was forced to succumb by the pressure of the most fundamental of all changes which he experienced, – that change whereby he finally found himself imprisoned within the confines of society and peace. It must have been no different for these semi-animals, happily adapted to the wilderness, war, the wandering life and adventure than it was for the sea animals when they were forced to either become land animals or perish – at one go, all instincts were devalued and 'suspended'. Now they had to walk on their feet and 'carry themselves', whereas they had been carried by the water up till then: a terrible heaviness bore down on them. They felt they were

---

[60] 'gladness'.

clumsy at performing the simplest task, they did not have their familiar guide any more for this new, unknown world, those regulating impulses that unconsciously led them to safety – the poor things were reduced to relying on thinking, inference, calculation, and the connecting of cause with effect, that is, to relying on their 'consciousness', that most impoverished and error-prone organ! I do not think there has ever been such a feeling of misery on earth, such a leaden discomfort, – and meanwhile, the old instincts had not suddenly ceased to make their demands! But it was difficult and seldom possible to give in to them: they mainly had to seek new and as it were underground gratifications. All instincts which are not discharged outwardly *turn inwards* – this is what I call the *internalization* of man: with it there now evolves in man what will later be called his 'soul'. The whole inner world, originally stretched thinly as though between two layers of skin, was expanded and extended itself and gained depth, breadth and height in proportion to the degree that the external discharge of man's instincts was *obstructed*. Those terrible bulwarks with which state organizations protected themselves against the old instincts of freedom – punishments are a primary instance of this kind of bulwark – had the result that all those instincts of the wild, free, roving man were turned backwards, *against man himself*. Animosity, cruelty, the pleasure of pursuing, raiding, changing and destroying – all this was pitted against the person who had such instincts: *that* is the origin of 'bad conscience'. Lacking external enemies and obstacles, and forced into the oppressive narrowness and conformity of custom, man impatiently ripped himself apart, persecuted himself, gnawed at himself, gave himself no peace and abused himself, this animal who battered himself raw on the bars of his cage and who is supposed to be 'tamed'; man, full of emptiness and torn apart with homesickness for the desert, has had to create from within himself an adventure, a torture-chamber, an unsafe and hazardous wilderness – this fool, this prisoner consumed with longing and despair, became the inventor of 'bad conscience'. With it, however, the worst and most insidious illness was introduced, one from which mankind has not yet recovered; man's sickness of *man*, of *himself*: as the result of a forcible breach with his animal past, a simultaneous leap and fall into new situations and conditions of existence, a declaration of war against all the old instincts on which, up till then, his strength, pleasure and formidableness had been based. Let us immediately add that, on the other hand, the prospect of an animal soul turning against itself, taking a part against itself, was something so new, profound, unheard-of, puzzling, contradictory and *momentous* [*Zukunftsvolles*] on earth that the whole character of the world changed in an essential way. Indeed, a divine audience was needed to appreciate the spectacle that began then, but the end of which is not yet in sight, – a spectacle too subtle, too wonderful, too paradoxical to be allowed to be played senselessly unobserved on some ridiculous planet! Since that time, man has been *included* among the most unexpected and exciting throws of dice played by Heraclitus' 'great child', call him Zeus or fate,[61] – he arouses interest, tension, hope, almost certainty for himself, as though something were being announced through him, were being prepared, as though man were not an end but just a path, an episode, a bridge, a great promise . . .

17

The first assumption in my theory on the origin of bad conscience is that the alteration was not gradual and voluntary and did not represent an organic assimilation into new circumstances, but was a breach, a leap, a compulsion, an inescapable fate that nothing could ward off, which occasioned no struggle, not even any *ressentiment*. A second assumption, however, is that the shaping of a population, which had up till now been unrestrained and shapeless, into a fixed form, as happened at the beginning with an act of violence, could only be concluded with acts of violence, – that consequently the oldest 'state' emerged as a terrible tyranny, as a repressive and ruthless machinery, and continued working until the raw material of people and semi-animals had been finally not just kneaded and made compliant, but *shaped*. I used the word 'state': it is obvious who is meant by this – some pack of blond beasts of prey, a conqueror and master race, which, organized on a war footing, and with the power to organize, unscrupulously lays its dreadful paws on a populace which, though it might be vastly greater in number, is still shapeless and shifting. In this way, the 'state' began on earth: I think I have dispensed with the fantasy which has it begin with a 'contract'. Whoever can command, whoever is a 'master' by nature, whoever appears violent in deed and gesture – what is he going to care about contracts! Such beings cannot be reckoned with, they come like fate, without cause, reason, consideration or pretext, they appear just like lightning appears, too terrible, sudden, convincing and 'other' even to be hated. What they do is to create and

---

[61] Heraclitus, Fragment 52.

imprint forms instinctively, they are the most involuntary, unconscious artists there are: – where they appear, soon something new arises, a structure of domination [*Herrschafts–Gebilde*] that *lives*, in which parts and functions are differentiated and related to one another, in which there is absolutely no room for anything that does not first acquire 'meaning' with regard to the whole. They do not know what guilt, responsibility, consideration are, these born organizers; they are ruled by that terrible inner artist's egoism which has a brazen countenance and sees itself justified to all eternity by the 'work', like the mother in her child. *They* are not the ones in whom 'bad conscience' grew; that is obvious – but it would not have grown *without* them, this ugly growth would not be there if a huge amount of freedom had not been driven from the world, or at least driven from sight and, at the same time, made *latent* by the pressure of their hammer blows and artists' violence. This *instinct of freedom*, forcibly made latent – we have already seen how – this instinct of freedom forced back, repressed, incarcerated within itself and finally able to discharge and unleash itself only against itself: that, and that alone, is *bad conscience* in its beginnings.

18

We must be wary of thinking disparagingly about this whole phenomenon because it is inherently ugly and painful. Fundamentally, it is the same active force as the one that is at work on a grand scale in those artists of violence and organizers, and that builds states, which here, internally, and on a smaller, pettier scale, turned backwards, in the 'labyrinth of the breast', as Goethe would say,[62] creates bad conscience for itself, and builds negative ideals, it is that very *instinct for freedom* (put into my language: the will to power): except that the material on which the formative and rapacious nature of this force vents itself is precisely man himself, his whole animal old self – and *not*, as in that greater and more eye-catching phenomenon, the *other* man, the *other* men. This secret self-violation, this artist's cruelty, this desire to give form to oneself as a piece of difficult, resisting, suffering matter, to brand it with a will, a critique, a contradiction, a contempt, a 'no', this uncanny, terrible but joyous labour of a soul voluntarily split within itself, which makes itself suffer out of the pleasure of making suffer, this whole *active* 'bad conscience' has finally – we have

[62] In the last strophe of his poem 'An den Mond' ('To the Moon') (1778).

already guessed – as true womb of ideal and imaginative events, brought a wealth of novel, disconcerting beauty and affirmation to light, and perhaps for the first time, beauty *itself* . . . What would be 'beautiful', if the contrary to it had not first come to awareness of itself, if ugliness had not first said to itself: 'I am ugly'? . . . At least, after this clue, one puzzle will be less puzzling, namely how an ideal, something beautiful, can be hinted at in self-contradictory concepts such as *selflessness, self-denial, self-sacrifice*, and furthermore, I do not doubt that we know one thing –, what kind of *pleasure* it is which, from the start, the selfless, the self-denying, the self-sacrificing feel: this pleasure belongs to cruelty. – So much, for the time being, on the descent of the 'unegoistic' as a *moral* value and on the delineation of the ground on which this value has grown: only bad conscience, only the will to self-violation provides the precondition for the *value* of the unegoistic. –

19

Bad conscience is a sickness, there is no point in denying it, but a sickness rather like pregnancy. Let us examine the conditions under which this sickness reached its most terrible and sublime peak: – we shall see what, with this, really entered the world. But we shall need a great deal of staying power, – and first we have to return to an earlier point. The relationship of a debtor to his creditor in civil law, about which I have written at length already, was for a second time transformed through interpretation, in a historically extremely strange and curious manner, into a relationship in which it is perhaps least comprehensible to us modern men: that is the relationship of the *present generation* to their *forebears*. Within the original tribal association – we are talking about primeval times – the living generation always acknowledged a legal obligation towards the earlier generation, and in particular towards the earliest, which founded the tribe (and this was not just a sentimental tie: this latter could, with good reason, be denied altogether for the longest period of the human race). There is a prevailing conviction that the tribe *exists* only because of the sacrifices and deeds of the forefathers, – and that these have to be *paid back* with sacrifices and deeds: people recognize an *indebtedness* [*Schuld*], which continually increases because these ancestors continue to exist as mighty spirits, giving the tribe new advantages and lending it some of their power. Do they do this for nothing, perhaps? But there is no 'for nothing' for those raw and 'spiritually impoverished' ages. What can people give them in return? Sacrifices (originally as food in the crudest sense), feasts, chapels, tributes, above all, obedience – for all traditions are, as works of the ancestors, also their rules and orders –: do people ever give them enough? This suspicion remains and grows: from time to time it exacts a payment on a grand scale, something immense as a repayment to the 'creditor' (the infamous sacrifice of the first-born, for example, blood, human blood in any case). Following this line of thought, the *dread* of the ancestor and his power, the consciousness of debts towards him, increases inevitably, in direct proportion to the increase in power of the tribe itself, that is, in proportion as the tribe itself becomes ever more victorious, independent, honoured and feared. And not the other way round! Every step towards the weakening of the tribe, all unfortunate calamities, all signs of degeneration and imminent disintegration, always *lessen* rather than increase the dread of the spirit of its founder, and lead to an ever lower opinion of his sagacity, providence and powerful presence. If you think this sort of crude logic through to the end: it follows that through the hallucination of the growing dread itself, the ancestors of the *most powerful* tribes must have grown to an immense stature and must have been pushed into the obscurity of divine mystery and transcendence: – inevitably the ancestor himself is finally transfigured into a *god*. Perhaps we have here the actual origin of gods, an origin, then, in *fear!* . . . And whoever should deem fit to add: 'but in piety, too!' would have difficulty in justifying the claim for the longest period of the human race, prehistory. All the more so, however, would he be right, for the *middle* period in which the noble tribes developed: – who actually did repay, with interest, their founders, their ancestors (heroes, gods) with all the attributes which, in the meantime, had become manifest in themselves, the *noble* attributes. Later, we shall take another look at the way gods are ennobled and exalted (which is not at all to say they were 'hallowed'): but let us, for the present, pursue the course of this whole development of the consciousness of guilt to its conclusion.

20

The awareness of having debts to gods did not, as history teaches, come to an end even after the decline of 'communities' organized on the principle of blood relationship; just as man inherited the concepts of 'good and bad' from the nobility of lineage (together with its psychological basic tendency to institute orders of rank), he also inherited, along with the divinities of tribes and clans, the burden of unpaid debts and the longing for them to be settled. (Those large populations of slaves and serfs who adapted themselves to the divinity cults of their masters, whether through compulsion, submission or mimicry, form the transitional stage: from them, the inheritance overflows in every direction.) The feeling of indebtedness towards a deity continued to grow for several millennia, and indeed always in the same proportion as the concept of and feeling for God grew in the world and was carried aloft. (The whole history of ethnic battles, victories, reconciliations and mergers, and everything that precedes the eventual rank-ordering of the diverse elements of the population in every great racial synthesis, is mirrored in the genealogical chaos of their gods, in the legends of their battles, victories and reconciliations; the progression to universal empires is always the progress to universal deities at the same time: despotism, with its subjugation of the independent nobility, always prepares the way for some sort of monotheism as well.) The advent of the Christian God as the maximal god yet achieved, thus also brought about the appearance of the greatest feeling of indebtedness on earth. Assuming that we have now started in the *reverse* direction, we should be justified in deducing, with no little probability, that from the unstoppable decline in faith in the Christian God there is, even now, a considerable decline in the consciousness of human debt; indeed, the possibility cannot be rejected out of hand that the complete and definitive victory of atheism might release humanity from this whole feeling of being indebted towards its beginnings, its *causa prima*. Atheism and a sort of *second innocence* belong together. –

21

So much for a brief and rough preliminary outline of the connection between the concepts 'debt/guilt' and 'duty' and religious precepts: I have so far intentionally set aside the actual moralization of these concepts (the way they are pushed back into conscience; more precisely, the way *bad* conscience is woven together with the concept of God), and at the conclusion of the last section I actually spoke as though this moralization did not exist, consequently, as though these concepts would necessarily come to an end once the basic premise no longer applied, the credence we lend our 'creditor', God. The facts diverge from this in a terrible way. With the moralization of the concepts debt/guilt and duty and their relegation to *bad* conscience, we have, in reality, an attempt to *reverse* the direction of the development I have described, or at least halt its movement: now the prospect for a once-and-for-all payment *is to be* foreclosed, out of pessimism, now our glance *is to* bounce and recoil disconsolately off an iron impossibility, now those concepts 'debt' and 'duty' *are to be* reversed – but against *whom?* It is indisputable: firstly against the 'debtor', in whom bad conscience now so firmly establishes itself, eating into him, broadening out and growing, like a polyp, so wide and deep that in the end, with the impossibility of paying back the debt, is conceived the impossibility of discharging the penance, the idea that it cannot be paid off (*'eternal* punishment'); ultimately, however, against the 'creditor', and here we should think of the *causa prima* of man, the beginning of the human race, of his ancestor who is now burdened with a curse ('Adam', 'original sin', 'the will in bondage'), or of nature, from whose womb man originated and to whom the principle of evil is imputed (diabolization of nature), or of existence in general, which is left standing as *inherently worthless* (a nihilistic turning-away from existence, the desire for nothingness or desire for the 'antithesis', to be other, Buddhism and such like) – until, all at once, we confront the paradoxical and horrifying expedient through which a martyred humanity has sought temporary relief, *Christianity's* stroke of genius: none other than God sacrificing himself for man's debt, none other than God paying himself back, God as the only one able to redeem man from what, to man himself, has become irredeemable – the creditor sacrificing himself for his debtor, out of love (would you credit it? –), out of *love* for his debtor! . . .

22

You will already have guessed *what* has really gone on with all this and *behind* all this: that will to torment oneself, that suppressed cruelty of animal man who has been frightened back into himself and given an inner life, incarcerated in the 'state' to be tamed, and has discovered bad conscience so that he can hurt himself, after the *more natural* outlet of this wish to hurt had been blocked, – this man of bad conscience has seized on religious presupposition in order to provide his self-torture with its most horrific hardness and sharpness. Debt towards *God*: this thought becomes an instrument of torture. In 'God' he seizes upon the ultimate antithesis he can find to his real and irredeemable animal instincts, he reinterprets these self-same animal instincts as debt/guilt before God (as animosity, insurrection, rebellion against the 'master', the 'father', the primeval ancestor and beginning of the world), he pitches himself into the contradiction of 'God' and 'Devil', he emits every 'no' which he says to himself, nature, naturalness and the reality of his being as a 'yes', as existing, living, real, as God, as the holiness of God, as God-the-Judge, as God-the-Hangman, as the beyond, as eternity, as torture without end, as hell, as immeasurable punishment and guilt. We have here a sort of madness of the will showing itself in mental cruelty which is absolutely unparalleled: man's *will* to find himself guilty and condemned without hope of reprieve, his *will* to think of himself as punished, without the punishment ever being equivalent to the level of guilt, his *will* to infect and poison the fundamentals of things with the problem of punishment and guilt in order to cut himself off, once and for all, from the way out of this labyrinth of 'fixed ideas', this *will* to set up an ideal – that of a 'holy God' –, in order to be palpably convinced of his own absolute worthlessness in the face of this ideal. Alas for this crazy, pathetic beast man! What ideas he has, what perversity, what hysterical nonsense, what *bestiality of thought* immediately erupts, the moment he is prevented, if only gently, from being a *beast in deed*! . . . This is all almost excessively interesting, but there is also a black, gloomy, unnerving sadness to it as well, so that one has to force oneself to forgo peering for too long into these abysses. Here is *sickness*, without a doubt, the most terrible sickness ever to rage in man: – and whoever is still able to hear (but people have no ear for it nowadays! –) how the shout of *love* has rung out during this night of torture and absurdity, the shout of the most yearning rapture, of salvation through *love*, turns away, gripped by an unconquerable horror . . . There is so much in man that is horrifying! . . . The world has been a madhouse for too long! . . .

23

That should be enough, once and for all, about the descent of the 'holy God'. – That the conception of gods does not, as *such*, necessarily lead to that deterioration of the imagination which we had to think about for a moment, that there are *nobler* ways of making use of the invention of gods than man's self-crucifixion and self-abuse, ways in which Europe excelled during the last millennia, – this can fortunately be deduced from any glance at the *Greek gods*, these reflections of noble and proud men in whom the *animal* in man felt deified, did *not* tear itself apart and did *not* rage against itself! These Greeks, for most of the time, used their gods expressly to keep 'bad conscience' at bay so that they could carry on enjoying their freedom of soul: therefore, the opposite of the way Christendom made use of its God. They went *very far* in this, these marvellous, lion-hearted children; and no less an authority than the Homeric Zeus gives them to understand that they are making it too easy for themselves. 'Strange!', he says on one occasion – he is talking about the case of Aegisthus, a *very* bad case –

> *Strange how much the mortals complain about the gods!* We alone cause evil, *they claim, but they themselves, through folly, bring about their own distress, even contrary to fate!*[63]

Yet we can immediately hear and see that even this Olympian observer and judge has no intention of bearing them a grudge for this and thinking ill of them: 'How foolish they are' is what he thinks when the mortals misbehave, – 'foolishness', 'stupidity', a little 'mental disturbance', this much even the Greeks of the strongest, bravest period *allowed* themselves as a reason for much that was bad or calamitous: – foolishness, *not* sin! you understand? . . . But even this mental disturbance was a problem – 'Yes, how is this possible? Where can this have actually come from with minds like *ours*, we men of high lineage, happy, well-endowed, high-born, noble and virtuous?' – for centuries, the noble Greek asked himself this in the face of any incomprehensible atrocity or crime with which one of his peers had sullied himself. 'A *god* must have confused him', he said to himself at last, shaking his head . . . This solution is *typical* for the Greeks . . . In this way, the gods served to justify man to a certain degree, even if he was in the wrong they served as causes of evil – they did not, at that time, take the punishment on themselves, but rather, as is *nobler*, the guilt . . .

24

– I shall conclude with three question marks, that much is plain. 'Is an ideal set up or destroyed here?' you might ask me . . . But have you ever asked yourselves properly how costly the setting up of *every* ideal on earth has been? How much reality always had to be vilified and misunderstood in the process, how many lies had to be sanctified, how much conscience had to be troubled, how much 'god' had to be sacrificed every time? If a

---

[63] *Odyssey* I. 32–4.

shrine is to be set up, a *shrine has to be destroyed*: that is the law – show me an example where this does not apply! . . . We moderns have inherited millennia of conscience-vivisection and animal-torture inflicted on ourselves: we have had most practice in it, are perhaps artists in the field, in any case it is our *raffinement* and the indulgence of our taste. For too long, man has viewed his natural inclinations with an 'evil eye', so that they finally came to be intertwined with 'bad conscience' in him. A reverse experiment should be possible *in principle* – but who has sufficient strength? – by this, I mean an intertwining of bad conscience with *perverse* inclinations, all those other-worldly aspirations, alien to the senses, the instincts, to nature, to animals, in short all the ideals which up to now have been hostile to life and have defamed the world. To whom should we turn with *such* hopes and claims today? . . . We would have none other than the *good* men against us; and, as is fitting, the lazy, the complacent, the vain, the zealous, the tired . . . What is more deeply offensive to others and separates us more profoundly from them than allowing them to realize something of the severity and high-mindedness with which we treat ourselves? And again – how co-operative and pleasant everyone is towards us, as soon as we do as everyone else does and 'let ourselves go' like everyone else! . . . For that purpose, we would need *another* sort of spirit than those we are likely to encounter in this age: spirits who are strengthened by wars and victories, for whom conquest, adventure, danger and even pain have actually become a necessity; they would also need to be acclimatized to thinner air higher up, to winter treks, ice and mountains in every sense, they would need a sort of sublime nastiness [*Bosheit*] itself, a final, very self-assured wilfulness of insight which belongs to great health, in brief and unfortunately, they would need precisely this *great health*! . . . Is this at all possible today? . . . But some time, in a stronger age than this mouldy, self-doubting present day, he will have to come to us, the *redeeming* man of great love and contempt, the creative spirit who is pushed out of any position 'outside' or 'beyond' by his surging strength again and again, whose solitude will be misunderstood by the people as though it were flight *from* reality –: whereas it is just his way of being absorbed, buried and immersed in reality so that from it, when he emerges into the light again, he can return with the *redemption* of this reality: redeem it from the curse which its ideal has placed on it up till now. This man of the future will redeem us, not just from the ideal held up till now, but also from those things *which had to arise from it*, from the great nausea, the will to nothingness, from nihilism, that stroke of midday and of great decision that makes the will free again, which gives earth its purpose and man his hope again, this Antichrist and anti–nihilist, this conqueror of God and of nothingness – *he must come one day* . . .

25

– But what am I saying? Enough! Enough! At this point just one thing is proper, silence: otherwise I shall be misappropriating something that belongs to another, younger man, one 'with more future', one stronger than me – something to which *Zarathustra* alone is entitled, *Zarathustra the Godless* . . .

Third essay: what do ascetic ideals mean?

Carefree, mocking, violent – this is how wisdom wants *us:* she is a woman, all she ever loves is a warrior.

Thus spoke Zarathustra

I

What do ascetic ideals mean? – With artists, nothing, or too many different things; with philosophers and scholars, something like a nose and sense for the most favourable conditions of higher intellectuality [*Geistigkeit*]; with women, at most, one *more* seductive charm, a little *morbidezza* on fair flesh, the angelic expression on a pretty, fat animal; with physiological causalities and the disgruntled (with the *majority* of mortals), an attempt to see themselves as 'too good' for this world, a saintly form of debauchery, their chief weapon in the battle against long-drawn-out pain and boredom; with priests, the actual priestly faith, their best instrument of power and also the 'ultimate' sanction of their power; with saints, an excuse to hibernate at last, their *novissima gloria cupido*,[64] their rest in nothingness ('God'), their form of madness. *That* the ascetic ideal has meant so much to man reveals a basic fact of human will, its *horror vacui; it needs an aim –*, and it prefers to will *nothingness* rather than *not* will. – Do I make myself understood? . . . Have I made myself understood? . . '*Absolutely not, sir!*' – So let us start at the beginning.

---

[64] 'the desire for glory, which is the last thing they will rid themselves of' (Tacitus, *Histories* Iv.6). Nietzsche cites the full phrase in §330 of *The Gay Science*.

2

What do ascetic ideals mean? – Or let me take an individual example, in connection with which my opinion has often been sought, what, for example, does it mean if an artist like Richard Wagner pays homage to chastity in his old age? I accept that he has always done this in a certain sense; but only at the very end in an ascetic sense. What does this change of 'sense' mean, this radical alteration of 'sense'? – because it was such a change, Wagner made a complete turnabout and became his exact opposite. What does it mean, if an artist makes such a turnabout? . . . Here we at once remember, providing we want to pause over the question a little, the best, strongest, most cheerful and *courageous* time which Wagner perhaps had in his life: it was when the idea of Luther's wedding pre-occupied him so deeply. Who knows what chance events actually had to occur for us to possess *Die Meistersinger* instead of that wedding music? And how much of the latter can still be heard in the former? But there's no doubt that even with 'Luther's Wedding', we would have had a praise of chastity. But also a praise of sensuality: – and that would have seemed to me to be quite right, it would have been quite 'Wagnerian' like that. For there is not, necessarily, an antithesis between chastity and sensuality; every good marriage, every real affair of the heart transcends this antithesis. I think Wagner would have done well to again remind his Germans of this *pleasant* fact with the help of a nice, plucky Luther comedy, because there always are and have been so many people amongst the Germans who slander sensuality; and perhaps Luther's achievement is nowhere greater than precisely in having had the courage of his own *sensuality* (– at the time it was delicately referred to as 'evangelical freedom' . . .). Even in a case where there really is an antithesis between chastity and sensuality, there is fortunately no need for it to be a tragic antithesis. This ought to be true for all healthy, cheerful mortals who are far from seeing their precarious balancing act between 'animal and angel' as necessarily one of the arguments against life, – the best and the brightest amongst them, like Goethe, like Hafiz, actually found in it one *more* of life's charms. Such 'contradictions' are what makes life so enticing . . . On the other hand, it is only too clear that if pigs who have fallen on hard times are made to praise chastity – and there are such pigs! – they will only see in it and praise the opposite of themselves, the opposite of pigs who have fallen on hard times – and oh! what a tragic grunting and excitement there will be! We can just imagine – that embarrassing and superfluous antithesis that Richard Wagner undeniably wanted to set to music and stage at the end of his life. *But why?* it is fair to inquire. For what were pigs to him, what are they to us? –

3

While we are here, we cannot avoid asking what concern that manly (oh-so-unmanly) 'country bumpkin', that poor devil and child of nature, Parsifal, was to Wagner, who ended up using such suspect means to turn him into a Catholic – and what? was this Parsifal meant to be taken *seriously?* We might be tempted to assume the opposite, even to wish, – that Wagner's *Parsifal* was meant to be funny, like an epilogue, or satyr play with which the tragedian Wagner wanted to take leave of us, of himself and above all of *tragedy* in a manner fitting and worthy of himself, namely by indulging in an excessive bout of the most extreme and deliberate parody of the tragic itself, of the whole, hideous, earthly seriousness and misery from the past, of the finally defeated, *crudest form* of perversion, of the ascetic ideal. This would have been, as I said, worthy of a great tragedian: in which capacity, like every artist, he only reaches the final summit of his achievement when he knows how to see himself and his art *beneath* him, – and knows how to *laugh* at himself. Is Wagner's *Parsifal* his secret, superior laugh at himself, his triumph at attaining the final, supreme freedom of the artist, his artistic transcendence? As I said, it would be nice to think so: because what would an *intentionally serious* Parsifal be like? Do we really need to see in him 'the spawn of an insane hatred of knowledge, mind and sensuality' (as someone once argued against me)? A curse on the senses and the mind in one breath of hate? An apostasy and return to sickly Christian and obscurantist ideals? And finally an actual self-denial, self-annulment on the part of an artist who had hitherto wanted the opposite with all the force of his will, namely for his art to be the *highest intellectualization and sensualization?* And not just his art: his life too. Recall how enthusiastically Wagner followed in the footsteps of the philosopher Feuerbach in his day: Feuerbach's dictum of 'healthy sensuality'[65] – that sounded like the pronouncement of salvation to the Wagner of the 1830s and 1840s, as to so many Germans (– they called themselves '*Young* Germans'). Did he finally *learn something different?* Because it at least seems that at the end, he had the will to *teach*

---

[65] Feuerbach's *Principle of the Philosophy of the Future* appeared in 1843. See esp. §§31 ff. of this work.

something different . . . and not just by having the trombones of *Parsifal*[66] sound out the way they do from the stage itself: – in the gloomy writings of his latter years, unfree and helpless as they are, we find a hundred passages revealing a secret desire and will, a hesitant, uncertain, unacknowledged will to preach a straightforward reversion, conversion, denial, Christianity, medievalism, and to say to his disciples: 'It is nothing! Seek salvation somewhere else!' Even the 'Redeemer's blood' is invoked once. . . . [67]

4

I have to speak my mind in a case like this, which is embarrassing in many ways – and it is a *typical* case – : it is certainly better if we separate an artist sufficiently far from his work as not immediately to take the man as seriously as his work. After all, he is merely the precondition for the work, the womb, the soil, sometimes the manure and fertilizer on which it grows, – and as such, he is something we have to forget about in most cases if we want to enjoy the work. The insight into the *descent* of a work concerns the physiologists and vivisectionists of the mind: but not aesthetic men and artists, and never will! The man who wrote and shaped *Parsifal* was as little spared the profound, thorough-going and indeed terrible tendency to sink and delve into medieval spiritual conflicts and the hostile falling-off from the sublimity, discipline and rigour of the spirit, a sort of intellectual *perversity* (if I may say so), as a pregnant woman is spared the reactions of nausea and odd cravings of pregnancy: which, as I said, must be *forgotten* if she is to enjoy the child. We should avoid the confusion to which the artist is only too prone, out of psychological contiguity, as the English say, of thinking he *were* identical with what he can portray, invent and express. In fact, *if* he really had that same identity he would simply not be able to portray, invent and express it; Homer would not have created Achilles and Goethe would not have created Faust, if Homer had been an Achilles and Goethe a Faust. A perfect and complete

---

[66] *Parsifal* is scored for three trombones in the orchestra and, quite unusually, six more off stage. Act I begins with the striking effect of all six off-stage trombones playing in unison and unaccompanied. They play a four-bar motif with a rather liturgical character which is one of the main structural elements of the work and which it is easy to associate with the aspiration to a specifically Christian form of love based on the renunciation of sexuality, an aspiration which is a central concern of the opera. Cf. R. Wagner, *Sämtliche Schriften und Dichtungen* (Leipzig, 1911), XII, p. 347.

[67] R. Wagner, *Gesammelte Schriften und Dichtungen* (Leipzig, 1907), X, pp. 280ff.

artist is cut off from what is 'real' and actual for all eternity; on the other hand, we can understand how he can occasionally be so tired of the eternal 'unreality' and falsity of his inner existence that he is driven to despair, – and that he will then probably try to reach into that area strictly forbidden to him, into reality, into real *being*. With what success? We can guess . . . it is the artist's *typical velleity*: that same velleity to which Wagner succumbed in old age and for which he had to pay so dearly and catastrophically (– through it he lost the more valuable amongst his circle of friends). Finally, however, quite apart from this velleity, who could not wish, for Wagner's sake, that he had taken leave of us and of his art in some *other* manner, not with a *Parsifal*, but in a more triumphant, self-confident, Wagnerian manner – in a manner less deceptive, less ambiguous with regard to his general intent, less Schopenhauerian, less nihilistic? . . .

5

– So what do ascetic ideals mean? In the case of an artist, we have concluded: *nothing at all!* . . . Or so many things that it is tantamount to nothing! . . . Let us put aside artists for the time being: their position in the world and *against* the world is far from sufficiently independent for their changing valuations *as such* to merit our attention! Down the ages, they have been the valets of a morality or philosophy or religion: quite apart from the fact that they were, unfortunately, often the all-too-glib courtiers of their hangers-on and patrons and sycophants with a nose for old or indeed up-and-coming forces. At the very least, they always need a defender, a support, an already established authority: artists never stand independently, being alone is against their deepest instincts. So, for example, Richard Wagner took the philosopher Schopenhauer as his front man, his defender, 'when the time came': – we can't even conceive of the possibility of him having the *courage* for an ascetic ideal without the support offered to him by Schopenhauer's philosophy, without the authority of Schopenhauer, which by the 1870s in Europe was *becoming dominant* (and we have not even raised the question whether an artist in the *new* Germany could even have existed at all without the milk of a pious [*fromm*] way of thinking[68] piously devoted to the Reich [*reichsfromm*]). – And with that we come to the more serious

---

[68] Schiller, F., *Wilhelm Tell* IV. 3. 2574. See also n. 3, p. 153.

question: what does it mean if a genuine *philosopher* pays homage to the ascetic ideal, a genuine, independent mind like Schopenhauer, a man and a knight with a brazen countenance who has the courage to be himself, knows how to stand alone and does not wait for the men in front and a nod from on high? – Let us immediately consider here the remarkable and, for many types of person, even fascinating stance of Schopenhauer towards *art*: because this is obviously what *first* caused Richard Wagner to go over to Schopenhauer (talked into it by a poet, as we all know, Herwegh),[69] and he did this to such a degree that a complete theoretical contradiction opened up between his earlier and later aesthetic beliefs, – the former, for example, expressed in *Opera and Drama*, and the latter in the writings published from 1870. In particular, and this is what is perhaps most disconcerting of all, Wagner ruthlessly altered his view of the value and place of *music* itself from then on: what did he care that up till now he had made music a means, a medium, a 'woman' which simply had to have a goal, a man in order to flourish – namely a drama! All at once, he grasped that with Schopenhauer's theory and innovation *more* could be done *in majorem musicae gloriam*,[70] – in fact, with the *sovereignty* of music as Schopenhauer understood it: music set apart from all the other arts, the inherently independent art, *not* providing reflections of the phenomenal world like the other arts, but instead, speaking the language *of the* will itself straight out of the 'abyss', as the latter's most unique, original, direct revelation. With this extraordinary increase in the value placed on music, which seemed to stem from Schopenhauer's philosophy, the *musician* himself suddenly had an unprecedented rise in price: from now on he became an oracle, a priest, in fact, more than a priest, a sort of mouthpiece of the 'in itself' of things, a telephone to the beyond [*ein Telephon des Jenseits*], – from now on, he did not just talk music, this ventriloquist of God, – he talked metaphysics: hardly surprising that one day he ended up talking *ascetic ideals*, is it? . . .

6

Schopenhauer made use of the Kantian version of the aesthetic problem, – although he definitely did not view it with Kantian eyes. Kant

---

[69] Cf. Wagner's autobiography *Mein Leben* (Munich, 1969), pp. 521f.
[70] 'For the greater glory of music'; parallel to the Christian slogan that all things should be done '*ad majorem Dei gloriam*' ('for the greater glory of God').

intended to pay art a tribute when he singled out from the qualities of beauty those which constitute the glory of knowledge: impersonality and universality. Whether or not this was essentially a mistake is not what I am dealing with here; all I want to underline is that Kant, like all philosophers, just considered art and beauty from the position of 'spectator', instead of viewing the aesthetic problem through the experiences of the artist (the creator), and thus inadvertently introduced the 'spectator' himself into the concept 'beautiful'. I just wish this 'spectator' had been sufficiently known to the philosophers of beauty! – I mean as a great *personal* fact and experience, as a fund of strong personal experiences, desires, surprises and pleasures in the field of beauty! But as I fear, the opposite has always been the case: and so we receive definitions from them, right from the start, in which the absence of more sensitive personal experience sits in the shape of a fat worm of basic error, as in that famous definition Kant gives of the beautiful. Kant said: 'Something is beautiful if it gives pleasure *without interest*'.[71] Without interest! Compare this definition with another made by a genuine 'spectator' and artist – Stendhal, who once called the beautiful *une promesse de bonheur*.[72] Here, at any rate, the thing that Kant alone accentuates in aesthetic matters: *le désintéressement*, is *rejected* and eliminated. Who is right, Kant or Stendhal? – However, as our aestheticians never tire of weighing in on Kant's side, saying that under the charm of beauty, *even* naked female statues can be looked at 'without interest', I think we are entitled to laugh a little at their expense: – the experiences of *artists* are 'more interesting' with regard to this tricky point and Pygmalion, at all events, was *not* necessarily an 'unaesthetic man'. Let us think all the better of the innocence of our aestheticians which we see reflected in such arguments, for example, let us pay tribute to Kant for expounding the peculiarities of the sense of touch with the naïvety of a country parson![73] – And now we come back to Schopenhauer, who stood much closer to the arts than Kant and still could not break free of the spell of Kant's definition: why not? The situation is very odd: he interpreted the phrase 'without interest' in the most personal way possible, from an experience which, in his case,

---

[71] I. Kant, *Critique of Judgment* (1790), §2 and 'General Remark on the Exposition of Aesthetic Reflective Judgments'.

[72] Stendhal, *De l'Amour*, ch. XVII (cf. also chs x, xi). Baudelaire also cites and discusses this view of the beautiful in *Le peintre de la vie moderne* (1863), ch. I.

[73] Kant does often sound like a country parson, but one would not have thought this trait particularly salient in his discussion of the sense of touch (*Anthropologie in pragmatischer Hinsicht*, 1st edn (1798), p. 48). Perhaps Nietzsche has some other passage in mind.

must have been one of the most frequently recurring. There are few things about which Schopenhauer speaks with such certainty as the effect of aesthetic contemplation: according to him, it counteracts *sexual* 'interestedness', rather like lupulin and camphor, and he never tired of singing the praises of *this* escape from the 'will' as the great advantage and use of the aesthetic condition. We might even be tempted to ask whether the basic conception of 'will and representation', the thought that redemption from the 'will' could only take place through 'representation', might not originate in a generalization of that sexual experience. (In all questions regarding Schopenhauer's philosophy, by the way, we must not overlook the fact that it is the conception of a twenty-six-year-old young man; so it reflects not just specific characteristics of Schopenhauer himself but also the specifics of that season of life.) For example, let us listen to one of the most explicit of the countless passages he wrote in honour of aesthetics (*World as Will and Representation* I, 231), let us listen to the tone, the suffering, the happiness, the gratitude with which such passages are written. 'This is the painless condition which Epicurus praises as the greatest good and as the condition of the gods; we are, for that moment, relieved of the base craving of the will, we celebrate the sabbath from the penal servitude of volition, the wheel of Ixion stands still' . . . What vehemence of speech! What images of torture and long-drawn-out fatigue! What an almost pathological juxtaposition of time between 'for that moment' and 'the wheel of Ixion', between 'penal servitude of volition' and 'base craving'! – Even granted that Schopenhauer was right about himself a hundred times over, what does this do for an insight into the nature of beauty? Schopenhauer described one effect of beauty, that of calming the will, – but is this even one that occurs regularly? As I said, Stendhal, no less a sensualist than Schopenhauer but with a more happily adjusted personality, emphasizes another effect of beauty: 'beauty *promises* happiness', to him, the fact of the matter is precisely the *excitement of the will* ('of interest') through beauty. And could we not, finally, accuse Schopenhauer himself of thinking, quite erroneously, that in this he was following Kant, and object that he did not understand the Kantian definition of beauty in a Kantian way at all – that beauty pleased him, too, out of 'interest', in fact, out of the strongest, most personal interest possible: that of the tortured person who frees himself from his torture? . . . And, to come back to our first question, 'what does it *mean* if a philosopher pays homage to ascetic ideals?' we get our first hint: he wants *to free himself from torture*–

7

Let us be careful not to pull gloomy faces as soon as we hear the word 'torture': in precisely this case, we have plenty to put down on the other side of the account, plenty to deduct – we even have some reason to laugh. For we must not underestimate the fact that Schopenhauer, who actually treated sexuality as a personal enemy (including its tool, woman, that '*instrumentum diaboli*'[74]), *needed* enemies to stay cheerful; that he loved wrathful, bilious, black-green words; that he got angry for the sake of it, passionately; that he would have become ill, a *pessimist* (– because he was not one, however much he wanted to be) without his enemies, without Hegel, women, sensuality and the whole existential will to existence, will to remain. Schopenhauer would otherwise *not* have stayed there, you can bet on that, he would have run away: but his enemies held him tight and kept seducing him back to existence; his anger was his solace, as with the ancient Cynics, his relaxation, his recompense, his *remedium* for nausea, his *happiness*. So much with regard to the most personal aspect in Schopenhauer's case; on the other hand, he is typical in one way, – and here, at last, we come back to our problem. Undeniably, as long as there are philosophers on earth and whenever there have been philosophers (from India to England, to take the opposite poles of a talent for philosophy), there exists a genuine philosophers' irritation and rancour against sensuality – Schopenhauer is just the most eloquent and, if you have an ear for it, he is also the most fascinating and delightful eruption amongst them –; similarly there exists a genuine partiality and warmth among philosophers with regard to the whole ascetic ideal, there should be no illusions on this score. Both these features belong, as I said, to the type; if both are lacking in a philosopher, he is always just a 'so-called' philosopher – you can be sure of that. What does that *mean*? For we must first interpret this state of affairs: *in himself*, he remains stupid for all eternity, like any 'thing in itself'. Every animal, including the *bête philosophe*, instinctively strives for an optimum of favourable conditions in which to fully release his power and achieve his maximum of power-sensation; every animal abhors equally instinctively, with an acute sense of smell that is 'higher than all reason', any kind of disturbance and hindrance that blocks or could block his path to the optimum (– it is *not* his path to 'happiness' I am talking about, but the path to power, action, the mightiest deeds, and in most cases, actually, his path to misery).

---

[74] Cf. Schopenhauer's famous misogynous essay 'Über die Weiber' in the second volume of his *Parerga et Paralipomena*.

Thus the philosopher abhors *marriage*, together with all that might persuade him to it, – marriage as hindrance and catastrophe on his path to the
optimum. Which great philosopher, so far, has been married? Heraclitus,
Plato, Descartes, Spinoza, Leibniz, Kant, Schopenhauer – were not;
indeed it is impossible to even *think* about them as married. A married
philosopher belongs to *comedy*, that is my proposition: and that exception,
Socrates, the mischievous Socrates, appears to have married *ironice*, simply
in order to demonstrate *this* proposition. Every philosopher would say
what Buddha said when he was told of the birth of a son:[75] 'Râhula is born
to me, a fetter is forged for me' (Râhula means here 'a little demon'); every
'free spirit' ought to have a thoughtful moment, assuming he has previously
had a thoughtless one, like the moment experienced by that same Buddha
– he thought to himself, 'living in a house, that unclean place, is cramped;
freedom is in leaving the house': so saying, he left the house. The ascetic
ideal points the way to so many bridges to *independence* that no philosopher
can refrain from inwardly rejoicing and clapping hands on hearing the story
of all those who, one fine day, decided to say 'no' to any curtailment of their
liberty, and go off into the *desert*: even granted they were just strong asses
and the complete opposite of a strong spirit. Consequently, what does the
ascetic ideal mean for a philosopher? My answer is – you will have guessed
ages ago: on seeing an ascetic ideal, the philosopher smiles because he sees
an optimum condition of the highest and boldest intellectuality
[*Geistigkeit*], – he does *not* deny 'existence' by doing so, but rather affirms
his existence and *only* his existence, and possibly does this to the point
where he is not far from making the outrageous wish: *pereat mundus, fiat
philosophia, fiat philosophus, fiam*! . . .[76]

8

As you see, they are hardly unbribed witnesses and judges of the *value*
of ascetic ideals, these philosophers! They are thinking of *themselves*, –
they don't care about 'the saint'! At the same time, they are thinking of
what, *to them*, is absolutely indispensable: freedom from compulsion,
disturbance, noise, business, duties, worries; clear heads; the dance,

[75] Nietzsche's source is H. Oldenburg's *Buddha: Sein Leben, seine Lehre, seine Gemeinde*
(Berlin 1881), pp. 122ff.
[76] 'Let the world perish, but let philosophy exist, let the philosopher exist, let me exist', mod-
elled on the common Latin saying 'Fiat justicia, pereat mundus' ('Let the world perish,
but let justice be done').

bounce and flight of ideas; good, thin, clear, free, dry air, like the air in the mountains, in which all animal existence becomes more spiritual and takes wings; peace in every basement; every dog nicely on the lead; no hostile barking and shaggy *rancune*; no gnawing worms of wounded ambition; bowels regular and under control, busy as a milling mechanism but remote; the heart alien, transcendent, expectant, posthumous, – all in all, they think of the ascetic ideal as the serene asceticism of a deified creature that has flown the nest and is more liable to roam above life than rest. We know what the three great catchwords of the ascetic ideal are: poverty, humility, chastity: let us now look at the life of all great, productive, inventive spirits close up, for once, – all three will be found in them, to a certain degree, every time. Of course, it goes without saying that they will definitely *not* be 'virtues' – this type of person cannot be bothered with virtues! – but as the most proper and natural prerequisites for their *best* existence and *finest* productivity. To do this, it is quite possible that their predominant intellect first had to bridle their unruly and tetchy pride or their wanton sensuality, or that they had to struggle hand and soul to maintain their will to the 'desert' in the face, perhaps, of an inclination towards luxury and finery or similarly, in the face of their extravagant generosity. But it did this precisely in its capacity of *predominant* instinct, which imposed its demands on all other instincts – it still does this; if it did not, it would not be predominant. So there is nothing 'virtuous' about it. Besides, the 'desert' I mentioned, to which strong, independent minds withdraw and become hermits – oh how different it looks from the desert which educated people imagined! – on occasion it is actually made up of these educated people themselves. What is certain is that none of the people playing at being intellectuals could survive in it at all, – it is not romantic enough, not Syrian enough, not enough of a stage desert for them! To be sure, there is no lack of camels: but there all similarity ends. A deliberate obscurity, perhaps; avoidance of self-confrontation; an aversion to noise, admiration, news, influence; a small position, daily routine, something that hides more than it uncovers; occasional association with harmless, happy animals and birds, which are refreshing to behold; mountains for company, not dead mountains, though, ones with *eyes* (by which I mean lakes); in some cases even a room in some crowded, run-of-the-mill hotel where one can be sure of not being recognized and can talk to anyone with impunity, – that is a 'desert': it is quite desolate enough, believe me! When Heraclitus withdrew into the courts and colonnades of the immense Temple of

Artemis,[77] I admit that this 'desert' was more dignified: why do we *lack* temples of that sort? (– maybe they are *not* lacking: I am just thinking of my nicest study, Piazza di San Marco,[78] spring, of course and in the morning, the time between ten and twelve). But what Heraclitus was trying to avoid is the same that *we* try to get away from: the noise and democratic tittle-tattle of the Ephesians, their politics, news of the 'Empire' (Persia, you understand), their market affairs of 'today', – because we philosophers need a rest from one thing above all: anything to do with 'today'. We appreciate peace, coldness, nobility, distance, the past, more or less everything at the sight of which the soul is not forced to defend itself and button up [*zuschnüren*], – something you can talk to without speaking *loudly*. Just listen to the sound of a spirit talking: every spirit has its own sound and likes to hear it. That one there, for example, is probably an agitator, meaning: empty head, empty vessel: whatever might go in, every single thing that comes out is dull-witted and dim-witted, laden with the echo of the great emptiness. That one there hardly says anything that is not hoarse: has he *thought* himself hoarse, perhaps? It could well be – ask the physiologists –, but whoever thinks in *words* thinks as a speaker and not a thinker (which indicates that basically he does not think in facts, factually, but in relation to facts, so that he is actually thinking about *himself* and his listeners). A third speaks importunately, he comes too physically close, we can feel his breath, – we involuntarily close our mouths, although he is talking to us through a book: the sound of his style betrays the reason, – that he has no time, that he has no confidence in himself, that it's now or never for him to get his word in. A spirit, however, which is sure of itself, speaks softly; it prefers to be hidden, keeps you waiting. You can recognize a philosopher by his avoidance of three shiny loud things, fame, princes, women: which does not mean that they avoid him. He shuns light that is too bright, so he shuns his time and its 'day'. He inhabits it like a shadow: the more the sun sinks, the bigger he becomes. With regard to his 'humility', he can stand a certain dependency and darkening in the same way that he can stand the dark: indeed, he dreads being disturbed by lightning, he shrinks at the lack of protection afforded by one all-too isolated and exposed tree which bears the brunt of the vagaries of the storm's temper and temper's storms. His 'motherly' instinct, that secret love towards

---

[77] Reported by Diogenes Laertius at the beginning of his life of Heraclitus (*Lives and Opinions of the Philosophers*, Book ix).

[78] A large public square in Venice.

what is growing inside him, shows him places where he can be relieved
of the necessity of thinking *about himself*; in the same sense that the
mother's instinct in woman has, generally, kept woman in her dependent
state up till now. In the last resort, they ask for little enough, these
philosophers, their slogan is, 'who possesses, is possessed' –: *not*, as I have
to say again and again, out of virtue, out of a creditable will to moderation and simplicity, but because their supreme master *so* demands, clev-
erly and inexorably: preoccupied with just one thing, collecting and
saving up everything – time, strength, love, interest – with that end in
view. This type of person dislikes being bothered with animosities or
even with friendships: he is quick to forget or despise. He thinks mar-
tyrdom is in bad taste; '*suffering* for the truth' – is something he leaves to
the ambitious and stage heroes of the spirit [*des Geistes*] and to anyone
else with the time (– they themselves, the philosophers, have to *do* something for the truth). They make sparing use of big words; I have heard
they do not even like the word 'truth': it sounds boastful . . . Finally, with
regard to the chastity of philosophers, this type of spirit obviously has a
different progeny than children, and perhaps maintains the survival of
its name, its bit of immortality, in some other way (in ancient India it was
said with even more presumption, 'why should the man whose soul is the
world need to procreate?'). This has nothing of chastity from ascetic
scruple or hatred of the senses, any more than it is chastity when an
athlete or jockey abstains from women: instead, it is their dominating
instinct, at least during periods when they are pregnant with something
great. Every artist knows how harmful sexual intercourse is at times of
great spiritual tension and preparation; for those with greatest power and
the surest instincts, it is not even a case of experience, bad experience, –
but precisely that *maternal* instinct ruthlessly takes charge of all other
stockpiles and reserves of energy, of animal vigour, to the advantage of
the work in progress: the greater energy *uses up* the lesser. – Let us now
apply this interpretation to what we were saying about Schopenhauer:
the sight of beauty clearly worked by stimulating the *main strength* in his
nature (the strength to contemplate and penetrate deeply); so that this
then exploded and suddenly took control of his consciousness. But this
certainly does not exclude the possibility that that remarkable sweetness
and fullness characteristic of the aesthetic condition might well descend
from the ingredient 'sensuality' (just as that 'idealism' characteristic of
nubile girls descends from the same source) – that in this way, sensuality
is not suspended as soon as we enter the aesthetic condition, as

Schopenhauer believed, but is only transfigured and no longer enters the consciousness as a sexual stimulus. (I shall return to this point on another occasion, in connection with even more delicate problems concerning the hitherto untouched and unexplored *physiology of aesthetics*.)

9

We have seen that a certain asceticism, a hard and hearty renunciation with a good will, belongs among the most favourable conditions for the highest spirituality, as well as being part of the most natural result of it, so it will come as no surprise that the ascetic ideal has never been treated by the philosophers without a certain partiality. A serious historical re-examination [*Nachrechnung*] actually reveals that the tie between the ascetic ideal and philosophy is very much closer and stronger. We could even say that it was only on the *leading-rein* of this ideal that philosophy ever learnt to take its first toddler steps on earth – still oh-so-clumsily, still with an oh-so-vexed expression, still oh-so-ready to fall and lie on its stomach, this clumsy little oaf and bandy-legged weakling! At first, philosophy began like all good things, – for a long time, everyone lacked self-confidence, looking round to see if anyone would come to their aid, even afraid of anyone who looked on. If we draw up a list of the particular drives and virtues of the philosopher – his drive to doubt, his drive to deny, his drive to prevaricate (his 'ephectic' drive),[79] his drive to analyse, his drive to research, investigate, dare, his drive to compare and counter-balance, his will to neutrality and objectivity, his will to every '*sine ira et studio*'[80] –: surely we realize that all these ran counter to the primary demands of morality and conscience for the longest period of time? (not to mention *reason* in general, which Luther was pleased to call Dame Shrewd, the shrewd whore). Would not a philosopher, assuming he *had* achieved an awareness of himself, practically feel he was the embodiment of '*nitimur in vetitum*'[81] – and wouldn't he consequently *guard* himself 'from feeling', from being aware of himself? . . . As I said, the case is no different with all the other good things we are so proud of nowadays; even using the

---

[79] 'The "ephectic" drive' is the drive to put off, delay, hold back, hesitate, suspend judgment. In Ch. III of the first book of his *Outlines of Pyrrhonism*, Sextus Empiricus says that another name for the sceptical method is the 'ephectic' method because of the state of suspension of judgment that results from it.

[80] At the beginning of his *Annals* (I, 1), Tacitus expresses his intention to write 'without anger or partisanship'.

[81] 'We have an inclination toward that which is forbidden' (Ovid *Amores* III.4.17).

yardstick of the ancient Greeks, our whole modern existence is nothing but *hubris* and godlessness, in so far as it is strength and awareness of strength rather than weakness: precisely the opposites of the things we admire today had conscience on their side and God as their watchman for the longest time. *Hubris* today characterizes our whole attitude towards nature, our rape of nature with the help of machines and the completely unscrupulous inventiveness of technicians and engineers; *hubris* characterizes our attitude to God, or rather to some alleged spider of purpose and ethics lurking behind the great spider's web of causality – we could echo what Charles the Bold said in his battle with Ludwig XI: '*je combats l'universelle araignée*'[82] –; *hubris* characterizes our attitude towards *ourselves*, – for we experiment on ourselves in a way we would never allow on animals, we merrily vivisect our souls out of curiosity: that is how much we care about the 'salvation' of the soul! Afterwards we heal ourselves: being ill is instructive, we do not doubt, more instructive than being well, – *people who make us ill* seem even more necessary for us today than any medicine men and 'saviours'. We violate ourselves these days, no doubt, we are nutcrackers of the soul, questioning and questionable, treating life as though it were nothing but cracking nuts; whereby we have to become daily more deserving of being questioned, more *deserving* of asking questions, more deserving – of living? . . . All good things used to be bad things at one time; every original sin has turned into an original virtue. Marriage, for example, was for a long time viewed as a crime against the rights of the community; people used to have to pay a fine for being so presumptuous as to claim one particular woman for themselves (there we include, for example, *jus primae noctis*,[83] still, in Cambodia, the prerogative of priests, those custodians of 'good old customs'). The gentle, benevolent, yielding, sympathetic feelings – so highly valued by now that they are almost 'values as such' – were undermined by self-contempt for most of the time: people were as ashamed of mildness as people are now ashamed of hardness (compare *Beyond Good and Evil*, IX, section 260[84]). Submission to *law*: – oh, how the consciences of nobler clans rebelled everywhere against having to give up their vendettas and accept the force of law over themselves! For a long time, 'law' was a *vetitum*,[85] a crime, a novelty; introduced with force, *as* a force to which man submitted, ashamed of himself. Each step on earth, even the smallest, was in the past a struggle that

---

[82] 'I struggle against a spider who is everywhere at once.'
[83] Right of spending the first night of marriage with the bride.
[84] See below, Supplementary material, pp. 154–7.
[85] Something forbidden.

was won with spiritual and physical torment: this whole attitude that, 'Not just striding forward, no! even the act of striding, moving, changing has required countless martyrs', sounds strange to us today, – I brought it to light in *Day-break*, I, section 18, where I say 'Nothing has been purchased more dearly than that little bit of human reason and feeling of freedom that now constitutes our pride.'[86] However, it is this pride that prevents us, almost completely, from having any empathy with those vast stretches of the 'morality of custom' which pre-date 'world history' as the genuine and decisive main historical period that determined man's character: where everywhere, suffering was viewed as virtue, cruelty as virtue, deceit as virtue, revenge as virtue, denial of reason as virtue, and conversely well-being was viewed as danger, curiosity as danger, peace as danger, compassion as danger, being pitied was viewed as disgrace, work as disgrace, madness was viewed as godlessness, *change* was viewed everywhere as being unethical and ruinous as such!' –

10

In the same book (section 42[87]), I examined in what kind of estimation the earliest race of contemplative men had to live, – widely despised when they were not feared! – and how *heavily* that estimation weighed down on them. Without a doubt: contemplation first appeared in the world in disguise, with an ambiguous appearance, an evil heart and often with an anxiety-filled head. All that was inactive, brooding and unwarlike in the instincts of contemplative men surrounded them with a deep mistrust for a long time: against which they had no other remedy than to conceive a pronounced *fear* of themselves. And the old Brahmins, for example, certainly knew how to do that! The earliest philosophers knew how to give their life and appearance a meaning, support and setting which would encourage people to learn to *fear* them: on closer inspection, from an even more fundamental need, namely in order to fear and respect themselves. Because they found in themselves all their value judgments turned *against* themselves, they had to fight off every kind of suspicion and resistance to the 'philosopher in themselves'. As men living in a terrible age, they did this with terrible methods: cruelty towards themselves, imaginative forms of self-mortification – these

---

[86] See below, Supplementary material, pp. 137–9.
[87] See below, Supplementary material, pp. 139–40.

were the main methods for these power-hungry hermits and thought-innovators, for whom it was necessary first to violate the gods and tradition in themselves, so they could *believe* in their own innovations. I remind you of the famous story about King Viçvamitra, who gained such a sense of power and self-confidence from a thousand-year-long self-martyrdom that he undertook to build a *new heaven*: the uncanny symbol of the most ancient and most recent story of philosophers on earth – anybody who has ever built a 'new heaven', only mustered the power he needed through his *own hell* . . . Let us set out the whole state of affairs briefly: the philosophic spirit has always had to disguise and cocoon itself among *previously established* types of contemplative man, as a priest, magician, soothsayer, religious man in general, in order for its existence *to be possible* at all: *the ascetic ideal* served the philosopher for a long time as outward appearance, as a precondition of existence, – he had to *play* that part [*darstellen*] in order to be a philosopher, he had to *believe* in it in order to be able to play it [*um es darstellen zu können*]. The peculiarly withdrawn attitude of the philosophers, denying the world, hating life, doubting the senses, desensualized, which has been maintained until quite recently to the point where it almost counted for the *philosophical attitude as such*, – this is primarily a result of the desperate conditions under which philosophy evolved and exists at all: that is, philosophy would have been *absolutely impossible* for most of the time on earth without an ascetic mask and suit of clothes, without an ascetic misconception of itself. To put it vividly and clearly: the *ascetic priest* has until the most recent times displayed the vile and dismal form of a caterpillar, which was the only one philosophers were allowed to adopt and creep round in . . . Have things really *changed?* Has the brightly coloured, dangerous winged-insect, the 'spirit' that the caterpillar hid within itself, really thrown off the monk's habit and emerged into the light, thanks to a sunnier, warmer and more enlightened world? Is there enough pride, daring, courage, self-confidence, will of spirit [*Wille des Geistes*], will to take responsibility, *freedom of will*, for 'the philosopher' on earth to be really – *possible?* . . .

I I

Only now that we have the *ascetic priest* in sight can we seriously get to grips with our problem: what does the ascetic ideal mean? – only now does it become 'serious': after all, we are face to face with the actual *represen-*

tative of seriousness. 'What is the meaning of all seriousness?' – this even more fundamental question is perhaps on our lips already: a question for physiologists, as is proper, but one we shall skirt round for the moment. The ascetic priest not only rests his faith in that ideal, but his will, his power, his interest as well. His *right* to exist stands and falls with that ideal: hardly surprising, then, that we encounter a formidable opponent in him, providing, of course, that we are opposed to that ideal? Such an opponent who fights for his life against people who deny that ideal? . . . On the other hand, it is *prima facie* not very likely that such a biased attitude to our problem would be of much use in attempting to solve it; the ascetic priest will hardly be the happiest defender of his own ideal, for the same reason that a woman always fails when she wants to justify 'woman as such', – there can be no question of his being the most objective assessor and judge of the controversy raised here. So, it is more a case of our having to help him – that much is obvious – to defend himself well against us than of our having to fear being refuted too well by him . . . The idea we are fighting over here is the *valuation* of our life by the ascetic priests: they relate this (together with all that belongs to it, 'nature', 'the world', the whole sphere of what becomes and what passes away), to a quite different kind of existence that it opposes and excludes, *unless* it should turn against itself and *deny itself*: in this case, the case of the ascetic life, life counts as a bridge to that other existence. The ascetic treats life as a wrong path that he has to walk along backwards till he reaches the point where he starts; or, like a mistake which can only be set right by action – *ought* to be set right: he *demands* that we should accompany him, and when he can, he imposes his valuation of existence. What does this mean? Such a monstrous method of valuation is not inscribed in the records of human history as an exception and curiosity: it is one of the most wide-spread and long-lived facts there are. Read from a distant planet, the majuscule script [*Majuskel-Schrift*] of our earthly existence would perhaps seduce the reader to the conclusion that the earth was the ascetic planet *par excellence*, an outpost of discontented, arrogant and nasty creatures who harboured a deep disgust for themselves, for the world, for all life and hurt themselves as much as possible out of pleasure in hurting: – probably their only pleasure. Let us consider how regularly and universally the ascetic priest makes his appearance in almost any age; he does not belong to any race in particular; he thrives everywhere; he comes from every social class. Not that he breeds and propagates his method of valuation through heredity: the opposite is the case, – a deep instinct forbids him to procreate, broadly speaking. It must be a necessity of the first rank which makes this species continually grow and prosper when it is *hostile to life*, – *life itself must have an interest* in preserving such a self-contradictory type. For an ascetic life is a self-contradiction: here an unparalleled *ressentiment* rules, that of an unfulfilled instinct and power-will that wants to be master, not over something in life, but over life itself and its deepest, strongest, most profound conditions; here, an attempt is made to use power to block the sources of the power; here, the green eye of spite turns on physiological growth itself, in particular the manifestation of this in beauty and joy; while satisfaction is *looked for* and found in failure, decay, pain, misfortune, ugliness, voluntary deprivation, destruction of selfhood, self-flagellation and self-sacrifice. This is all paradoxical in the extreme: we are faced with a conflict [*Zwiespältigkeit*] that *wills* itself to be conflicting [*zwiespältig*], which *relishes* itself in this affliction and becomes more self-assured and triumphant to the same degree as its own condition, the physiological capacity to live, *decreases*. 'Triumph precisely in the final agony': the ascetic ideal has always fought under this exaggerated motto; in this seductive riddle, this symbol of delight and anguish, it recognized its brightest light, its salvation, its ultimate victory. *Crux, nux, lux*[88] – with the ascetic ideal, these are all one. –

12

Assuming that such a personified will to contradiction and counternature can be made to *philosophize:* on what will it vent its inner arbitrariness? On that which is experienced most certainly to be true and real: it will look for *error* precisely where the actual instinct of life most unconditionally judges there to be truth. For example, it will demote physicality to the status of illusion, like the ascetics of the Vedânta philosophy did, similarly pain, plurality, the whole conceptual antithesis 'subject' and 'object' – errors, nothing but errors! To renounce faith in one's own ego, to deny one's own 'reality' to oneself – what a triumph! – and not just over the senses, over appearance, a much higher kind of triumph, an act of violation and cruelty inflicted on *reason*: a voluptuousness which reaches its peak when ascetic self-contempt decrees the self-ridicule of reason: 'there *is* a realm of truth and being, but reason is firmly *excluded* from it!' . . .

---

[88] 'Cross, nut, light'. Meaning unclear, unless 'nux' is a misprint for 'nox' ('night') or unless the Greek word (= 'night') is intended.

(By the way: even in the Kantian concept of 'the intelligible character of things',[89] something of this lewd ascetic conflict [*Zwiespältigkeit*] still lingers, which likes to set reason against reason: 'intelligible character' means, in Kant, a sort of quality of things about which all that the intellect can comprehend is that it is, for the intellect – *completely incomprehensible*.) – Finally, as knowers, let us not be ungrateful towards such resolute reversals of familiar perspectives and valuations with which the mind has raged against itself for far too long, apparently to wicked and useless effect: to see differently, and to *want* to see differently to that degree, is no small discipline and preparation of the intellect for its future 'objectivity' – the latter understood not as 'contemplation [*Anschauung*] without interest' (which is, as such, a non-concept and an absurdity), but as *having in our power* the ability to engage and disengage our 'pros' and 'cons': we can use the *difference* in perspectives and affective interpretations for knowledge. From now on, my philosophical colleagues, let us be more wary of the dangerous old conceptual fairy-tale which has set up a 'pure, will-less, painless, timeless, subject of knowledge', let us be wary of the tentacles of such contradictory concepts as 'pure reason', 'absolute spirituality', 'knowledge as such': – here we are asked to think an eye which cannot be thought at all, an eye turned in no direction at all, an eye where the active and interpretative powers are to be suppressed, absent, but through which seeing still becomes a seeing-something, so it is an absurdity and non-concept of eye that is demanded. There is *only* a perspectival seeing, *only* a perspectival 'knowing'; the *more* affects we are able to put into words about a thing, the *more* eyes, various eyes we are able to use for the same thing, the more complete will be our 'concept' of the thing, our 'objectivity'. But to eliminate the will completely and turn off all the emotions without exception, assuming we could: well? would that not mean to *castrate* the intellect? . . .

13

But to return. A self-contradiction such as that which seems to occur in the ascetic, 'life *against* life', is – so much is obvious – seen from the physiological, not just the psychological standpoint, simply nonsense. It can only be *apparent*; it has to be a sort of provisional expression, an explanation, formula, adjustment, a psychological misunderstanding of

---

[89] *Critique of Pure Reason* B 564ff.

something, the real nature of which was far from being understood, was far from being able to be designated as it is *in itself*, – a mere word wedged into an old *gap* in human knowledge. Allow me to present the real state of affairs in contrast to this: *the ascetic ideal springs from the protective and healing instincts of a degenerating life*, which uses every means to maintain itself and struggles for its existence; it indicates a partial physiological inhibition and exhaustion against which the deepest instincts of life, which have remained intact, continually struggle with new methods and inventions. The ascetic ideal is one such method: the situation is therefore the precise opposite of what the worshippers of this ideal imagine, – in it and through it, life struggles with death and *against* death, the ascetic ideal is a trick for the *preservation* of life. The fact that, as history tells us, this ideal could rule man and become powerful to the extent that it did, especially everywhere where the civilization and taming of man took place, reveals a major fact, the *sickliness* of the type of man who has lived up till now, at least of the tamed man, the physiological struggle of man with death (to be more exact: with disgust at life, with exhaustion and with the wish for the 'end'). The ascetic priest is the incarnate wish for being otherwise, being elsewhere, indeed, he is the highest pitch of this wish, its essential ardour and passion: but the *power* of his wishing is the fetter which binds him here, precisely this is what makes him a tool, who now has to work to create more favourable conditions for our being here and being human, – it is precisely with this *power* that he makes the whole herd of failures, the disgruntled, the under-privileged, the unfortunate, and all who suffer from themselves, retain their hold on life by instinctively placing himself at their head as their shepherd. You take my meaning already: this ascetic priest, this apparent enemy of life, this *negating one*, – he actually belongs to the really great *conserving* and *yes-creating* forces of life . . . What causes this sickliness? For man is more ill, uncertain, changeable and unstable than any other animal, without a doubt, – he is *the* sick animal: what is the reason for this? Certainly he has dared more, innovated more, braved more, and has challenged fate more than all the rest of the animals taken together: he, the great experimenter with himself, the unsatisfied and insatiable, struggling for supreme control against animals, nature and gods, – man, the still-unconquered eternal-futurist who finds no more rest from the pressure of his own strength, so that his future mercilessly digs into the flesh of every present like a spur: – how could such a courageous and rich animal not be the most endangered as well, of all sick animals the one most seriously ill, and for longest? . . . Man is often enough fed up, there are whole epidemics of this state of being fed up (– like the one around 1348, at the time of the Dance of Death): but even this nausea, this weariness, this fatigue, this disgust with himself – everything manifests itself so powerfully in him that it immediately becomes a new fetter. His 'no' that he says to life brings a wealth of more tender 'yeses' [*eine Fülle zarterer Ja's (sic)*] to light as though by magic; and even when he *wounds* himself, this master of destruction, self-destruction, – afterwards it is the wound itself that forces him *to live* . . .

14

The more normal this sickliness is in man – and we cannot dispute this normality –, the higher we should esteem the unusual cases of spiritual and physical powerfulness, man's *strokes of luck*, and the better we should protect the successful from the worst kind of air, that of the sick-room. Do we do that? . . . The sick are the greatest danger for the healthy; harm comes to the strong *not* from the strongest but from the weakest. Do people realize this? . . . Broadly speaking, it is not the fear of man that we should wish to see diminished: for this fear forces the strong to be strong, on occasions terrible, – it *maintains* a type of man who is successful. What is to be feared and can work more calamitously than any other calamity is not great fear of, but great *nausea* at man; similarly, great *compassion* for man. Assuming that these might one day mate, then immediately and unavoidably something most uncanny would be produced, the 'last will' of man, his will to nothingness, nihilism. And in fact: a great deal has been done to prepare for this. Whoever still has a nose to smell with as well as eyes and ears, can detect almost everywhere he goes these days something like the air of the madhouse and hospital, – I speak, as is appropriate, of man's cultural domains, of every kind of 'Europe' that still exists on this earth. The *sickly* are the greatest danger to man: *not* the wicked, *not* the 'beasts of prey'. Those who, from the start, are the unfortunate, the downtrodden, the broken – these are the ones, the *weakest*, who most undermine life amongst men, who introduce the deadliest poison and scepticism into our trust in life, in man, in ourselves. Where can we escape the surreptitious glance imparting a deep sadness, the backward glance of the born misfit revealing how such a man communes with himself, – that glance which is a sigh. 'If only I were some other person!' is what this glance sighs: 'but there's no hope of that.

I am who I am: how could I get away from myself? And oh – *I'm fed up with myself*!' . . . In such a soil of self-contempt, such a veritable swamp, every kind of weed and poisonous plant grows, all of them so small, hidden, dissembling and sugary. Here, the worms of revenge and rancour teem all round; here, the air stinks of things unrevealed and unconfessed; here, the web of the most wicked conspiracy is continually being spun, – the conspiracy of those who suffer against those who are successful and victorious, here, the sight of the victorious man is *hated*. And what mendacity to avoid admitting this hatred as hatred! What expenditure of big words and gestures, what an art of 'righteous' slander! These failures: what noble eloquence flows from their lips! How much sugared, slimy, humble humility swims in their eyes! What do they really want? At any rate, to *represent* justice, love, wisdom, superiority, that is the ambition of these who are 'the lowest', these sick people! And how skilful such an ambition makes them! In particular, we have to admire the counterfeiter's skill with which the stamp of virtue, the ding-a-ling golden ring of virtue is now imitated. They have taken out a lease on virtue to keep it just for themselves, these weak and incurably sick people, there is no doubt about it: 'Only we are good and just' is what they say, 'only we are the *homines bonæ voluntatis*'.[90] They promenade in our midst like living reproaches, like warnings to us, – as though health, success, strength, pride and the feeling of power were in themselves depravities for which penance, bitter penance will one day be exacted: oh, how ready they themselves are, in the last resort, to *make* others penitent, how they thirst to be *hangmen*! Amongst them we find plenty of vengeance-seekers disguised as judges, with the word justice continually in their mouth like poisonous spittle, pursing their lips and always at the ready to spit at anybody who does not look discontented and who cheerfully goes his own way. Among their number there is no lack of that most disgusting type of dandy, the lying freaks who want to impersonate 'beautiful souls'[91] and put their wrecked sensuality on the market, swaddled in verses and other nappies, as 'purity of the heart': the type of moral onanists and 'self-gratifiers' [*die Species der moralischen Onanisten und 'Selbstbefriediger'*]. The will of the sick to appear superior in *any* way, their instinct for secret paths, which lead to tyranny over the healthy, – where can it not be found, this will to power of precisely the weakest! In particular, the sick woman: nobody can outdo

---

[90] 'men of good will', Gospel according to Luke 2.14.
[91] Cf. Goethe's *Wilhelm Meister*, Book 6. Cf. also Hegel, *Phenomenology of Spirit* VI.C.c.

her refinements in ruling, oppressing, tyrannizing. The sick woman spares nothing, either living or dead, to this end, she digs up the things most deeply buried (the Bogos say: 'woman is a hyena'). You can look behind every family, every corporate body, every community: everywhere, the struggle of the sick against the healthy – mostly a silent struggle with small doses of poison, pinpricks, spiteful, long-suffering looks, but also interspersed with the *loud* gesture of the sick Pharisee playing his favourite role of 'righteous indignation'. The hoarse, indignant baying of sick hounds, the vicious mendacity and rage of such 'noble' Pharisees, can be heard right into the hallowed halls of learning (– I again remind readers who have ears to hear of that apostle of revenge from Berlin, Eugen Dühring, who makes the most indecent and disgusting use of moral clap-trap of anyone in Germany today: Dühring, today's biggest loudmouth of morality, even amongst his kind, the anti-Semites). These worm-eaten physiological casualties are all men of *ressentiment*, a whole, vibrating realm of subterranean revenge, inexhaustible and insatiable in its eruptions against the happy, and likewise in masquerades of revenge and pretexts for revenge: when will they actually achieve their ultimate, finest, most sublime triumph of revenge? Doubtless if they succeeded in *shoving* their own misery, in fact all misery, *on to the conscience* of the happy: so that the latter eventually start to be ashamed of their happiness and perhaps say to one another: 'It's a disgrace to be happy! *There is too much misery!*' . . . But there could be no greater or more disastrous misunderstanding than for the happy, the successful, those powerful in body and soul to begin to doubt their *right to happiness* in this way. Away with this 'world turned upside down'! Away with this disgraceful mollycoddling of feeling! That the sick should *not* make the healthy sick – and this would be that kind of mollycoddling – ought to be the chief concern on earth: – but for that, it is essential that the healthy should remain *separated* from the sick, should even be spared the sight of the sick so that they do not confuse themselves with the sick. Or would it be their task, perhaps, to be nurses and doctors? . . . But they could not be more mistaken and deceived about *their task*, – the higher *ought* not to abase itself as the tool of the lower, the pathos of distance *ought* to ensure that their tasks are kept separate for all eternity! Their right to be there, the priority of the bell with a clear ring over the discordant and cracked one, is clearly a thousand times greater: they alone are *guarantors* of the future, they alone have a *bounden duty* to man's future. What *they* can do, what *they* should do, is something the sick must never do: but *so that* they can do what only *they* should, why should they still be free to play doctor, comforter and 'saviour' to the sick? . . . And so we need good air! good air! At all events, well away from all madhouses and hospitals of culture! And so we need good company, *our* company! Or solitude, if need be! But at all events, keep away from the evil fumes of inner corruption and the secret, worm-eaten rottenness of disease! . . . So that we, my friends, can actually defend ourselves, at least for a while yet, against the two worst epidemics that could possibly have been set aside just for us – against *great nausea at man*! Against *deep compassion for man*! . . .

15

If you have comprehended in full – and right here I demand *profound apprehension*, profound comprehension – why it can absolutely *not* be the task of the healthy to nurse the sick, to make the sick healthy, then another necessity has also been comprehended, – the necessity of doctors and nurses *who are sick themselves*: and now we have and hold with both hands the meaning of the ascetic priest. The ascetic priest must count as pre-destined saviour, shepherd and defender of the sick herd in our eyes: only then do we understand his immensely historic mission. *Rule over the suffering* is his domain, his instinct directs him towards it and his own special skill, mastery and brand of happiness are to be had in it. He must be sick himself, he must really be a close relative of the sick and the destitute in order to understand them, – in order to come to an understanding with them; but he has to be strong, too, more master of himself than of others, actually unscathed in his will to power, so that he has the trust and fear of the sick and can be their support, defence, prop, compulsion, disciplinarian, tyrant, God. He has to defend his herd, – against whom? Against the healthy, no doubt, but also against envy of the healthy; he must be the natural opponent and *despiser* of all crude, stormy, unbridled, hard, violently predatory health and mightiness. The priest is the first form of the *more delicate* animal which despises more easily than it hates. He will not be spared from waging war with predators, a war of cunning (of the 'spirit') rather than of force, it goes without saying, – in addition he will, if necessary, practically have to make himself into a new kind of predator, or at least *signify it*, – a new animal ferocity in which the polar bear, the lissom, cold tiger-cat on the watch and not least the fox, appear to be combined in a unity as attractive as it is frightening. If forced by necessity, he would probably even step among the other kind of beast of prey themselves, in all likelihood with bearish solemnity, venerable, clever, cold, deceptively superior, as the herald and mouthpiece of more mysterious powers, determined to sow suffering, division and self-contradiction on this ground wherever he can, and only too certain of his skill at being master of the *suffering* at any time. He brings ointments and balms with him, of course; but first he has to wound so that he can be the doctor; and whilst he soothes the pain caused by the wound, *he poisons the wound at the same time* – for that is what he is best trained to do, this magician and tamer of beasts of prey, whose mere presence necessarily makes everything healthy, sick, and everything sick, tame. Actually, he defends his sick herd well enough, this strange shepherd, – he even defends it against itself and against the wickedness, deceit, malice and everything else characteristic of all those who are diseased and sick, all of which smoulders in the herd itself, he carries out a clever, hard and secret struggle against anarchy and the ever-present threat of the inner disintegration of the herd, where that most dangerous of blasting and explosive materials, *ressentiment*, continually piles up. His particular trick, and his prime use, is to detonate this explosive material without blowing up either the herd or the shepherd; if we wanted to sum up the value of the priestly existence in the shortest formula, we would immediately say: the priest is the *direction-changer* of *ressentiment*. For every sufferer instinctively looks for a cause of his distress; more exactly, for a culprit, even more precisely for a *guilty* culprit who is receptive to distress, – in short, for a living being upon whom he can release his emotions, actually or in effigy, on some pretext or other: because the release of emotions is the greatest attempt at relief, or should I say, at *anaesthetizing* on the part of the sufferer, his involuntarily longed-for narcotic against pain of any kind. In my judgment, we find here the actual physiological causation of *ressentiment*, revenge and their ilk, in a yearning, then, to *anaesthetize pain through emotion*: – people generally look for the same thing, wrongly in my view, in the defensive return of a blow, a purely protective reaction, a 'reflex movement' in the case of any sudden injury or peril, such as that performed even by a headless frog to ward off corrosive acid. But the difference is fundamental: in the one case, the attempt is made to prevent further harm being done, in the other case, the attempt is made to *anaesthetize* a tormenting, secret pain that is becoming unbearable with a more violent emotion of any sort, and at least rid the consciousness of it for the moment, – for this, one needs an emotion, the wildest possible emotion and, in order to arouse it, the first available pretext. 'Someone or other must be to blame that I feel ill' – this kind of conclusion is peculiar to all sick people, and in fact becomes more insistent, the more they remain in ignorance of the true reason, the physiological one, why they feel ill (this can, perhaps, be a disease of the *nervus sympaticus*, or lie in an excessive secretion of bile, or in a deficiency of potassium sulphate and phosphate in the blood, or in abdominal stricture interrupting the blood circulation, or in degeneration of the ovaries and such like). The sufferers, one and all, are frighteningly willing and inventive in their pretexts for painful emotions; they even enjoy being mistrustful and dwelling on wrongs and imagined slights: they rummage through the bowels of their past and present for obscure, questionable stories that will allow them to wallow in tortured suspicion, and intoxicate themselves with their own poisonous wickedness – they rip open the oldest wounds and make themselves bleed to death from scars long-since healed, they make evil-doers out of friend, wife, child and anyone else near to them. 'I suffer: someone or other must be guilty' – and every sick sheep thinks the same. But his shepherd, the ascetic priest, says to him, 'Quite right, my sheep! Somebody must be to blame: but you yourself are this somebody, you yourself alone are to blame for it, *you yourself alone are to blame for yourself* . . . That is bold enough, wrong enough: but at least one thing has been achieved by it, the direction of *ressentiment* is, as I said – *changed*.

16

You can now guess what, in my opinion, the healing instinct of life has at least *tried* to do through the ascetic priest and what purpose was served by a temporary tyranny of such paradoxical and paralogical concepts [*solcher paradoxer und paralogischer Begriffe*] as 'guilt', 'sin', 'sinfulness', 'corruption', 'damnation': to make the sick *harmless* to a certain degree, to bring about the self-destruction of the incurable, to direct the less ill strictly towards themselves, to give their *ressentiment* a backwards direction ('one thing is needful'[92] –) and in this way to *exploit* the bad instincts of all sufferers for the purpose of self-discipline, self-surveillance and self-overcoming. It goes without saying that 'medication' of this sort, mere affect-medication, cannot possibly yield a real *cure* of the sick in the physiological sense; we do not even have the right to claim that in this instance, the instinct of life in any way expects or intends a cure. On the

---

[92] Gospel according to Luke 10.42.

one hand, the sick packed together and organized (– the word 'church' is the most popular name for it), on the other hand a sort of provisional safeguarding of those in better health, the physically better-developed, thus the opening of a *cleft* between healthy and sick – and for a long time that was all! And it was a great deal! It was a *very great deal!* . . . [In this essay I proceed, as you see, on an assumption that I do not first have to justify with regard to readers of the kind I need: that 'sinfulness' in man is not a fact, but rather the interpretation of a fact, namely a physiological upset, – the latter seen from a perspective of morals and religion which is no longer binding on us. – The fact that someone *feels* 'guilty', 'sinful', by no means proves that he is right in feeling this way; any more than someone is healthy just because he feels healthy. Just remember the notorious witch-trials: at the time, the most perspicacious and humane judges did not doubt that they were dealing with guilt; the witches *themselves did not doubt it*, – and yet there was no guilt. – To expand upon that assumption: even 'psychic suffering' does not seem to be a fact to me at all, but simply an interpretation (causal interpretation) of facts that could not be formulated exactly up till now: thus, as something which is still completely in the air and has no scientific standing – actually just a fat word in place of a spindly question mark. If someone cannot cope with his 'psychic suffering', this does *not* stem from his psyche, to speak crudely; more probably from his stomach (I did say I would speak crudely: which does not in any way signify a desire for it to be heard crudely, understood crudely . . .). A strong and well-formed man digests his experiences (including deeds and misdeeds) as he digests his meals, even when he has hard lumps to swallow. If he 'cannot cope' with an experience, this sort of indigestion is as much physiological as any other – and often, in fact, just one of the consequences of that other – with such a point of view we can, between ourselves, still be the severest opponents of all materialism . . .]

17

But is he really a *doctor*, this ascetic priest? – We already saw the degree to which it is hardly admissible to call him a doctor, much as he feels himself to be a 'saviour', and likes to be honoured as 'saviour'. It is only suffering itself, the discomfort of the sufferer, that he combats, *not* its cause, *not* the actual state of being ill, – this must constitute our most fundamental objection to priestly medication. But if we just put ourselves into the only perspective known to the priests for a moment, it is hard to stop admiring how much he has seen, sought and found within this perspective. The *alleviation* of suffering, 'consolation' of every kind, – that is where his genius lies: how imaginatively he has understood his task as consoler, how unscrupulously and boldly he has chosen the means to do it! We have every right to call Christianity in particular a large treasure-trove of the most ingenious means of consolation, so much to refresh, soothe and narcotize is piled up inside it, so many of the most dangerous and most daring risks are taken for the purpose, it has been so especially subtle, so refined, so southerly refined in guessing which emotions to stimulate in order to conquer the deep depression, the leaden fatigue and the black melancholy of the physiologically obstructed, at least temporarily. For, to speak generally: with all great religions, the main concern is the fight against a certain weariness and heaviness that has become epidemic. We can regard it as inherently probable that from time to time, at certain places on earth, almost from necessity, a *physiological feeling of obstruction* will rule amongst large masses of people which, however, is not consciously perceived as such, through lack of physiological knowledge, so that its 'cause' and its cure can be sought and tested only on the psychological-moral level (– actually, this is my most general formula for what is usually called a *'religion'*). Such a feeling of obstruction can be of the most diverse descent: for example, as a result of crossing races that are too heterogeneous (or estates – estates always indicate differences in descent and race as well: the European *'Weltschmerz'*, the pessimism of the nineteenth century, is essentially the result of a foolishly sudden mixing of estates); or it could be brought about by unsound emigration – a race ending up in a climate for which its powers of adaptation are inadequate (the case of the Indians in India); or by the after-effects of a race's age and fatigue (Parisian pessimism from 1850 on); or by a faulty diet (alcoholism of the Middle Ages; the nonsense of the vegetarians who at least have the authority of Sir Christopher[93] in Shakespeare on their side); or by corruption of the blood, malaria, syphilis and such like (German depression after the Thirty Years' War, which infected half of Germany with ruinous diseases and thus prepared the ground for German servility, German faint-heartedness). In such a case, an attempt is made every time to *fight against the feeling of lethargy* on a grand scale; let us briefly

---

[93] Nietzsche read Shakespeare in the Schlegel/Tieck translation. This translation calls 'Sir Andrew Aguecheek', who believes that excessive beef-eating has harmed his wits (*Twelfth Night* I.iii), 'Junker Christoph von Bleichenwang'.

examine its principle methods and forms. (As is fitting, I leave to one side the actual fight of the *philosophers* against the feeling of lethargy, which always has taken place at the same time – it is interesting enough, but too absurd, too trivial in practice, too prone to gathering cobwebs and loafing around, as when pain is supposed to be proved to be an error, using the naïve premise that pain would *have to* vanish as soon as the error it contains is recognized – but lo and behold! it refused to vanish . . .) *Firstly*, we fight against that dominating lethargy with methods that reduce the awareness of life to the lowest point. If possible, absolutely no more wanting, no more wishing; everything that arouses the emotions and 'blood' must be avoided (no eating salt: hygiene of the Fakirs); no loving, no hating; equanimity; no taking of revenge; no getting rich; no working; begging; if possible, no consorting with women or as little as possible of this; in spiritual matters, Pascal's principle '*il faut s'abêtir*'[94]. The result in psychological and moral terms: '*loss of self*', 'sanctification', in physiological terms: hypnotization, – the attempt to achieve for man something akin to what *hibernation* is for some kinds of animal and *estivation* is for many plants in hot climates, a minimum of expenditure of energy and metabolism, where life can just about be maintained without actually entering consciousness. To this end, an amazing amount of human energy has been expended – perhaps in vain? . . . We can have absolutely no doubt that these sportsmen of 'holiness' who are so abundant at all times, in almost all peoples, have actually found a real deliverance from what they fought against with such a rigorous training, – they finally *rid* themselves of that deep, physiological depression with the help of a system of hypnotizing methods in countless cases: for which reason their methodology belongs among the most general ethnological facts. Similarly, it is completely inappropriate to count the mere intention to starve out physicality and desire as symptoms of insanity (as a clumsy type of roast beef-eating 'free thinker' and Sir Christopher are wont to do[95]). It is all the more certain that it leads, or can lead, the *way* to all sorts of spiritual disturbances, [*geistige[n] Störungen*] for example, to 'inner lights' as with the Hesychasts[96] of Mount Athos, to hallucinations of sound and sight, to voluptuous

---

[94] 'One must make oneself stupid'. Cf. Pascal's *Pensées*, section III.
[95] Cf. the note on p. 96.
[96] Sect that flourished in the twelfth to fourteenth centuries whose members aimed at attaining 'quietude' ('hesuchia' in Greek, hence the name of the sect). The use of various ascetic techniques was thought to culminate in a vision of the divine light.

excesses and ecstasies of sensuality (the story of Saint Theresa). The interpretation placed on these states by those subject to them has always been as fanatically incorrect as possible, this goes without saying: but we should not overlook the tone of the most convinced gratitude resounding in the mere *will* to such a kind of interpretation. The supreme state, that of *salvation* itself, that finally achieved state of total hypnosis and silence, is always seen by them as mystery as such, which even the supreme symbols are inadequate to express, as a journey home and into the heart of things, as a liberation from all delusion, as 'knowledge', 'truth', 'being', as an escape from every aim, every wish, every action, as a beyond good and evil as well. 'Good and evil', says the Buddhist, '– both are fetters: the perfect One [*der Vollendete*] has mastered both'; a man of the Vedânta faith says 'he cannot be hurt by anything done or not done; as a wise man, he shakes off good and evil; no action can damage his domain; he has gone beyond good and evil, beyond both': – so, a conception found throughout India, as much Brahminic as Buddhist.[97] (Neither in the Indian nor Christian way of thinking is that 'salvation' regarded as *attainable* through virtue, through moral improvement, however high the value of virtue is set by them as a means of hypnosis: we should mark this well, – moreover, it simply corresponds to the facts of the matter. To have remained *true* in this may perhaps be regarded as the best piece of realism in the three greatest religions otherwise so thoroughly steeped in moralizing. 'For the man of knowledge there is no duty' . . . 'Salvation does not come about by *accumulating* virtues: since it consists of being one with Brahma, whose perfection admits of no addition; still less does it consist of *taking away* mistakes: because Brahma, with whom being one constitutes salvation, is eternally pure' – these passages from the commentary of Shankara, quoted by the first real *expert* on Indian philosophy in Europe, my friend Paul Deussen.) So we want to pay due respect to 'salvation' in the great religions; on the other hand, it is a little difficult for us to remain serious, in view of the value placed on *deep sleep* by these people so weary of life that they are too weary even to dream, – that same deep sleep as the entry to Brahma, as a *unio mystica* with God *achieved*. 'When he has completely fallen asleep' – it says on the matter in the oldest, most venerable 'scripture' – 'and completely come to rest, so that he sees no more

---

[97] Nietzsche's sources are Paul Deussen's *Das System der Vedânta* (Leipzig, 1883) and *Die Sutras des Vedânta aus dem Sanskrit übersetzt* (Leipzig, 1887).

dream images, then, dearly beloved, he is united with being, and has entered into himself, – embraced by the cognitive self, he no longer has any consciousness of what is outside him or within him. This bridge is not crossed by day or night, age, death, suffering, good work nor evil work.' 'In deep sleep', likewise say the faithful of this deepest of the three great religions, 'the soul lifts itself out of the body, enters the supreme light and emerges in its true form: there it is the highest spirit itself [*der höchste Geist selbst*], roaming round joking and playing and enjoying itself, with women, carriages, friends or whatever, without a thought for this appendage of a body to which prâna (the breath of life) is harnessed like a beast to a cart.' Nevertheless, we want to remain aware, here as with the case of 'salvation', that fundamentally, in spite of the splendour of Oriental exaggeration, the same value is expressed as that by the clear, cool, Greek-cool but suffering Epicurus: the hypnotic feeling of nothingness, the repose of deepest sleep, in short, *absence of suffering* – this may be counted as the highest good, the value of values, by the suffering and by those who are deeply depressed, it *has* to be valued positively by them and found to be *the* positive itself. (According to the same logic of feeling, nothingness is called *God* in all pessimistic religions.)

18

Much more often than such a hypnotic total dampening of sensibility, of susceptibility to pain, which presupposes unusual powers, above all courage, contempt of opinion, 'intellectual stoicism', another training is tried to combat the condition of depression, which at all events is easier: *mechanical activity*. It is beyond doubt that with this, an existence of suffering is alleviated to a not inconsiderable extent: today people call this fact, rather dishonestly, 'the blessing of work'. The alleviation consists of completely diverting the interest of the sufferer from the pain, – so that constantly an action and yet another action enters consciousness and consequently little room is left for suffering: because this chamber of human consciousness is *small*! Mechanical activity and what goes with it – like absolute regularity, punctual, mindless obedience, one's way of life fixed once and for all, time-filling, a certain encouragement, indeed discipline, to be 'impersonal', to forget oneself, to be in a state of '*incuria sui*'[98] –: how

---

[98] 'lack of concern for self'; this is Geulincx's definition of the virtue of humility.

thoroughly, how accurately the ascetic priest has exploited these in the fight against pain! And when he had to deal with the suffering of the lower orders, with work slaves or prisoners (or with women: who are, after all, mostly both at the same time, work slaves and prisoners), all he had to do was switch names round a bit, some rebaptizing, so that in future they would view a hated thing as a benefit, as relative happiness: in any case, – the slaves' discontent with their lot was *not* invented by the priests. – An even higher-valued means of fighting depression is the prescription of a *small pleasure* which is readily accessible and can be made into normal practice; this medication is often used in conjunction with those just discussed. The most frequent form in which a pleasure of this type is prescribed as a cure is the pleasure of *giving pleasure* (as doing good, giving gifts, bringing relief, helping, encouraging, comforting, praising, honouring); the ascetic priest thereby prescribes, when he prescribes 'love thy neighbour', what is actually the arousal of the strongest, most life-affirming impulse, albeit in the most cautious dose, – the *will to power*. The happiness of even the 'smallest superiority' such as that which accompanies all doing good, being useful, helping, honouring, is the most ample consolation used by the physiologically inhibited, provided they are well advised: otherwise they hurt one another, naturally in obedience to the same fundamental instinct. If we look for the beginnings of Christianity in the Roman world, we find associations for mutual support, associations for the poor, the sick, for burials, which have sprouted on the lowest level of that society, where the chief means to counter depression, that of the small pleasure, of mutual do-gooding, was deliberately nurtured, – perhaps this was something new then, an actual discovery? This 'will to reciprocity', to form a herd, a 'community', a 'conventicle', called forth in such a manner is bound to lead, if only in miniature, to a new and much fuller outbreak of the will to power: the *formation of a herd* is an essential step and victory in the fight against depression. With the growth of the community, a new interest is kindled for the individual as well, which often enough will lift him out of the most personal element in his discontent, his aversion to *himself* (Geulincx's *'despectio sui'*[99]). All the sick and sickly strive instinctively for a herd-organization, out of a longing to shake off dull lethargy and the feeling of weakness: the ascetic priest senses this instinct and promotes it; wherever there are herds, it is the instinct of weakness that has willed the herd and the cleverness of the

---

[99] 'contempt of self'.

priests that has organized it. For it should not be overlooked: the strong are as naturally inclined to strive to be *apart* as the weak are to strive to be *together*, when the former unite, this takes place only with a view to an aggressive collective action and collective satisfaction of their will to power, with much resistance from their individual consciences; the latter, on the contrary, gather together with *pleasure* at this very gathering, – their instinct is just as satisfied in doing this as the instinct of the born 'masters' (I mean here the solitary species of human beast of prey) is basically irritated and unsettled by organization. Behind every oligarchy – the whole of history informs us – the lust for *tyranny* always lurks; every oligarchy constantly quakes at the tension that each individual has to exert in order to remain in control of this desire. (For example, it was like that with the *Greeks*: Plato testifies to it in a hundred places, Plato, who knew his peers – *and* himself . . .)

19

The ascetic priest's methods that we have been getting to know – the total dampening of the awareness of life, mechanical activity, the small pleasure, above all the pleasure of 'loving one's neighbour', herd-organization, the awakening of the communal feeling of power, consequently the individual's dissatisfaction with himself is overridden by his delight at the prosperity of the community – these, measured in modern terms, are his *innocent* means in the fight against displeasure: now let us turn to the more interesting, the 'guilty' means. They are all concerned with one thing: some kind of *excess of feeling*, – which is used as the most effective anaesthetic for dull, crippling, long-drawn-out pain; that is why the ingenuity of the priests has been practically inexhaustible in thinking out the implications of this one question: '*how* can one achieve excess of feeling?' . . . That sounds hard: obviously it would sound more pleasant and sound better on the ears if I were to say 'the ascetic priest has always made use of the *enthusiasm* that lies in all strong affects'. But why caress the effeminate ears of our modern weaklings? Why, *for our part*, should we give in, even by an inch, to their verbal tartuffery? For us psychologists, this would constitute a tartuffery of *deed*; apart from the fact that it would nauseate us. Actually, a psychologist today shows his *good* taste, if he shows any at all (others might say: his integrity), by resisting the scandalously *over-moralistic* language with which practically all modern judgments about men and things are smeared. For we must make no mistake about it: the most characteristic feature of modern souls, modern books, is not their lies but the deep-rooted *innocence* in their moralistic mendaciousness. To have to rediscover this 'innocence' everywhere – that is, perhaps, the most revolting task among the somewhat dubious tasks a psychologist today has to perform; it is part of *our* great danger, – it is a path that, perhaps, leads *us*, too, to the great nausea . . . I do not doubt for *what* use alone modern books (assuming they last, which certainly is not to be feared, and likewise assuming that one day there will be posterity with stricter, harder, *more healthy* taste) – what use *everything* modern in general will serve, could serve, for this posterity: as an emetic, – and that on account of its moral sugariness and falsity, its innermost feminism, which is pleased to call itself 'idealism' and at all events believes itself to be idealism. Our educated people today, our 'good' men, do not lie – that is true, but it does them *no* credit! The actual lie, the genuine, resolute 'honest' lie (listen to Plato about its value[100]) would be something far too tough and strong for them; it would demand something of them that one *must not* demand, that they open their eyes to themselves, that they come to know how to distinguish between 'true' and 'false' with regard to themselves. The *dishonest lie* is the only thing fitting for them; everyone who feels himself to be a 'good person' today is completely incapable of approaching any thing except in a *dishonestly mendacious* way, in a way that was mendacious right down to its very depths, but innocently mendacious, true-heartedly mendacious, blue-eyed mendacious, virtuously mendacious. These 'good people', – all of them now moralized root and branch and disgraced as far as honesty is concerned and ruined for all eternity: which of them could stand a single *truth* 'about man'! . . . Or, to ask more pertinently: which of them could bear a *true* biography! . . . A few hints: Lord Byron wrote some extremely personal things about himself, but Thomas Moore was 'too good' for this: he burnt his friend's papers. The same is said to have happened with Dr Gwinner, Schopenhauer's executor: for Schopenhauer had written a few things about himself as well and perhaps against himself too ('εἰς ῞εαυτόν'). The industrious American Thayer, Beethoven's biographer, suddenly called his work to a halt: having reached some point or other in this honourable and naïve life, he could no longer stand it . . . moral: what prudent man would write an honest word about himself these days? – he would have to belong to the Order of Holy Daredevils. We are promised Richard Wagner's autobiography: who can doubt but that it will be a

---

[100] *Republic* 382c, 389b, 414b–c, 459c–d.

prudent autobiography? . . . Let us, think of the comical horror which the Catholic priest Janssen[101] aroused with his incredibly down-to-earth and innocuous picture of the German Reformation; what would people do next if someone told the story *differently* for once, if a real psychologist told us about the real Luther, no longer with the moralistic simplicity of a country pastor, no longer with the sugary, deferential modesty of Protestant historians, but instead with the intrepidity of a *Taine*, from *strength of soul* and not from a shrewd indulgence toward strength . . . (The Germans, by the way, have finally produced an agreeable enough classical specimen of the latter, – they have every right to claim him as one of their own, and be proud of him: one Leopold Ranke, this born classical *advocatus* of every *causa fortior*,[102] this most prudent of all prudent 'realists'.)

20

But you will have already understood me: – surely reason enough, do you not think, all in all, why we psychologists of today cannot get rid of a certain mistrust *towards ourselves?* . . . Probably we, too, are still 'too good' for our trade, probably we, too, are still the victims, the prey, the sick of this contemporary taste for moralization, much as we feel contempt towards it, – it probably infects *us* as well. What warning did that diplomat[103] give when he spoke to his peers? 'Above all, gentlemen, we must mistrust our first impulses!' he said, *'they are nearly always good'* . . . Every psychologist ought to speak to his peers like that today . . . And with that, we return to our problem, which really does require a certain discipline from us, a certain mistrust, especially towards our 'first impulses'. *The ascetic ideal utilized to produce excess of feelings:* – if you can remember the last essay, you will be able to extrapolate the essentials of what follows from the meaning compressed in these nine words. To throw the human soul out of joint, plunging it into terror, frosts, fires and raptures to such an extent that it rids itself of all small and petty forms of lethargy, apathy and depression, as though hit by lightning: what paths lead to *this* goal? And which are most certain to do so? . . . Basically, all strong emotions have this capacity, providing they are released suddenly: anger, fear, voluptuousness, revenge, hope, triumph, despair, cruelty; in fact, the ascetic priest has insouciantly taken into his service the *whole*

---

[101] Johannes Janssen, *Geschichte des deutschen Volkes seit dem Mittelalter* (Freiburg/Br., 1877).
[102] 'Stronger case'.
[103] allusion to Charles Maurice de Talleyrand (1754–1838).

pack of wild hounds in man, releasing now one, then another, always with the same purpose of waking man out of his long-drawn-out melancholy, of putting to flight, at least temporarily, his dull pain, his lingering misery, always with a religious interpretation and 'justification' as well. Every such excess of emotion has to be *paid* for afterwards, it goes without saying – it makes the sick person even sicker –: and therefore this type of remedy for pain is a 'guilty' one, measured against the modern yardstick. However, we have to insist all the more firmly, as fairness demands, that this remedy was applied with a *good conscience*, that the ascetic priest prescribed it with the utmost faith in its efficacy, indeed its indispensability, – often enough nearly collapsing himself at the distress he caused; similarly that the vehement physiological revenge taken by such excesses, perhaps even mental disturbance, is fundamentally not actually inconsistent with the general idea of this type of medication: which did *not*, as I have already shown, set out to heal diseases but rather to fight the lethargy of depression, to alleviate and anaesthetize it. *In this way*, too, the aim was achieved. The main contrivance which the ascetic priest allowed himself to use in order to make the human soul resound with every kind of heart-rending and ecstatic music was – as everyone knows – his utilization of the *feeling of guilt*. The previous essay indicated the descent of this feeling briefly – as a piece of animal-psychology, no more: there we encountered the feeling of guilt in its raw state, as it were. Only in the hands of the priest, this real artist in feelings of guilt, did it take shape – and what a shape! 'Sin' – for that is the name for the priestly reinterpretation of the animal 'bad conscience' (cruelty turned back on itself) – has been the greatest event in the history of the sick soul up till now: with sin, we have the most dangerous and disastrous trick of religious interpretation. Man, suffering from himself in some way, at all events physiologically, rather like an animal imprisoned in a cage, unclear as to why? what for? and yearning for reasons – reasons bring relief –, yearning for cures and narcotics as well, finally consults someone who knows hidden things too – and lo and behold! from this magician, the ascetic priest, he receives the *first* tip as to the 'cause' of his suffering: he should look for it within *himself*, in *guilt*, in a piece of the past, he should understand his suffering itself as a *condition of punishment* . . . The unhappy man has heard, has understood; he is like a hen around which a line has been drawn. He cannot get out of this drawn circle: the sick man has been made into 'the sinner' . . . And now we shall not be rid of the sight of this new sick person, 'the sinner', for a few thousand years, – shall we ever be rid of him? – wherever we look, everywhere the hypnotic glance of the sinner always moving in the one direction (in the direction of 'guilt' as the *sole* cause of suffering); everywhere, bad conscience, that 'abominable beast', as Luther called it; everywhere, the past regurgitated, the deed distorted, the green eye on every action; everywhere, the *will* to misunderstand suffering made into the content of life, suffering reinterpreted as feelings of guilt, fear, punishment; everywhere, the scourge, the hair shirt, the starving body, contrition; everywhere, the sinner breaking himself on the cruel wheel of a restless and morbidly lustful conscience; everywhere, dumb torment, the most extreme fear, the agony of the tortured heart, the paroxysms of unknown happiness, the cry for 'redemption'. In fact, the old depression, heaviness and fatigue were thoroughly *overcome* by this system of procedures, life became *very* interesting again: awake, eternally awake, sleepless, glowing, burned out, exhausted and yet not tired, – this is how man, the 'sinner', looked when initiated into *these* mysteries. That great old magician fighting lethargy, the ascetic priest – had obviously won, *his* kingdom had come: already people were no longer making complaints *against* pain, they *thirsted* for it; '*more pain! more* pain' screamed the desire of his disciples and initiates for centuries. Every excess of feeling that hurt, everything that broke, overthrew, crushed, entranced and enraptured, the secret of the torture chamber, the ingenuity of hell itself – all this was now discovered, guessed at and utilized, everything was at the magician's service, from now on, everything served towards the victory of his ideal, the ascetic ideal . . . 'My kingdom is not of *this* world'[104] – is what he kept on saying: did he really have the right to talk like that? . . . Goethe claimed there were only thirty-six tragic situations:[105] from this we gather, if we did not know already, that Goethe was not an ascetic priest. He – knows more . . .

21

With regard to *this* whole type of priestly medication, the 'guilty' kind, every word of criticism is too much. That such an excess of feeling as prescribed by the ascetic priest to his patient (under the holiest of names, as goes without saying, and likewise impregnated with the sanctity of his purpose) should in any way have been really of *use* to any patient, who

---

[104] Gospel according to John 18.36.
[105] *Conversations with Eckermann*, 14 February 1830.

would want to justify a claim of this kind? At least we should be clear about the word 'use'. If we want to imply by it that such a system of treatment *improved* man, I shall not argue: I merely add what 'improved' means to me – exactly the same as tamed, weakened, discouraged, refined, molly-coddled, emasculated (so, almost the same as *injured* . . .). If, however, it is mainly a question of the sick, the disgruntled, the depressed, a system like this makes the sick patient *more* sick in every case, even if it makes him 'better'; just ask the doctors dealing with lunatics what always accompanies systematic application of penitential torments, contrition and spasms of redemption. Likewise, study history: everywhere where the ascetic priest has prevailed with this treatment of the sick, the sickness has increased in depth and breadth at a terrific speed. What was in each case the 'successful result'? A shattered nervous system added on to the sickness; and that applied on the largest and smallest scale, with individuals and with masses. We find terrible epileptic epidemics in the wake of training in penance and redemption, the greatest known to history such as those of the dancers of St Vitus and St John in the Middle Ages; another form its after-effect takes is terrible paralyses and long-term depressions, which can bring about, under certain circumstances, a permanent reversal of the temperament of a people or a town (Geneva, Basel); – the witch-hysteria belongs here, related somewhat to sleep-walking (eight great epidemic outbreaks of hysteria between 1564 and 1605 alone) –; in its wake we find, likewise, that death-seeking mass delirium, whose dreadful cry *'evviva la morte'*[106] could be heard over the whole of Europe, interrupted now by voluptuous, now by manic-destructive idiosyncrasies: and the same alternation of emotions, with the same intervals and reversals, can still be observed everywhere today in every case where the ascetic doctrine of sin has another great success (religious neurosis *appears* as a form of 'The Evil One': there is no doubt about it. What is it? *Quæritur.*[107]). Broadly speaking, the ascetic ideal and its sublimely moral cult, this most ingenious, unscrupulous and dangerous systematization of all the methods of emotional excess under the protection of holy intentions, has inscribed itself, in a terrible and unforgettable way, into the whole history of man, and unfortunately *not just* into his history . . . I can think of hardly anything that has sapped the *health* and racial strength of precisely the Europeans so destructively as this ideal; without any exaggeration we are

---

[106] 'Long live death'.
[107] 'That is the question'.

entitled to call it the *real catastrophe* in the history of the health of European man. The only thing that can be compared with its influence is the specifically Germanic influence: I mean the alcoholic-poisoning of Europe, which has strictly kept pace so far with the political and racial predominance of the Germans (– where they injected their blood, they injected their vice as well). – Third in line would be syphilis – *magno sed proxima intervallo.*[108]

22

The ascetic priest has ruined spiritual health wherever he has come to rule, consequently he has ruined taste *in artibus et litteris*[109] – he is still ruining it. 'Consequently'? – I hope you will simply allow me this 'consequently'; at any rate, I do not want to prove it. One single pointer: it refers to the basic text of Christian literature, its model, its 'book of books'. Even during the era of Græco-Roman splendour, which was also a splendour of books, in the face of an ancient world of writings that had not yet succumbed to decay and ruin, at a time when you could still read a few books we would nowadays give half of whole literatures to possess, the simplicity and vanity of Christian agitators – we call them Church Fathers – dared to decree: 'we have our own classical literature, *we don't need that of the Greeks*', and so saying, they proudly pointed to books of legends, letters of the apostles and apologetic little tracts, rather similar to the way the English 'Salvation Army' today fights Shakespeare and other 'heathens' with similar literature. I do not like the New Testament, you have worked that out by now; it almost disturbs me to be so very isolated in my taste regarding this most valued, over-valued work (the taste of two millenia is *against* me): but it is no use! 'Here I stand, I can do no other',[110] – I have the courage of my bad taste. The *Old* Testament – well, that is something quite different: every respect for the Old Testament! I find in it great men, heroic landscape and something of utmost rarity on earth, the incomparable naïvety of the *strong heart*; even more, I find a people. In contrast, in the New Testament I find nothing but petty sectarian groupings, nothing but rococo of the soul, nothing but arabesques, crannies and oddities, nothing but the air of the conventicle, not to forget the occasional breath of bucolic sugariness which belongs to the epoch (*and* to the Roman

---

[108] 'next but after a large interval'.

[109] 'in arts and letters'.

[110] Luther's reputed answer at the Diet of Worms (1521) to the demand that he recant.

province) and is neither Jewish nor Hellenistic. Humility and pomposity right next to each other; a garrulousness of feeling that almost stupefies; ostensibly passionate but lacking passion; embarrassing gesticulation; obviously breeding is lacking here. What right have people to make such a fuss about their little failings, like these pious little men do? No cock is going to crow over it; still less, God. Finally, they even want to have the 'crown of eternal life',[111] all these little provincial people: what for? why? it is the ultimate in presumption. An 'immortal' Peter: who could stand *him*? They have an ambition which makes you laugh: people like *that* regurgitating their most personal affairs, stupidities, sorrows and lingering worries, as if the in-itself of things were duty-bound to concern itself with all that, people like *that* never tire of involving God in the most trivial trouble they are in. And this continual use of first-name-terms with God, in the worst taste! This Jewish, not just Jewish pawing and nuzzling impertinence towards God! . . . There are small, despised 'heathen peoples' in East Asia who could have taught these first Christians something essential, some *tact* in reverence; the former do not permit themselves even to mention the name of their god, as Christian missionaries testify. This seems to me to be delicate enough; it is certainly too delicate and not just for the 'first' Christians: so that you can appreciate the contrast, think of Luther, the 'most eloquent' and most presumptuous peasant Germany has had, think of the Lutheran tone that he was pleased to adopt in his conversations with God. Luther's resistance to the mediating saints in the Church (in particular to the 'devil's sow, the Pope') was, no doubt, basically the resistance of a lout irritated by the Church's *good etiquette*, that reverential etiquette of hieratic taste, which only admits the more consecrated and silent into the holy of holies, and closes it to louts. These were absolutely not going to be allowed a voice here – but Luther, the peasant, wanted a complete change, it wasn't *German* enough for him: above all, he wanted to speak directly, in person and 'without ceremony' to his God . . . Well, he did it. – The ascetic ideal, you have guessed, was never anywhere a school of good taste, still less of good manners, – at best it was a school for hieratic manners, –: which means it contains within itself something that is the deadly enemy of all good manners, – lack of moderation, dislike of moderation, being itself a '*non plus ultra*'.[112]

---

[111] Revelation 2.10.
[112] 'unsurpassable extreme'.

23

The ascetic ideal not only spoilt health and taste, it spoilt a third, fourth, fifth, sixth thing as well – I shall refrain from saying what they all were (I would never reach the end!). I do not want to bring to light what the ideal *did*; rather simply what it *means*, what it indicates, what lies hidden behind, beneath and within it and what it expresses in a provisional, indistinct way, laden with question marks and misunderstandings. And only in regard to *this* purpose could I not spare my readers a glimpse of the monstrosity of its effects, and of how calamitous those effects are: to prepare them, as a matter of fact, for the final, terrible aspect that the question of the meaning of this ideal has for me. What does the *power* of that ideal mean, the *monstrosity* of its power? Why has it been given so much space? why has more effective resistance not been offered to it? The ascetic ideal expresses a will: *where* is the opposing will, in which an *opposing ideal* might express itself? The ascetic ideal has a *goal*, – this being so general that all the interests of human existence appear petty and narrow when measured against it; it inexorably interprets epochs, peoples, man, all with reference to this one goal, it permits of no other interpretation, no other goal, and rejects, denies, affirms, confirms only with reference to *its* interpretation (– and was there ever a system of interpretation more fully thought through?); it does not subject itself to any power, in fact, it believes in its superiority over any power, in its unconditional *superiority of rank* over any other power, – it believes there is nothing on earth of any power that does not first have to receive a meaning, a right to existence, a value from it, as a tool to *its* work, as a way and means to *its* goal, to *one* goal . . . Where is the *counterpart* to this closed system of will, goal and interpretation? Why is the counterpart *lacking*? . . . Where is the *other* 'one goal'? . . . But I am told it is *not* lacking, not only has it fought a long, successful fight with that ideal, but it has already mastered that ideal in all essentials: all our modern *science* is witness to that, – modern science which, as a genuine philosophy of reality, obviously believes only in itself, obviously possesses the courage to be itself, the will to be itself, and has hitherto got by well enough without God, the beyond and the virtues of denial. However, I am not impressed by such noise and rabble-rousers' claptrap: these people who trumpet reality are bad musicians, it is easy enough to hear that their voices do *not* come from the depths, the abyss of scientific conscience does *not* speak from them – for the scientific conscience today is an abyss –, the word 'science' is quite simply an obscenity in the traps of such trumpeters, an abuse, an indecency.

Precisely the opposite of what they are declaring here is the truth: science today has absolutely *no* faith in itself, let alone in an ideal *above* it, – and where it is still passion, love, fire, *suffering*, it is not the opposite of the ascetic ideal but rather the latter's own *most recent and noble manifestation*. Does that sound strange to you? . . . There are enough worthy and modest workers even amongst the scholars of today, who like their little corner and therefore, because they like being there, are occasionally somewhat presumptuous in making their demand heard that people today *ought* to be content in general, especially with science – there being so much useful work to be done. I do not deny it: I am the last to want to spoil the pleasure of these honest workers in their craft: for I delight in their work. But the fact that nowadays people are working hard in science, and that they are contented workmen, does *not* at all prove that today, science as a whole has a goal, a will, an ideal, a passion of great faith. The opposite, as I said, is the case: where it is not the most recent manifestation of the ascetic ideal – there are too few noble, exceptional cases for the general judgment to be deflected – then science today is a *hiding place* for all kinds of ill-humour, unbelief, gnawing worms, *despectio sui*,[113] bad conscience – it is the *disquiet* of the lack of ideals itself, the suffering from a *lack* of great love, the discontent over *enforced* contentedness. Oh, what does science not conceal today! how much it is *supposed* to conceal, at any rate! The industry of our best scholars, their unreflective diligence, heads smoking night and day, their very mastery of their craft – how often does all that mean trying to conceal something from themselves? Science as a means of self-anaesthetic: *do you know that?* . . . Everyone in contact with scholars has the experience that they are sometimes wounded to the marrow by a harmless word, we anger our scholarly friends at the very moment when we want to honour them, we make them lose their temper and control simply because we were too coarse to guess who we were actually dealing with, with *sufferers* who do not want to admit what they are to themselves, with people drugged and dazed who fear only one thing: *coming to consciousness* . . .

24

– And now consider the rarer cases of which I spoke, the last idealists we have today amongst philosophers and scholars: do we perhaps have, in them, the sought-for *opponents* of ascetic ideals, the latter's *counter-idealists?*

[113] 'contempt of self'.

In fact, they *believe* themselves to be, these 'unbelievers' (because that is what they all are); that seems to be their last remnant of faith, to be opponents of this ideal, so serious are they on this score, so passionate is their every word and gesture: – does what they believe therefore need to be *true?* . . . We 'knowers' are positively mistrustful of any kind of believers; our mistrust has gradually trained us to conclude the opposite to what was formerly concluded: namely, to presuppose, wherever the strength of a belief becomes prominent, a certain weakness, even *improbability* of proof. Even we do not deny that faith 'brings salvation':[114] *precisely for that reason* we deny that faith *proves* anything, – a strong faith which brings salvation is grounds for suspicion of the object of its faith, it does not establish truth, it establishes a certain probability – of *deception*. What now is the position in this case? – These 'no'-sayers and outsiders of today, those who are absolute in one thing, their demand for intellectual rigour [*Sauberkeit*], these hard, strict, abstinent, heroic minds who make up the glory of our time, all these pale atheists, Antichrists, immoralists, nihilists, these sceptics, ephectics,[115] *hectics* of the mind [*des Geistes*] (they are one and all the latter in a certain sense), these last idealists of knowledge in whom, alone, intellectual conscience dwells and is embodied these days, – they believe they are all as liberated as possible from the ascetic ideal, these 'free, *very* free spirits': and yet, I will tell them what they themselves cannot see – because they are standing too close to themselves – this ideal is quite simply *their* ideal as well, they themselves represent it nowadays, and perhaps no one else, they themselves are its most intellectualized product, its most advanced front-line troops and scouts, its most insidious, delicate and elusive form of seduction: – if I am at all able to solve riddles, I wish to claim to do so with *this* pronouncement! . . . These are very far from being *free* spirits: *because they still believe in truth* . . . When the Christian Crusaders in the East fell upon that invincible order of Assassins, the order of free spirits *par excellence*, the lowest rank of whom lived a life of obedience the like of which no monastic order has ever achieved, somehow or other they received an inkling of that symbol and watchword that was reserved for the highest ranks alone as their *secretum*: 'nothing is true, everything is permitted' . . . Certainly *that* was *freedom* of the mind [*des Geistes*], *with that* the termination of the belief in truth was *announced*. . . . Has a European or a Christian free-thinker [*Freigeist*] ever strayed into this proposition and

[114] Gospel according to Luke 1.45; Gospel according to John 20.29.
[115] Cf. note p. 81.

the labyrinth of its *consequences*? Does he know the Minotaur of this cave *from experience*? . . . I doubt it, indeed, I know otherwise: – nothing is stranger to these people who are absolute in one thing, these *so-called* 'free spirits', than freedom and release in that sense, in no respect are they more firmly bound; precisely in their faith in truth they are more rigid and more absolute than anyone else. Perhaps I am too familiar with all this: that venerable philosopher's abstinence prescribed by such a faith like that commits one, that stoicism of the intellect which, in the last resort, denies itself the 'no' just as strictly as the 'yes', that *will* to stand still before the factual, the *factum brutum*, that fatalism of '*petits faits*'[116] (*ce petit faitalisme*,[117] as I call it) in which French scholarship now seeks a kind of moral superiority over the German, that renunciation of any interpretation (of forcing, adjusting, shortening, omitting, filling-out, inventing, falsifying and everything else *essential* to interpretation) – on the whole, this expresses the asceticism of virtue just as well as any denial of sensuality (it is basically just a *modus* of this denial). However, the *compulsion* towards it, that unconditional will to truth, is *faith in the ascetic ideal itself*, even if, as an unconscious imperative, make no mistake about it, – it is the faith in a *metaphysical* value, a *value as such of truth* as vouched for and confirmed by that ideal alone (it stands and falls by that ideal). Strictly speaking, there is no 'presuppositionless' knowledge, the thought of such a thing is unthinkable, paralogical: a philosophy, a 'faith' always has to be there first, for knowledge to win from it a direction, a meaning, a limit, a method, a *right* to exist. (Whoever understands it the other way round and, for example, tries to place philosophy 'on a strictly scientific foundation', must first *stand on its head* not just philosophy, but also truth itself: the worst offence against decency which can occur in relation to two such respectable ladies!) Yes, there is no doubt – and here I let my *Gay Science* have a word, see the fifth book (section 344) – 'the truthful man, in that daring and final sense which faith in science presupposes, *thus affirms another world* from the one of life, nature and history; and inasmuch as he affirms this "other world", must he not therefore deny its opposite, this world, *our* world, in doing so? . . . Our faith in science is still based on a *metaphysical faith*, – even we knowers of today, we godless anti-metaphysicians, still take *our* fire from the blaze set alight by a faith thousands of years old, that faith of the Christians, which was also Plato's faith, that God is truth, that truth is *divine* . . . But what if precisely

[116] 'small facts'.
[117] 'this petty factualism' (with a rather lame pun: 'fatalisme' 'faitalisme').

this becomes more and more unbelievable, when nothing any longer turns out to be divine except for error, blindness and lies – and what if God himself turned out to be our oldest lie?' – – At this point we need to stop and take time to reflect. Science itself now *needs* a justification (which is not at all to say that there is one for it). On this question, turn to the most ancient and most modern philosophies: all of them lack a consciousness of the extent to which the will to truth itself needs a justification, here is a gap in every philosophy – how does it come about? Because the ascetic ideal has so far been *master* over all philosophy, because truth was set as being, as God, as the highest authority itself, because truth was not *allowed* to be a problem. Do you understand this 'allowed to be'? – From the very moment that faith in the God of the ascetic ideal is denied, *there is a new problem as well*: that of the *value* of truth. – The will to truth needs a critique – let us define our own task with this –, the value of truth is tentatively to be *called into question* . . . (Anyone who finds this put too briefly is advised to read that section of *Gay Science* with the title 'To what extent even we are still pious' (section 344[118]) better still, the whole fifth book of that work, similarly the preface to *Daybreak*.)

25

No! Do not come to me with science when I am looking for the natural antagonist to the ascetic ideal, when I ask: 'Where is the opposing will in which its *opposing ideal* expresses itself?' Science is not nearly independent enough for that, in every respect it first needs a value-ideal, a value-creating power, in whose *service* it *can believe* in itself, – science itself never creates values. Its relationship to the ascetic ideal is certainly not yet inherently antagonistic; indeed, it is much more the case, in general, that it still represents the driving force in the inner evolution of that ideal. Its repugnance and pugnacity are, on closer inspection, directed not at the ideal itself but at its outworks, its apparel and disguise, at the way the ideal temporarily hardens, solidifies, becomes dogmatic – science liberates what life is in it by denying what is exoteric in this ideal. Both of them, science and the ascetic ideal, are still on the same foundation – I have already explained –; that is to say, both overestimate truth (more correctly: they share the same faith that truth can*not* be assessed or criticized), and this makes them both *necessarily* allies, – so that, if they

---

[118] See below, Supplementary material, pp. 158–60.

must be fought, they can only be fought and called into question together. A depreciation of the value of the ascetic ideal inevitably brings about a depreciation of the value of science: one must keep one's eyes open and prick up one's ears for this in time! (*Art*, let me say at the outset, since I shall deal with this at length some day, – art, in which *lying* sanctifies itself and the *will to deception* has good conscience on its side, is much more fundamentally opposed to the ascetic ideal than science is: this was sensed instinctively by Plato, the greatest enemy of art Europe has yet produced. Plato *versus* Homer:[119] that is complete, genuine antagonism – on the one hand, the sincerest 'advocate of the beyond', the great slanderer of life, on the other hand, its involuntary idolater, the *golden* nature. Artistic servitude in the service of the ascetic ideal is thus the specific form of artistic *corruption*, unfortunately one of the most common: for nothing is more corruptible than an artist.) And when we view it physiologically, too, science rests on the same base as the ascetic ideal: the precondition of both the one and the other is a certain *impoverishment of life*, – the emotions cooled, the tempo slackened, dialectics in place of instinct, *solemnity* stamped on faces and gestures (solemnity, that most unmistakable sign of a more sluggish metabolism and of a struggling, more toiling life). Look at the epochs in the life of a people where scholars predominated: they are times of exhaustion, often of twilight, of decline, – gone are the overflowing energy, the certainty of life, the certainty as to the *future*. The preponderance of the mandarins never indicates anything good: any more than the rise of democracy, international courts of arbitration instead of wars, equal rights for women, the religion of compassion and everything else that is a symptom of life in decline. (Science conceived as a problem: what does science mean? – compare the Preface to *The Birth of Tragedy* on this.) No! – open your eyes! – this 'modern science' is, for the time being, the *best* ally for the ascetic ideal, for the simple reason that it is the most unconscious, involuntary, secret and subterranean! The 'poor in spirit'[120] and the scientific opponents of this ideal have up till now played the same game (by the way, beware of thinking that they are its opposite, i.e. the *rich* in spirit: – they are *not* that, I called them the hectics of the spirit). These famous *victories* of the latter: undoubtedly they are victories – but over what? The ascetic ideal was decidedly not conquered, it was, on the contrary, made stronger, I mean more elusive, more spiritual,

---

[119] See especially Plato's *Republic*, Books II, III, and X.
[120] Gospel according to Matthew 5.3.

more insidious by the fact that science constantly and unsparingly detached and broke off a wall or outwork that had attached itself to it and *coarsened* its appearance. Do you really think that, for example, the defeat of theological astronomy meant a defeat of that ideal? . . . Has man perhaps become less *in need* of a transcendent solution to the riddle of his existence because this existence has since come to look still more arbitrary, loiterer-like, and dispensable in the *visible* order of things? Has not man's self-deprecation, his *will* to self-deprecation, been unstoppably on the increase since Copernicus? Gone, alas, is his faith in his dignity, uniqueness, irreplaceableness in the rank-ordering of beings, – he has become *animal*, literally, unqualifiedly and unreservedly an animal, man who in his earlier faiths was almost God ('child of God', 'man of God') . . . Since Copernicus, man seems to have been on a downward path, – now he seems to be rolling faster and faster away from the centre – where to? into nothingness? into the '*piercing* sensation of his nothingness'? – Well! that would be the straight path – to the *old* ideal? . . . *All* science (and not just astronomy alone, the humiliating and degrading effects of which Kant singled out for the remarkable confession that 'it destroys my importance'[121] . . .), all science, natural as well as *unnatural* – this is the name I would give to the self-critique of knowledge – is nowadays seeking to talk man out of his former self-respect as though this were nothing but a bizarre piece of self-conceit; you could almost say that its own pride, its own austere form of stoical ataraxy, consisted in maintaining this laboriously won *self-contempt* of man as his last, most serious claim to self-respect (in fact, rightly so: for the person who feels contempt is always someone who 'has not forgotten how to respect' . . .). Does this really *work against* the ascetic ideal? Do people in all seriousness still really believe (as theologians imagined for a while), that, say, Kant's *victory* over theological conceptual dogmatism ('God', 'soul', 'freedom', 'immortality') damaged that ideal? – we shall not, for the moment, concern ourselves with whether Kant himself had anything like that in view. What is certain is that every sort of transcendentalist since Kant has had a winning hand, – they are emancipated from the theologians: what good luck! – he showed them the secret path on which, from now on, they could, independently, and with the best scientific decorum, pursue 'their heart's desires'. Likewise: who would blame the agnostics if, as worshippers of the unknown and the secret, they worship *the question mark* itself as God.

---

[121] *Critique of Pure Reason* A 289.

(Xaver Doudan on one occasion speaks of the ravages caused by *'l'habi-tude* d'admirer *l'inintelligible au lieu de rester tout simplement dans l'in-connu*';[122] he thinks the ancients avoided this.) Suppose that everything man 'knows' does not satisfy his desires but instead contradicts them and arouses horror, what a divine excuse it is to be permitted to lay the guilt for this at the door of 'knowing' rather than 'wishing'! . . . 'There is no knowing: *consequently* – there is a God': what a new *elegantia syllogismi*![123] What a *triumph* for the ascetic ideal! –

26

– Or did the whole of modern historiography take a more confident pos-ition regarding life and ideals? Its noblest claim nowadays is that it is a *mirror*, it rejects all teleology, it does not want to 'prove' anything any more; it scorns playing the judge, and shows good taste there, – it affirms as little as it denies, it asserts and 'describes' . . . All this is ascetic to a high degree; but to an even higher degree it is *nihilistic*, make no mistake about it! You see a sad, hard but determined gaze, – an eye *peers out*, like a lone explorer at the North Pole (perhaps so as not to peer in? or peer back? . . .). Here there is snow, here life is silenced; the last crows heard here are called 'what for?', 'in vain', *'nada'*[124] – here nothing flourishes or grows any more, except, perhaps, for St Petersburg metapolitics and Tolstoi's 'compassion'. With regard to that other type of historian, perhaps an even more 'modern', pleasure-seeking, voluptuous type who flirts with life as much as with the ascetic ideal, who uses the word 'artist' as a glove and comman-deers for himself the praise of contemplation: oh, how thirsty these cloying wits make me even for ascetics and winter landscapes! No! Let such 'con-templative' people go to the devil! I would vastly prefer to wander through the most sombre, grey, cold mists with those historic nihilists! – indeed, if I had to choose, I might even lend an ear to someone quite unhistorical, anti-historical (such as Dühring, whose voice enraptures a hitherto shy and unacknowledged species of 'beautiful souls' in Germany today, the species *anarchistica* within the educated proletariat). The 'contemplatives' are a hundred times worse –: I know of nothing as nauseating as this type of 'objective' armchair scholar and perfumed sensualist towards history,

---

[122] 'the habit of transforming the unintelligible into an object of admiration rather than remaining simply in the unknown'.

[123] 'elegant form of inference'.

[124] nothing.

half-priest, half-satyr, Renan-scented, who reveals, by the mere falsetto of his approval, all that he lacks, *where* he lacks it, *where* the fates in his case have been, alas! rather too surgical with their cruel scissors! I have neither taste nor patience for this: the person with nothing to lose by doing so can keep patient at such sights, – I become angry at them, such 'spectators' make me more embittered towards the 'play' than the play itself does (history itself, you understand), anacreontic moods seize me unexpectedly. Nature, which gave the bull its horn and the lion its χάσμ' ὀδόντων,[125] gave me a foot – what for? . . . To kick, by holy Anacreon! not just to run away: to kick to pieces the rotten armchairs, this cowardly contemplative-ness, this lewd eunuchism towards history, this flirting with ascetic ideals, this tartuffery of fairness that results from impotence! I have every respect for the ascetic ideal *in so far as it is honest*! so long as it believes in itself and does not tell us bad jokes! But I dislike all these coquettish bedbugs, with their insatiable ambition to smell out infinity until finally infinity smells of bedbugs; I dislike the whitewashed graves which portray life; I dislike the tired and worn-out who cocoon themselves in wisdom and look 'objective'; I dislike agitators dressed up as heroes who wear a magic cap of ideals around their straw heads; I dislike the ambitious artists who want to be taken for ascetics and priests and are basically just pathetic clowns; I also dislike the latest speculators in idealism, the anti-Semites, who nowadays roll their Christian-Aryan-Philistine eyes and try to stir up the bovine elements in the population through a misuse, which exhausts all patience, of the cheapest means of agitating, the moralistic attitude (– the fact that *every* type of charlatanism in today's Germany is rewarded with success is related to the practically undeniable, already palpable *desolation* of the German spirit [*des deutschen Geistes*], the cause of which I look for in the almost exclusive diet of newspapers, politics, beer and Wagnerian music, in addition, the precondition for this regimen: namely the national constrict-edness and vanity, the strong but narrow-minded principle of *Deutschland Deutschland über alles*, as well as the *paralysis agitans*[126] of 'modern ideals'). Europe is rich and inventive nowadays, especially in methods of stimula-tion, nothing seems more essential than *stimulantia* and strong liquor: which explains the enormous hypocrisy in ideals, spirit's strongest liquor, and therefore, also, the disgusting, foul-smelling, mendacious,

---

[125] 'yawning gap of teeth'. This is from number 26 of the poems in the collection ascribed to 'Anacreon'. (Modern scholarship no longer attributes these poems to the sixth-century poet of Teos.)

[126] 'shaking palsy'.

pseudo–alcoholic air everywhere. I want to know how many shiploads of sham idealism, hero-outfits and tinny rattle of great words, how many tons of sugared, alcoholic sympathy (distillery: *la religion de la souffrance*[127]), how many stilts of 'noble indignation' to help the spiritually flat-footed, how many *comedians* of the Christian moral ideal Europe would have to export for its air to smell cleaner . . . Obviously, a new type of *trade* possibility is opened up with regard to this overproduction, obviously, 'business' can be made out of little idolatrous ideals and related 'idealists': do not let this opportunity slip by! Who has enough courage for it? – it is in our *hands* whether we 'idealize' the whole earth! . . . But why am I talking about courage: one thing only is needful, a hand, an uninhibited, very uninhibited hand . . .

27

– Enough! Enough! Let us leave these curiosities and complexities of the most modern spirit, which have as many ridiculous as irritating aspects: *our* problem, indeed, can do without them, the problem of the *meaning* of the ascetic ideal, – what has that to do with yesterday and today! These things will be addressed by me more fully and seriously in another connection (with the title 'On the History of European Nihilism'; for which I refer you to a work I am writing, *The Will to Power. Attempt at a Revaluation of all Values*). The only reason I have alluded to this is that the ascetic ideal has, for the present, even in the most spiritual sphere, only one type of real enemy and *injurer*: these are the comedians of this ideal – because they arouse mistrust. Everywhere else where spirit is at work in a rigorous, powerful and honest way, it now completely lacks an ideal – the popular expression for this abstinence is 'atheism' –: *except for its will to truth*. But this will, this *remnant* of an ideal, if you believe me, is that ideal itself in its strictest, most spiritual formulation, completely esoteric, totally stripped of externals, and thus not so much its remnant as its *kernel*. Unconditional, honest atheism (– *its* air alone is what we breathe, we more spiritual men of the age!) is therefore *not* opposed to the ascetic ideal as it appears to be; instead, it is only one of the ideal's last phases of development, one of its final forms and inherent logical conclusions, – it is the awe-inspiring *catastrophe* of a two-thousand-year discipline in truth-telling, which finally forbids itself the *lie entailed in the belief in*

---

[127] 'the religion of suffering'.

God. (The same process of development in India, completely independently, which therefore proves something; the same ideal forcing the same conclusion; the decisive point was reached five centuries before the European era began, with Buddha or, more precisely: already with the Sankhya philosophy subsequently popularized by Buddha and made into a religion.) *What*, strictly speaking, has actually *conquered* the Christian God? The answer is in my *Gay Science* (section 357):[128] 'Christian morality itself, the concept of truthfulness which was taken more and more seriously, the confessional punctiliousness of Christian conscience, translated and sublimated into scientific conscience, into intellectual rigour at any price. Regarding nature as though it were a proof of God's goodness and providence; interpreting history in honour of divine reason, as a constant testimonial to an ethical world order and ethical ultimate purpose; explaining all one's own experiences in the way pious folk have done for long enough, as though everything were providence, a sign, intended, and sent for the salvation of the soul: now all that is *over*, it has conscience *against* it, every sensitive conscience sees it as indecent, dishonest, as a pack of lies, feminism, weakness, cowardice, – this severity makes us *good Europeans* if anything does, and heirs to Europe's most protracted and bravest self-overcoming!' . . . All great things bring about their own demise through an act of self-sublimation: that is the law of life, the law of *necessary* 'self-overcoming' in the essence of life, – the lawgiver himself is always ultimately exposed to the cry: '*patere legem, quam ipse tulisti*'.[129] In this way, Christianity *as a dogma* was destroyed by its own morality, in the same way Christianity *as a morality* must also be destroyed, – we stand on the threshold of *this* occurrence. After Christian truthfulness has drawn one conclusion after another, it will finally draw the *strongest conclusion*, that *against* itself; this will, however, happen when it asks itself, '*What does all will to truth mean?*' . . . and here I touch on my problem again, on our problem, my *unknown* friends (– because I don't *know* of any friend as yet): what meaning does *our* being have, if it were not that that will to truth has become conscious of itself *as a problem* in us? . . . Without a doubt, from now on, morality will be *destroyed* by the will to truth's becoming-conscious-of-itself: that great drama in a hundred acts reserved for Europe in the next two centuries, the most terrible, most questionable drama but perhaps also the one most rich in hope . . .

[128] See below Supplementary material, pp. 160–3.
[129] 'Submit to the law you have yourself made'.

28

Except for the ascetic ideal: man, the *animal* man, had no meaning up to now. His existence on earth had no purpose; 'What is man for, actually?' – was a question without an answer; there was no *will* for man and earth; behind every great human destiny sounded the even louder refrain 'in vain!' *This* is what the ascetic ideal meant: something was *missing*, there was an immense *lacuna* around man, – he himself could think of no justification or explanation or affirmation, he *suffered* from the problem of what he meant. Other things made him suffer too, in the main he was a *sickly* animal: but suffering itself was *not* his problem, instead, the fact that there was no answer to the question he screamed, 'Suffering for *what*?' Man, the bravest animal and most prone to suffer, does *not* deny suffering as such: he *wills* it, he even seeks it out, provided he is shown a *meaning* for it, a *purpose* of suffering. The meaninglessness of suffering, *not* the suffering, was the curse that has so far blanketed mankind, – and *the ascetic ideal offered man a meaning!* Up to now it was the only meaning, but any meaning at all is better than no meaning at all; the ascetic ideal was, in every respect, the ultimate *'faute de mieux' par excellence*. Within it, suffering was interpreted; the enormous emptiness seemed filled; the door was shut on all suicidal nihilism. The interpretation – without a doubt – brought new suffering with it, deeper, more internal, more poisonous suffering, suffering that gnawed away more intensely at life: it brought all suffering within the perspective of *guilt* . . . But in spite of all that – man was *saved*, he had a *meaning*, from now on he was no longer like a leaf in the breeze, the plaything of the absurd, of 'non-sense'; from now on he could *will* something, – no matter what, why and how he did it at first, the *will itself was saved*. It is absolutely impossible for us to conceal what was actually expressed by that whole willing that derives its direction from the ascetic ideal: this hatred of the human, and even more of the animalistic, even more of the material, this horror of the senses, of reason itself, this fear of happiness and beauty, this longing to get away from appearance, transience, growth, death, wishing, longing itself – all that means, let us dare to grasp it, a *will to nothingness*, an aversion to life, a rebellion against the most fundamental prerequisites of life, but it is and remains a *will*! . . . And, to conclude by saying what I said at the beginning: man still prefers to *will nothingness*, than *not* will . . .

SUPPLEMENTARY MATERIAL TO ON THE GENEALOGY OF MORALITY

The following section includes full translation of all the material which Nietzsche either refers to or partly cites from in the *Genealogy of Morality*.

Human, All Too Human

Volume 1, Section 45

Twofold prehistory of good and evil. – The concept good and evil has a two-fold prehistory: *firstly* in the soul of the ruling tribes and castes. He who has the power to requite, good with good, evil with evil, and also actually practises requital – is, that is to say, grateful and revengeful – is called good; he who is powerless and cannot requite counts as bad. As a good man one belongs to the 'good', a community which has a sense of belonging together because all the individuals in it are combined with one another through the capacity for requital. As a bad man one belongs to the 'bad', to a swarm of subject, powerless people who have no sense of belonging together. The good are a caste, the bad a mass like grains of sand. Good and bad is for a long time the same thing as noble and base, master and slave. On the other hand, one does not regard the enemy as evil: he can requite. In Homer the Trojan and the Greek are both good. It is not he who does us harm but he who is contemptible who counts as bad. In the community of the good goodness is inherited; it is impossible that a bad man could grow up out of such good soil. If, however, one of the good should do something unworthy of the good, one looks for excuses; one ascribes the guilt to a god, for example, by saying he struck the good man with madness and rendered him blind. – *Then* in the soul of the subjected, the powerless. Here every *other* man, whether he be noble or base, counts as inimical, ruthless, cruel, cunning, ready to take advantage. Evil is the characterizing expression for man, indeed for every living being one supposes to exist, for a god, for example; human, divine mean the same thing as diabolical, evil. Signs of goodness, benevolence, sympathy are received fearfully as a trick, a prelude with a dreadful termination, a means of confusing and outwitting, in short as refined wickedness. When this disposition exists in the individual a community can hardly arise, at best the most rudimentary form of community: so that wherever this conception of good and evil reigns the downfall of such individuals, of their tribes and races, is near. – Our present morality has grown up in the soil of the *ruling* tribes and castes.

I, 92

Origin of justice. – Justice (fairness) originates between parties of approximately *equal power*, as Thucydides correctly grasped (in the terrible colloquy between the Athenian and Melian ambassadors): where there is no clearly recognizable superiority of force and a contest would result in mutual injury producing no decisive outcome the idea arises of coming to an understanding and negotiating over one another's demands: the characteristic of *exchange* is the original characteristic of justice. Each satisfies the other, inasmuch as each acquires what he values more than the other does. One gives to the other what he wants to have, to be henceforth his own, and in return receives what one oneself desires. Justice is thus requital and exchange under the presupposition of an approximately equal power position: revenge therefore belongs originally within the domain of justice, it is an exchange. Gratitude likewise. – Justice goes back naturally to the viewpoint of an enlightened self-preservation, thus to the egoism of the reflection: 'to what end should I injure myself uselessly and perhaps even then not achieve my goal?' – so much for the *origin* of justice. Since, in accordance with their intellectual habit, men have *forgotten* the original purpose of so-called just and fair actions, and especially because children have for millennia been trained to admire and imitate such actions, it has gradually come to appear that a just action is an unegoistic one: but it is on this appearance that the high value accorded it depends; and this high value is, moreover, continually increasing, as all valuations do: for something highly valued is striven for, imitated, multiplied through sacrifice, and grows as the worth of the toil and zeal expended by each individual is added to the worth of the valued thing – How little moral would the world appear without forgetfulness! A poet could say that God has placed forgetfulness as a doorkeeper on the threshold of the temple of human dignity.

1, 96

Custom and what is in accordance with it. – To be moral, to act in accordance with custom, to be ethical means to practise obedience towards a law or tradition established from of old. Whether one subjects oneself with effort or gladly and willingly makes no difference, it is enough that one does it. He is called 'good' who does what is customary as if by nature, as a result of a long inheritance, that is to say easily and gladly, and this is so whatever what is customary may be (exacts revenge, for example, when exacting revenge is part of good custom, as it was with the ancient Greeks). He is called good because he is good 'for something'; since, however, benevolence, sympathy and the like have throughout all the changes in customs always been seen as 'good for something', as useful, it is now above all the benevolent, the helpful who are called 'good'. To be evil is 'not to act in accordance with custom', to practise things not sanctioned by custom, to resist tradition, however rational or stupid that tradition may be; in all the laws of custom of all times, however, doing injury to one's neighbour has been seen as injurious above all else, so that now at the word 'evil' we think especially of voluntarily doing injury to one's neighbour. 'Egoistic' and 'unegoistic' is not the fundamental antithesis which has led men to make the distinction between 'in accordance with custom' and 'in defiance of custom', between good and evil, but adherence to a tradition, a law, and severance from it. How the tradition has *arisen* is here a matter of indifference, and has in any event nothing to do with good and evil or with any kind of immanent categorical imperative; it is above all directed at the preservation of a *community*, a people; every superstitious usage which has arisen on the basis of some chance event mistakenly interpreted enforces a tradition which it is in accordance with custom to follow; for to sever oneself from it is dangerous, and even more injurious to the *community* than to the individual (because the gods punish the community for misdeeds and for every violation of their privileges and only to that extent punish the individual). Every tradition now continually grows more venerable the farther away its origin lies and the more this origin is forgotten; the respect paid to it increases from generation to generation, the tradition at last becomes holy and evokes awe and reverence; and thus the morality of piety is in any event a much older morality than that which demands unegoistic actions.

I, 99

The innocent element in so-called evil acts. – All 'evil' acts are motivated by the drive to preservation or, more exactly, by the individual's intention of procuring pleasure and avoiding displeasure; so motivated, however, they are not evil. 'Procuring pain as such' *does not exist*, except in the brains of philosophers, neither does 'procuring pleasure as such' (compassion[1] in the Schopenhauerian sense). In conditions obtaining *before* the existence of the state we kill the creature, be it ape or man, that seeks to deprive us of a fruit of the tree if we happen to be hungry and are making for the tree ourself: as we would still do to the animals even now if we were travelling in inhospitable regions. – The evil acts at which we are now most indignant rest on the error that he who perpetrates them against us possesses free will, that is to say, that he could have *chosen* not to cause us this harm. It is this belief in choice that engenders hatred, revengefulness, deceitfulness, all the degrading our imagination undergoes, while we are far less censorious towards an animal because we regard it as unaccountable. To do injury not from the drive to preservation but as requital – is the consequence of a mistaken judgment and therefore likewise innocent. In conditions obtaining before the existence of the state the individual can act harshly and cruelly for the purpose of *frightening* other creatures: to secure his existence through such fear-inspiring tests of his power. Thus does the man of violence, of power, the original founder of states, act when he subjugates the weaker. His right to do so is the same as the state now relegates to itself; or rather, there exists no right that can prevent this from happening. The ground for any kind of morality can then be prepared only when a greater individual or a collective individuality, for example society, the state, subjugates all other individuals, that is to say draws them out of their isolation and orders them within a collective. Morality is preceded by *compulsion*, indeed it is for a time itself still compulsion, to which one accommodates oneself for the avoidance of what one regards as unpleasurable. Later it becomes custom, later still voluntary obedience, finally almost instinct: then, like all that has for a long time been habitual and natural, it is associated with pleasure – and is now called *virtue*.

I, 136

Of Christian asceticism and holiness. – However much individual thinkers have exerted themselves to represent those strange phenomena

---

[1] *Mitleid*: changed to compassion, and on following pages to page 144.

of morality usually called asceticism and holiness as a marvel and miracle to attempt a rational explanation of which is almost a sacrilege and pro-fanation: the urge to commit this sacrilege is, on the other hand, every bit as strong. A mighty drive of *nature* has at all times prompted a protest against these phenomena as such; science, insofar as it is, as aforesaid, an imitation of nature, permits itself at least to register a protest against the alleged inexplicability, indeed inapproachability, of the said phenomena. So far, to be sure, it has done so in vain: they are still unexplained, a fact that gives great satisfaction to the above-mentioned votaries of the morally miraculous. For, speaking quite generally, the unexplained is to be altogether inexplicable, the inexplicable altogether unnatural, super-natural, miraculous – thus sounds the demand in the souls of all religious people and metaphysicians (in those of the artists, too, when they are also thinkers); while the scientific man sees in this demand the 'evil principle'. – The first general probability one arrives at when reflecting on holiness and asceticism is that its nature is a *complex* one: for almost everywhere, within the physical world as well as in the moral, the supposedly marvel-lous has successfully been traced back to the complex, to the multiply caused. Let us therefore venture first to isolate individual drives in the soul of the saint and ascetic and then conclude by thinking of them entwined together.

Volume 11, *Assorted Opinions and Maxims*, section 89

Custom and its sacrifices. – The origin of custom lies in two ideas: 'the community is worth more than the individual' and 'an enduring advan-tage is to be preferred to a transient one'; from which it follows that the enduring advantage of the community is to take unconditional prece-dence over the advantage of the individual, especially over his momentary well-being but also over his enduring advantage and even over his sur-vival. Even if the individual suffers from an arrangement which benefits the whole, even if he languishes under it, perishes by it – the custom must be maintained the sacrifice offered up. Such an attitude *originates*, however, only in those who are *not* the sacrifice – for the latter urges that, in his own case, the individual could be worth more than the many, like-wise that present enjoyment, the moment in paradise, is perhaps to be rated higher than an insipid living-on in a painless condition of comfort. The philosophy of the sacrificial beast, however, is always noised abroad too late: and so we continue on with custom and *morality* [*Sittlichkeit*]: which latter is nothing other than simply a feeling for the whole content of those customs under which we live and have been raised – and raised, indeed, not as an individual, but as a member of the whole, as a cipher in a majority. – So it comes about that through his morality the individual *outvotes* himself.

Volume 11, *The Wanderer and His Shadow*, section 22

Principle of equilibrium. – The brigand and the man of power who promises to defend a community against the brigand are probably at bottom very similar beings, except that the latter obtains what he wants in a different way from the former: namely through regular tributes paid to him by the community and not by imposts levied by force. (It is the same relationship as that between merchant and pirate, who are for a long time one and the same person: where one function does not seem to him advisable he practises the other. Even now, indeed, merchant's morality is really, only a *more* prudent form of pirate's morality: to buy as cheap as possible – where possible for no more than the operational costs – to sell as dear as possible.) The essential thing is: this man of power promises to maintain an *equilibrium* with the brigand; in this the weaker perceive a possibility of living. For they must either combine together to produce an *equivalent* power or subject themselves to one already possessing this equivalent power (perform services for him in exchange for his protection). The latter proceeding is easily the preferred one, because at bottom it holds *two* dangerous beings in check: the former through the latter, the latter through considerations of advantage; for the latter derives benefit from treating the subject community with kindness or restraint so that they may feed not only themselves but their master too. In reality the people can still have a hard enough time of it even under this arrangement, but when they compare it with the perpetual possibility of complete *destruction* that preceded it they find even this condition endurable. – The community is originally the organization of the weak for the production of an *equilibrium* with powers that threaten it with danger. An organization to produce preponderance would be more advisable if the community could thereby become strong enough to *destroy* the threatening power once and for all: and if it were a matter of a single powerful depredator this would certainly be *attempted*. If, however, he is the head of a clan or has a large following his speedy and decisive destruction is unlikely to be accomplished and what is to be expected is a long-drawn-out *feud*: but this state of things is the least desirable one for the community, since it must deprive them of the time they need for the pro-vision of their subsistence with the regularity it requires and be attended by the ever-present threat that they will be deprived of all the products of their labours. That is why the community prefers to bring its power of defence and attack up to precisely the point at which the power possessed by its dangerous neighbour stands and then to give him to understand that the scales are now evenly balanced: why, in that event, should they not be good friends with one another? – *Equilibrium* is thus a very import-ant concept for the oldest theory of law and morality; equilibrium is the basis of justice. When in ruder ages justice says: 'An eye for an eye, a tooth for a tooth', it presupposes that equilibrium has been attained and seeks through this retribution to *preserve* it: so that when one man now trans-gresses against another, the other no longer takes on him the revenge of blind animosity. On the contrary, by virtue of the *jus talionis* the equilib-rium of the disturbed power relationship is *restored*: for in such primeval conditions one eye, one arm *more* is one piece of power more, one weight more in the scales. – Within a community in which all regard themselves as equivalent there exist *disgrace* and punishment as measures against transgressions, that is to say against disruptions of the principle of equi-librium: disgrace as a weight placed in the scales against the encroaching individual who has procured advantages for himself through his encroachment and now through the disgrace he incurs experiences dis-advantages which abolish these earlier advantages and *outweigh* them. The same applies to punishment: against the preponderance which every criminal promises himself it imposes a far greater counter-weight, enforced imprisonment for acts of violence, restitution and punitive fines for theft. In this way the transgressor is *reminded* that through his act he has *excluded* himself from the community and its moral *advantages*: the community treats him as one who is not equivalent, as one of the weak standing outside it; that is why punishment is not only retribution but contains something *more*, something of the *harshness of the state of nature*; it is precisely *this* that it wants to *recall*.

11, 26

Rule of law as a means. – *Law*, reposing on compacts between *equals*, continues to exist for so long as the power of those who have concluded these compacts remains equal or similar; prudence created law to put an end to feuding and to *useless* squandering between forces of similar strength. But *just as definitive* an end is put to them if one party has *become* decisively *weaker* than the other: then subjection enters in and law *ceases*, but the consequence is the same as that previously attained through the rule of law. For now it is the *prudence* of the dominant party which advises that the strength of the subjected should be *economized* and not uselessly squandered: and often the subjected find themselves in more favourable circumstances than they did when they were equals. – The rule of law is thus a temporary means advised by prudence, not an end.

II, 33

Elements of revenge. – The word 'revenge' is said so quickly it almost seems as if it could contain no more than one conceptual and perceptional root. And so one continues to strive to discover it: just as our economists have not yet wearied of scenting a similar unity in the word 'value' and of searching after the original root-concept of the word. As if every word were not a pocket into which now this, now that, now several things at once have been put! Thus 'revenge', too, is now this, now that, now something more combined. Distinguish first of all that defensive return blow which one delivers even against lifeless objects (moving machinery, for example) which have hurt us: the sense of our counter-action is to put a stop to the injury by putting a stop to the machine. To achieve this the violence of the counter-blow sometimes has to be so great as to shatter the machine; if, however, it is in fact too strong to be instantly destroyed by a single individual, the latter will nonetheless still deliver the most vigorous blow of which he is capable – as a last-ditch effort, so to speak. One behaves in a similar way towards people who have harmed us when we feel the injury directly; if one wants to call this an act of revenge, all well and good; only let it be considered that *self-preservation* alone has here set its clockwork of reason in motion, and that one has fundamentally been thinking, not of the person who caused the injury, but only of oneself: we act thus *without* wanting to do harm in return, but only so as *to get out* with life and limb. – One needs *time* if one is to transfer one's thoughts from oneself to one's opponent and to ask oneself how he can be hit at most grievously. This happens in the second species of revenge: its presupposition is a reflection over the other's vulnerability and capacity for suffering: one wants to hurt. To secure himself against further harm is here so far from the mind of the revenger that he almost always brings further harm upon himself and very often cold-bloodedly anticipates it. If in the case of the first species of revenge it was fear of a second blow which made the counter-blow as vigorous as possible, here there is almost complete indifference to what the opponent *will* do; the vigour of the counterblow is determined only by that which he *has* done to us. What, then, has he done? And of what use is it to us if our opponent now suffers after we have suffered through him? It is a question of *restitution*: while the act of revenge of the first species serves only *self-preservation*. Perhaps we lost property, rank, friends, children through our opponent – these losses are not made good by revenge, the restitution applies only to an *attendant loss* occasioned by the other losses referred to. Restitutional revenge does not protect one from further harm, it does not make good the harm one has suffered – except in one case. If our *honour* has suffered through our opponent revenge is capable of *restoring* it. But our honour has suffered harm in every case in which someone has done us a deliberate injury: for our opponent proved thereby that he did not *fear* us. By revenging ourself on him we prove that we do not fear him either: it is in this that the compensation, the restitution lies. (The objective of demonstrating the complete absence of *fear* goes so far in the case of some people that the danger to themselves involved in the revenge – loss of health or life or other deprivations – counts as an indispensable condition of the revenge. That is why they choose the path of the duel even when the courts offer them a means of acquiring compensation for the offence they have sustained: they refuse to regard as sufficient a restitution of their honour that involves no risk because it cannot serve to demonstrate their lack of fear.) – In the first species of revenge it is precisely fear which directs the counter-blow: here, on the contrary, it is the absence of fear which, as stated, *wants to prove itself* through the counter-blow. – Nothing, therefore, could appear more different than the inner motives of these two modes of action which are called by the common word 'revenge': and yet it very often happens that the revenger is unclear as to what has really determined his action; perhaps he delivered the counter-blow out of fear and to preserve himself but afterwards, when he has had time to reflect on the motive of wounded honour, convinces himself he has exacted revenge on account of his honour: – this motive is, after all, *nobler* than the other. An essential element in this is whether he sees his honour as having been injured in the eyes of others (the world) or only in the eyes of him who injured it: in the latter case he will prefer secret revenge, in the former public. His revenge will be the more incensed or the more moderate according to how deeply or weakly he can think his way into the soul of the perpetrator and the witnesses of his injury; if he is wholly lacking in this kind of imagination he will not think of revenge at all, since the feeling of 'honour' will not be present in him and thus cannot be wounded. He will likewise not think of revenge if he *despises* the perpetrator and the witnesses: because, as people he despises, they cannot accord him any honour and consequently cannot take any honour from him either. Finally, he will refrain from revenge in the not uncommon case that he loves the perpetrator: he will thus lose honour in the perpetrator's eyes, to be sure, and will perhaps become less worthy of being loved in return. But to renounce even all claim to love in return is a sacrifice which love is prepared to make if only it does not *have to hurt* the beloved being: this would mean hurting himself more than any sacrifice hurts. – Thus: everyone will revenge himself, except if he is without honour or full of contempt or full of love for the person who has harmed and offended him. Even when he turns to the courts he desires revenge as a private person: *additionally*, however, as a fore-thoughtful man of society, he desires the revenge of society on one who does not *honour* it. Through judicial punishment, private honour as well as the honour of society is thus *restored:* that is to say – punishment is revenge. – Undoubtedly there is also in it those other elements of revenge already described, insofar as through punishment society serves its own *self-preservation* and delivers a counterblow in *self-defence*. Punishment serves to prevent *further* injury, it wishes to *deter*. Two such various elements of revenge are thus actually *united* in punishment, and the main effect of this may be to sustain the confusion of concepts referred to by virtue of which the individual who takes revenge usually does not know what he really wants.

Daybreak

Book 1, section 9

Concept of morality of custom. – In comparison with the mode of life of whole millennia of mankind we present-day men live in a very immoral age: the power of custom is astonishingly enfeebled and the moral sense so rarefied and lofty it may be described as having more or less evaporated. That is why the fundamental insights into the origin of morality are so difficult for us latecomers, and even when we have acquired them we find it impossible to enunciate them, because they sound so uncouth or because they seem to slander morality! This is, for example, already the case with the *chief proposition*: morality is nothing other (therefore *no more!*) than obedience to customs, of whatever kind they may be; customs, however, are the *traditional* way of behaving and evaluating. In things in which no tradition commands there is no morality; and the less life is determined by tradition, the smaller the circle of morality. The free human being is immoral because in all things he is *determined* to depend upon himself and not upon a tradition: in all the original conditions of mankind, 'evil' signifies the same as 'individual', 'free', 'capricious', 'unusual', 'unforeseen', 'incalculable'. Judged by the standard of these conditions, if an action is performed *not* because tradition commands it but for other motives (because of its usefulness to the individual, for example), even indeed for precisely the motives which once founded the tradition, it is called immoral and is felt to be so by him who performed it: for it was not performed in obedience to tradition. What is tradition? A higher authority which one obeys, not because it commands what is *useful* to us, but because it *commands*. – What distinguishes this feeling in the presence of tradition from the feeling of fear in general? It is fear in the presence of a higher intellect which here commands, of an incomprehensible, indefinite power, of something more than personal – there is *superstition* in this fear. – Originally all education and care of health, marriage, cure of sickness, agriculture, war, speech and silence, traffic with one another and with the gods belonged within the domain of morality: they demanded one observe prescriptions *without thinking of oneself* as an individual. Originally, therefore, everything was custom, and whoever wanted to elevate himself above it had to become lawgiver and medicine man and a kind of demi-god: that is to say, he had to *make customs* – a dreadful, mortally dangerous thing! Who is the most moral man? *First*, he who obeys the law most frequently: who, like the Brahmin, bears a consciousness of the law with him everywhere and into every minute division of time, so that he is continually inventive in creating opportunities for obeying the law. *Then*, he who obeys it even in the most difficult cases. The most moral man is he who *sacrifices* the most to custom: what, however, are the greatest sacrifices? The way in which this question is answered determines the development of several diverse kinds of morality; but the most important distinction remains that which divides the morality of *most frequent obedience* from that of the *most difficult* obedience. Let us not deceive ourselves as to the motivation of that morality which demands difficulty of obedience to custom as the mark of morality! Self-overcoming is demanded, *not* on account of the useful consequences it may have for the individual, but so that the hegemony of custom, tradition, shall be made evident in despite of the private desires and advantages of the individual: the individual is to sacrifice himself – that is the commandment of morality of custom. – Those moralists, on the other hand, who, following in the footsteps of Socrates, offer the *individual* a morality of self-control and temperance as a means to his own *advantage*, as his personal key to happiness, *are the exceptions* – and if it seems otherwise to us that is because we have been brought up in their after-effect: they all take a new path under the highest disapprobation of all advocates of morality of custom – they cut themselves off from the community, as immoral men, and are in the profoundest sense evil. Thus to a virtuous Roman of the old stamp every *Christian* who 'considered first of all his *own* salvation' appeared – evil. – Everywhere that a community, and consequently a morality of custom exists, the idea also predominates that punishment for breaches of custom will fall before all on the community: that supernatural punishment whose forms of expression and limitations are so hard to comprehend and are explored with so much superstitious fear. The community can compel the individual to compensate another individual or the community for the immediate injury his action has brought in its train; it can also take a kind of revenge on the individual for having, as a supposed after-effect of his action, caused the clouds and storms of divine anger to have gathered over the community – but it feels the individual's guilt above all as *its own* guilt and bears the punishment as *its own* punishment –: 'customs have grown lax', each wails in his soul, 'if such actions as this are possible'. Every individual action, every individual mode of thought arouses dread; it is impossible to compute what precisely the rarer, choicer, more original spirits in the whole course of history have had to suffer through being felt as evil and dangerous; indeed through *feeling themselves to be so*. Under the dominion of the morality of custom, originality of every kind has acquired a bad conscience; the sky above the best men is for this reason to this very moment gloomier than it need be.

I, 14

Significance of madness in the history of morality. – When in spite of that fearful pressure of 'morality of custom' under which all the communities of mankind have lived, many millennia before the beginnings of our calendar and also on the whole during the course of it up to the present day (we ourselves dwell in the little world of the exceptions and, so to speak, in the evil zone): – when, I say, in spite of this, new and deviate ideas, evaluations, drives again and again broke out, they did so accompanied by a dreadful attendant: almost everywhere it was madness which prepared the way for the new idea, which broke the spell of a venerated usage and superstition. Do you understand why it had to be madness which did this? Something in voice and bearing as uncanny and incalculable as the demonic moods of the weather and the sea and therefore worthy of a similar awe and observation? Something that bore so visibly the sign of total unfreedom as the convulsions and froth of the epileptic, that seemed to mark the madman as the mask and speaking-trumpet of a divinity? Something that awoke in the bearer of a new idea himself reverence for and dread of himself and no longer pangs of conscience and drove him to become the prophet and martyr of his idea? – while it is constantly suggested to us today that, instead of a grain of salt, a grain of the spice of madness is joined to genius, all earlier people found it much more likely that wherever there is madness there is also a grain of genius and wisdom – something 'divine', as one whispered to oneself. Or rather: as one said aloud forcefully enough. 'It is through madness that the greatest good things have come to Greece', Plato said, in concert with all ancient mankind. Let us go a step further: all superior men who were irresistibly drawn to throw off the yoke of any kind of morality and to frame new laws had, if they were not actually mad, no alternative but to make themselves or pretend to be mad – and this indeed applies to innovators in every domain and not only in the domain of priestly and political dogma: – even the innovator of poetical metre had to establish his credentials by madness. (A certain convention that they were mad continued to adhere to poets even into much gentler ages: a convention of which Solon, for example, availed himself when he incited the Athenians to reconquer Salamis.) – 'How can one make oneself mad when one is not mad and does not dare to appear so?' – almost all the significant men of ancient civilization have pursued this train of thought; a secret teaching of artifices and dietetic hints was propagated on this subject, together with the feeling that such reflections and purposes were innocent, indeed holy. The recipes for becoming a medicine-man among the Indians, a saint among the Christians of the Middle Ages, an angekok among Greenlanders, a pajee among Brazilians are essentially the same: senseless fasting, perpetual sexual abstinence, going into the desert or ascending a mountain or a pillar, or 'sitting in an aged willow tree which looks upon a lake' and thinking of nothing at all except what might bring on an ecstasy and mental disorder. Who would venture to take a look into the wilderness of bitterest and most superfluous agonies of soul in which probably the most fruitful men of all times have languished! To listen to the sighs of these solitary and agitated minds: 'Ah, give me madness, you heavenly powers! Madness, that I may at last believe in myself! Give deliriums and convulsions, sudden lights and darkness, terrify me with frost and fire such as no mortal has ever felt with deafening din and prowling figures, make me howl and whine and crawl like a beast: so that I may only come to believe in myself! I am consumed by doubt, I have killed the law, the law anguishes me as a corpse does a living man: if I am not *more* than the law I am the vilest of all men. The new spirit which is in me, whence is it if it is not from you? Prove to me that I am yours; madness alone can prove it.' And only too often this fervour achieved its goal all too well: in that age in which Christianity proved most fruitful in saints and desert solitaries, and thought it was proving itself by this fruitfulness, there were

in Jerusalem vast madhouses for abortive saints, for those who had sur-
rendered to it their last grain of salt.

1, 16

First proposition of civilization. Among barbarous peoples there exists
a species of customs whose purpose appears to be custom in general:
minute and fundamentally superfluous stipulations (as for example those
among the Kamshadales forbidding the scraping of snow from the shoes
with a knife, the impaling of a coal on a knife, the placing of an iron in the
fire – and he who contravenes them meets death!) which, however,
keep continually in the consciousness the constant proximity of custom,
the perpetual compulsion to practise customs: so as to strengthen the
mighty proposition with which civilization begins: any custom is better
than no custom.

1, 18

The morality of voluntary suffering. – Of all pleasures, which is the
greatest for the men of that little, constantly imperilled community which
is in a constant state of war and where the sternest morality prevails? –
for souls, that is to say, which are full of strength, revengefulness, hostility, deceit and suspicion, ready for the most fearful things and made hard
by deprivation and morality? The pleasure of *cruelty*: just as it is reckoned
a *virtue* in a soul under such conditions to be inventive and insatiable in
cruelty. In the act of cruelty the community refreshes itself and for once
throws off the gloom of constant fear and caution. Cruelty is one of the
oldest festive joys of mankind. Consequently it is imagined that the gods
too are refreshed and in festive mood when they are offered the spectacle
of cruelty – and thus there creeps into the world the idea that *voluntary
suffering*, self-chosen torture, is meaningful and valuable. Gradually,
custom created within the community a practice corresponding to this
idea: all excessive well-being henceforth aroused a degree of mistrust, all
hard suffering inspired a degree of confidence; people told themselves: it
may well be that the gods frown upon us when we are fortunate and smile
upon us when we suffer – though certainly they do not feel compassion!
For compassion is reckoned contemptible and unworthy of a strong,
dreadful soul; – they smile because they are amused and put into a good
humour by our suffering: for to practise cruelty is to enjoy the highest

gratification of the feeling of power. Thus the concept of the 'most moral man' of the community came to include the virtue of the most frequent suffering, of privation, of the hard life, of cruel chastisement – *not*, to repeat it again and again, as a means of discipline, of self-control, of satisfying the desire for individual happiness – but as a virtue which will put the community in good odour with the evil gods and which steams up to them like a perpetual propitiatory sacrifice on the altar. All those spiritual leaders of the peoples who were able to stir something into motion within the inert but fertile mud of their customs have, in addition to madness, also had need of voluntary torture if they were to inspire belief – and first and foremost, as always, their own belief in themselves! The more their spirit ventured on to new paths and was as a consequence tormented by pangs of conscience and spasms of anxiety, the more cruelly did they rage against their own flesh, their own appetites and their own health – as though to offer the divinity a substitute pleasure in case he might perhaps be provoked by this neglect of and opposition to established usages and by the new goals these paths led to. Let us not be too quick to think that we have by now freed ourselves completely from such a logic of feeling! Let the most heroic souls question themselves on this point. Every smallest step in the field of free thought, of a life shaped personally, has always had to be fought for with spiritual and bodily tortures: not only the step forward, no! the step itself, movement, change of any kind has needed its innumerable martyrs through all the long path-seeking and foundation-laying millennia which, to be sure, are not what one has in mind when one uses the expression 'world history' – that ludicrously tiny portion of human existence; and even within this so-called world history, which is at bottom merely much ado about the latest news, there is no more really vital theme than the age-old tragedy of the martyrs *who wanted to stir up the swamp*. Nothing has been purchased more dearly than that little bit of human reason and feeling of freedom that now constitutes our pride. It is this pride, however, which now makes it almost impossible for us to empathise with those tremendous eras of '*morality of custom*' which precede 'world history' as the *actual and decisive eras of history which determined the character of mankind*: the eras in which suffering counted as virtue, cruelty counted as virtue, dissembling counted as virtue, revenge counted as virtue, denial of reason counted as virtue, while on the other hand well-being was accounted a danger, desire for knowledge was accounted a danger, peace was accounted a danger, compassion was accounted a danger, being pitied was accounted an affront, work was accounted an affront, madness was accounted godliness, and change was accounted immoral and pregnant with disaster! – Do you think all this has altered and that mankind must therefore have changed its character? O observers of mankind, learn better to observe yourselves!

1, 42

Origin of the vita contemplativa. – In rude ages, where pessimistic judgments as to the nature of man and world prevail, the individual in the feeling of possessing all his powers is always intent upon acting in accordance with these judgments and thus translating idea into action through hunting, robbing, attacking, mistreatment and murder, including the paler reflections of these actions such as are alone tolerated within the community. But if his powers decline, if he feels weary or ill or melancholy or satiated and as a consequence for the time being devoid of desires and wishes, he is then a relatively better, that is to say less harmful man, and his pessimistic ideas discharge themselves only in words and thoughts, for example about the value of his comrades or his wife or his life or his gods – his judgments will be *unfavourable* judgments. In this condition he becomes thinker and prophet, or he expands imaginatively on his superstition and devises new usages, or he mocks his enemies – but whatever he may think about, all the products of his thinking are bound to reflect the condition he is in, which is one in which fear and weariness are on the increase and his valuation of action and active enjoyment on the decrease; the content of these products of his thinking must correspond to the content of these poetical, thoughtful, priestly moods; unfavourable judgment is bound to predominate. Later on, all those who continually acted as the single individual had formerly acted while in this condition, and who thus judged unfavourably and whose lives were melancholy and poor in deeds, came to be called poets or thinkers or priests or medicine-men – because they were so inactive one would have liked to have despised such men and ejected them from the community; but there was some danger attached to that – they were versed in superstition and on the scent of divine forces, one never doubted that they commanded unknown sources of power. This is the estimation under which *the oldest race of contemplative natures* lived – despised to just the extent they were not dreaded! In this muffled shape, in this ambiguous guise, with an evil heart and often an anguished head, did contemplation first appear on earth, at once weak and fearsome, secretly despised and publicly loaded with superstitious reference! Here, as always, it is a case of *pudenda origo!*.

I, 77

On the torments of the soul. – Everyone now exclaims loudly against torment inflicted by one person on the body of another; indignation is at once ignited against a person capable of doing it; indeed, we tremble at the mere idea of a torment which could be inflicted on a man or an animal, and suffer quite dreadfully when we hear of a definitely attested fact of this kind. But we are still far from feeling so decisively and with such unanimity in regard to torments of the soul and how dreadful it is to inflict them. Christianity has made use of them on an unheard-of scale and continues to preach this species of torture; indeed, it complains quite innocently of falling-off and growing lukewarm when it encounters those who are not in this state of torment – all with the result that even today mankind regards spiritual death-by-fire, spiritual torture and instruments of torture, with the same anxious toleration and indecision as it formerly did the cruelties inflicted on the bodies of men and animals. Hell has, in truth, been more than merely a word: and the newly created and genuine fear of Hell has been attended by a new species of pity corresponding to it, a horrible, ponderously heavy feeling of compassion, unknown to former ages, for those 'irrevocably damned to Hell' – a condition, for example, which the stone guest gives Don Juan to understand he is in, and which had no doubt often before during the Christian centuries wrung tears even from stones. Plutarch gives a gloomy picture of the state of a superstitious man in the pagan world: this picture pales when contrasted with the Christian of the Middle Ages who *supposes* he is no longer going to escape 'eternal torment'. Dreadful portents appear to him: perhaps a stork holding a snake in its beak but *hesitating* to swallow it. Or nature suddenly blanches or fiery colours flutter across the ground. Or he is approached by the figures of dead relatives, their faces bearing the traces of fearful sufferings. Or when he is asleep the dark walls of his room grow bright and there appear on them in a yellow exhalation the images of torture-instruments and a confusion of snakes and devils. Indeed, what a dreadful place Christianity had already made of the earth when it everywhere erected the crucifix and thereby designated the earth as the place 'where the just man is *tortured* to death'! And when the powerful oratory of great Lenten preachers for once fetched into the light of publicity all the hidden suffering of the individual, the torments of the 'closet'; when a Whitefield, for instance, preached 'like a dying man to the dying', now violently weeping, now stamping loudly, and passionately and unashamedly, in the most abrupt and cutting tones, directed the whole weight of his attack upon some one individual present and in a fearful manner excluded him from the community – then the earth really did seem to want to transform itself into the 'vale of misery'! Whole masses then come together appeared to fall victim to a madness; many were paralysed with fear; others lay unconscious and motionless; some were seized with violent trembling or rent the air for hours with piercing cries. Everywhere a loud breathing, as of people half-choked gasping for air. 'And truly', says one eye-witness of such a sermon, 'almost all the sounds to be heard were those of people *dying in bitter torment.*' – Let us never forget that it was Christianity which made of the *death-bed* a bed of torture, and that with the scenes that have since then been enacted upon it, with the terrifying tones which here seemed to be realized for the first time, the senses and the blood of countless witnesses have been poisoned for the rest of their life and for that of their posterity! Imagine a harmless human being who cannot get over once having heard such words as these: 'Oh eternity! Oh that I had no soul! Oh that I had never been born! I am damned, damned, lost for ever. A week ago you could have helped me. But now it is all over. Now I belong to the Devil. I go with him to Hell. Break, break, poor hearts of stone! Will you not break? What more can be done for hearts of stone? I am damned that you may be saved! There he is! Yes, there he is! Come, kind Devil! Come!' –

11, 112

On the natural history of rights and duties. – Our duties – are the rights of others over us. How have they acquired such rights? By taking us to be capable of contracting and of requiring, by positing us as similar and equal to them, and as a consequence entrusting us with something, educating, reproving, supporting us. We fulfil our duty – that is to say: we justify the idea of our power on the basis of which all these things were bestowed upon us, we give back in the measure in which we have been given to. It is thus our pride which bids us do our duty – when we do something for others in return for something they have done for us, what we are doing is restoring our self-regard – for in doing something for us, these others have impinged upon our sphere of power, and would have continued to have a hand in it if we did not with the performance of our 'duty' practise a requital, that is to say impinge upon their power. The rights of others can relate only to that which lies within our power; it would be unreasonable if they wanted of us something we did not possess. Expressed more precisely: only to that which they believe lies within our power, provided it is the same thing we believe lies within our power. The same error could easily be made on either side: the feeling of duty depends upon our having the same *belief* in regard to the extent of our power as others have: that is to say, that we *are able* to promise certain things and bind ourselves to perform them ('freedom of will'). – My rights – are that part of my power which others have not merely conceded me, but which they wish me to preserve. How do these others arrive at that? First: through their prudence and fear and caution: whether in that they expect something similar from us in return (protection of their own rights); or in that they consider that a struggle with us would be perilous or to no purpose; or in that they see in any diminution of our force a disadvantage to themselves, since we would then be unsuited to forming an alliance with them in opposition to a hostile third power. *Then*: by donation and cession. In this case, others have enough and more than enough power to be able to dispose of some of it and to guarantee to him they have given it to the portion of it they have given: in doing so they presuppose a feeble sense of power in him who lets himself be thus donated to. That is how rights originate: recognized and guaranteed degrees of power. If power-relationships undergo any material alteration, rights disappear and new ones are created – as is demonstrated in the continual disappearance and reformation of rights between nations. If our power is materially diminished, the feeling of those who have hitherto guaranteed our rights changes: they consider whether they can restore us to the full possession we formerly enjoyed – if they feel unable to do so, they henceforth deny our 'rights'. Likewise, if our power is materially increased, the feeling of those who have hitherto recognized it but whose recognition is no longer needed changes: they no doubt attempt to suppress it to its former level, they will try to intervene and in doing so will allude to their 'duty' – but this is only a useless playing with words. Where rights *prevail*, a certain condition and degree of power is being maintained, a diminution and increment warded off. The rights of others constitute a concession on the part of our sense of power to the sense of power of those others. If our power appears to be deeply shaken and broken, our rights cease to exist: conversely, if we have grown very much more powerful, the rights of others, as we have previously conceded them, cease to exist for us. – The 'man who wants to be fair' is in constant need of the subtle tact of a balance: he must be able to assess degrees of power and rights, which, given the transitory nature of human things, will never stay in equilibrium for very long but will usually be rising or sinking: – being fair is consequently difficult and demands much practice and good will, and very much very good *sense*. –

11, 113

The striving for distinction. – The striving for distinction keeps a constant eye on the next man and wants to know what his feelings are: but the empathy which this drive requires for its gratification is far from being harmless or sympathetic or kind. We want, rather, to perceive or divine how the next man outwardly or inwardly *suffers* from us, how he loses control over himself and surrenders to the impressions our hand or even merely the sight of us makes upon him; and even when he who strives after distinction makes and wants to make a joyful, elevating or cheering impression, he nonetheless enjoys this success not inasmuch as he has given joy to the next man or elevated or cheered him, but inasmuch as he has *impressed* himself on the soul of the other, changed its shape and ruled over it at his own sweet will. The striving for distinction is the striving for domination over the next man, though it be a very indirect domination and only felt or even dreamed. There is a long scale of degrees of this secretly desired domination, and a complete catalogue of them would be almost the same thing as a history of culture, from the earliest, still grotesque barbarism up to the grotesqueries of over-refinement and morbid idealism. The striving for distinction brings with it *for the next man* – to name only a few steps on the ladder: torment, then blows, then terror, then fearful astonishment, then wonderment, then envy, then admiration, then elevation, then joy, then cheerfulness, then laughter, then derision, then mockery, then ridicule, then giving blows, then imposing torment: – here at the end of the ladder stands the *ascetic* and martyr, who feels the highest enjoyment by himself enduring, as a consequence of his drive for distinction, precisely that which, on the first step of the ladder, his counterpart the *barbarian* imposes on others on whom and before whom he wants to distinguish himself. The triumph of the ascetic over himself, his glance turned inwards which beholds man split asunder into a sufferer and a spectator, and henceforth gazes out into the outer world only in order to gather as it were wood for his own pyre, this final tragedy of the drive for distinction in which there is only one character burning and consuming himself – this is a worthy conclusion and one appropriate to the commencement: in both cases an unspeakable happiness at the *sight of torment*! Indeed, happiness, conceived of as the liveliest feeling of power, has perhaps been nowhere greater on earth than in the souls of superstitious ascetics. The Brahmins give expression to this in the story of King Viçvamitra, who derived such strength from *practising penance* for a thousand years that he undertook to construct a new *Heaven*. I believe that in this whole species of inner experience we are now incompetent novices groping after the solution of riddles: they knew more about these infamous refinements of self-enjoyment 4,000 years ago. The creation of the world: perhaps it was then thought of by some Indian dreamer as an ascetic operation on the part of a god! Perhaps the god wanted to banish himself into active and moving nature as into an instrument of torture, in order thereby to feel his bliss and power doubled! And supposing it was a god of love: what enjoyment for such a god to create *suffering* men, to suffer divinely and superhumanly from the ceaseless torment of the sight of them, and thus to tyrannize over himself! And even supposing it was not only a god of love, but also a god of holiness and sinlessness: what deliriums of the divine ascetic can be imagined when he creates sin and sinners and eternal damnation and a vast abode of eternal affliction and eternal groaning and sighing! – It is not altogether impossible that the souls of Dante, Paul, Calvin and their like may also once have penetrated the gruesome secrets of such voluptuousness of power – and in face of such souls one can ask: is the circle of striving for distinction really at an end with the ascetic? Could this circle not be run through again from the beginning, holding fast to the basic disposition of the ascetic and at the same time that of the compassionate god? That is to say, doing hurt to others in order thereby to hurt *oneself*, in order then to triumph over oneself and one's compassion and to revel in an extremity of power! – Excuse these extravagant reflections on all that may have been possible on earth through the psychical extravagance of the lust for power!

Beyond Good and Evil

195

The Jews – a people 'born for slavery',[1] as Tacitus and the whole ancient world says, 'the chosen people among peoples' as they themselves say and believe – the Jews brought about that miracle of a reversal of values, thanks to which life on earth received a new and dangerous attraction for a few thousand years: – their prophets have smelted 'rich', 'godless', 'evil', 'violent' and 'sensual' into one and coined the word 'world' as a term of abuse for the first time. In this reversal of values (in which it is right and proper to use the word 'poor' as a synonym for 'holy' and 'friend') lies the importance of the Jewish people: with them begins the *slaves' revolt in morality*.

197

We completely misunderstand the beast of prey and man of prey (for example, Cesare Borgia), we misunderstand 'nature', as long as we seek something 'pathological' at the core of these healthiest of all tropical monsters and growths, or even a kind of 'hell' innate to them –: as almost all moralists have done so far. It seems that the moralists harbour a hatred against the primeval forest and against the tropics? And that 'tropical man' must be discredited at all cost, whether as sickness and human degeneracy or as his own hell and self-torture? But why? In favour of the 'moderate zones'? In favour of moderate men? Of the 'moral'? Of the mediocre? – This for the chapter 'Morality as Timidity'. –

---

[1] Tacitus, *Histories* v. 8.

198

All these moralities that address themselves to the individual person purportedly for the purpose of his 'happiness', – what else are they but the rules of behaviour relative to the level of *danger* in which the individual person lives with himself; recipes against his passions, his good and bad inclinations in so far as they all have the will to power and want to play master; small and large wisdoms and artifices imbued with the closet smell of old household remedies and old wives' tales; the whole lot baroque and unreasonable in form – because they address themselves to 'all', because they generalize where generalization should not take place –, making unconditional statements and taking themselves as unconditional, the whole lot not seasoned with just *one* grain of salt, but rather only bearable and sometimes even seductive when they learn to smell over-seasoned and dangerous, especially when they smell 'of the other world': all that, measured intellectually, is worth little and is far from being 'science', let alone 'wisdom', but, to say it again and say it three times: cleverness, cleverness, cleverness mixed with stupidity, stupidity, stupidity, – whether it be that indifference and statuesque coldness which the Stoics counselled and administered against the heated folly of the affects; or that no-more-laughing and no-more-crying of Spinoza, his so naïvely recommended destruction of the affects through analysis and vivisection of the same; or that relegation of the affects to a harmless mediocrity, at which level they may be satisfied, the Aristotelianism of morality; even morality as the enjoyment of the affects in a deliberate dilution and spiritualization through the symbolism of art, as music, perhaps, or as love towards God and towards man for God's sake – for in religion the passions again have civil rights, providing that .....; finally, even that accommodating and deliberate surrender to the affects, as taught by Hafiz and Goethe, that bold dropping of the reins, that physical and spiritual *licentia morum* in the exceptional case of wise old owls and drunkards, where there is 'no longer much danger'. This, too, for the chapter 'Morality as Timidity'.

199

Since at all times at which there have been people at all, there have also been herds of people (clans, communities, tribes, peoples, states, churches) and always a great number of those obeying in comparison to those giving orders, – in consideration, then, of the fact that obedience has been practised and cultivated best and longest amongst men, one may justifiably conclude that on average now the need for it is inborn in everyone as a kind of *formal conscience* which commands: 'Thou shalt do something unconditionally, thou shalt unconditionally refrain from doing something', in short, 'thou shalt'. This need seeks to satisfy itself and to fill its form with a content; it tucks in fairly indiscriminately according to its strength, impatience and state of suspense as a crude appetite, and accepts whatever is shouted into its ear by those who command – parents, teachers, laws, social prejudices [*Standesvorurtheile* (*n*)], public opinion. The strange limitation of human development, its hesitant, long-drawn-out, frequently recoiling and cyclic nature, is due to the fact that the herd instinct of obedience is inherited most easily and at the expense of the art of giving commands. If one imagines this instinct progressing to its final excesses, in the end precisely those in command and those who are independent will be lacking; or they suffer inwardly from bad conscience and need, first of all, to exercise self-deception in order to be able to command: as though they too were only obeying. This state of affairs actually exists in Europe today: I call it the moral hypocrisy of those who command. They know no other method of protecting themselves from their bad conscience than passing themselves off as the executors of older or higher commands (of their ancestors, of the constitution, of the laws or even of God), or even borrowing herd maxims from the herd way of thinking, for example passing themselves off as 'first servants of the people' or as 'instruments of the common weal'. On the other hand, the herd man in Europe tries to create the impression that he is the only permitted type of man, and glorifies as the really human virtues the attributes which make him tame, agreeable and useful to the herd: to wit, public-spiritedness, benevolence, consideration, industriousness, moderation, modesty, understanding and compassion. However, in those cases where one regards leaders and bellwethers as indispensable, one tries again and again today to replace those in command with an accumulation of clever herd men: for example, all representative constitutions have this origin. In spite of all this, what a relief, what a release from a pressure which was becoming intolerable, is the appearance of someone who commands unconditionally for these herd-animal Europeans, the last great proof of which was the effect which Napoleon's appearance made: – the history of the effect of Napoleon is practically the history of the highest happiness that this whole century has produced amongst its worthiest men and moments.

200

Man, in an age of disintegration in which the races are mixed, who has in his body the legacy of diverse origins, which is to say contradictory and often not even only contradictory drives and standards of valuation, which fight each other and seldom give each other peace, – such a man of late cultures and refracted lights will, on average, be a weaker man: his most fundamental desire is that the war, which he *is*, should finally have an end; happiness appears to him, in accordance with a tranquillizing medicine and way of thought (for example, the Epicurean or the Christian), principally to be the happiness of rest, of being undisturbed, of repleteness, of being finally at one, as the 'Sabbath of Sabbaths', to speak with the holy rhetorician Augustine,[2] who was himself such a man. – If, however, contradiction and war in such a nature have the effect of being one *more* stimulus to life and one *more* thrill, and if, in addition to the powerful and irreconcilable drives, the actual mastery and finesse in waging war on oneself, I mean self-control, self-outwitting, is inherited and cultivated: then those enigmatic, magically elusive and incomprehensible people develop, predestined to victory and seduction, the finest example of whom are Alcibiades and Caesar (– in whose company I would like to rank that *first* European to my taste, the Hohenstaufen Friedrich the Second), and perhaps amongst artists Leonardo da Vinci. They appear at precisely the same time in which that weaker type, with its desire to rest, steps into the foreground: both types belong together and arise from the same causes.

201

As long as the usefulness which predominates in moral value judgments is only herd-usefulness, as long as the gaze is fixed only on preserving the community, and the immoral is precisely and exclusively sought in what appears dangerous to the survival of the community: there cannot be any 'morality of love of one's neighbour'. Suppose, even there, one were to find a continual, minor exercise of consideration, compassion, equity, leniency, mutuality of assistance, suppose, too, that in that

---

[2] Augustine ends both his *Confessions* and *The City of God* with the image of a state of perfect rest at the end of time which he calls a 'Sabbath' 'without evening' or 'without end'. The expression 'Sabbath of Sabbaths' is used in the Greek translation of the Old Testament known as the *Septuagint* at Leviticus 16.31 and 23.3.

state of society all those drives were active which are later honoured with the name 'virtues', and finally almost collapsed into one with the concept 'morality': in that period of time they still do not yet belong in the realm of moral valuations – they are still *extra-moral*. For example, an act of compassion is not in the best days of the Romans called either good or evil, either moral or immoral; and even if the act is praised, this praise is still most consistent with a kind of grudging disdain as soon as it is compared with an act which serves to promote the *res publica*. In the final analysis, 'love of one's neighbour' is always something secondary, partly conventional and arbitrarily illusory in relation to *fear of the neighbour*. After the structure of society as a whole appears determined and secure against external dangers, it is this fear of the neighbour which creates new perspectives of moral evaluation. Certain strong and powerful drives like the enterprising spirit, daring, vengeance, cunning, rapacity and the desire to dominate, which in the sense of social usefulness not only had to be honoured – under names different, of course, from the ones chosen above – but also had to be trained and cultivated (because when the whole was in danger they were always needed against its enemies), are now felt as dangerous with increased intensity – now, when their proper channels have disappeared – and are step by step branded as immoral and given over to vilification. Now the opposite drives and inclinations come to receive moral honours; step by step the herd instinct draws its conclusion. How much or how little that is dangerous to the community, dangerous to equality, lies in an opinion, in a state [*Zustand*] and affects, in a will, in a talent, that is now the moral perspective: here, too, fear is again the mother of morality. When the highest and strongest drives, erupting passionately, drive the individual far beyond and above the average range of the herd conscience, they destroy the self-confidence of the community, its belief in itself, breaking as it were its spine: consequently it is just these drives which are branded and vilified most. High and independent spirituality [*Geistigkeit*], the will to stand alone, even reason on a grand scale are conceived to be a danger; everything that raises the individual above the herd and causes one's neighbour to be afraid is called *evil* from now on; the equitable, modest, adaptive, conforming mentality, the *mediocrity* of desires, acquires the names and honours of morality. Finally, under very peaceful conditions, there is an increasing lack of the opportunity and necessity of training one's feelings in severity and hardness; and now any severity, even severity in exercising justice, begins to disturb consciences; a high and hard nobility and self-responsibility is almost insulting and arouses mistrust, 'the lamb', even more, 'the sheep', gains respect. There comes a point in the history of a society that has become pathologically rotten and soft, when it even sides with its attacker, the *criminal*, and indeed, in a genuine and serious way. Punishment: that seems unfair to it somehow, – what is certain is that it hurts and frightens society to imagine 'punishment' and 'having to punish'. Is it not sufficient to render the criminal *undangerous*? Why punish as well? Punishment itself is terrible! – with this question, herd morality, the morality of timidity, draws its final conclusion. Assuming one could completely get rid of the danger, the reason for being afraid, one would have got rid of this morality at the same time: it would no longer be necessary, *it would no longer regard itself* as necessary any more! – Whoever tests the conscience of today's European will always have to draw out the same imperative from a thousand moral folds and hiding places, the imperative of herd timidity: 'our desire is for there to be *nothing more to fear* some time or other!' Some time or other – the will and the way *there* is called 'progress' everywhere in Europe today.

202

Let us immediately say once more what we have already said a hundred times already: for the ears are not well-disposed to such truths – to *our* truths – these days. We know well enough already how insulting it sounds when someone includes man, unadorned [*ungeschminkt*] and literally, amongst the animals; but it will almost be reckoned as *guilt* on our part that precisely regarding the man of 'modern ideas' we constantly use the expressions 'herd', 'herd instincts' and the like. What's the use! We cannot do otherwise: for precisely here is where our new insight lies. We found that in all major moral judgments, Europe has become unanimous, including the countries where Europe's influence dominates: one plainly *knows* in Europe what Socrates thought he did not know, and what that famous old snake once promised to teach, – one 'knows' today what good and evil are. Now it must sound harsh and jar on the ear when we repeatedly insist: that which here believes it knows, which here glorifies itself with praise and blame, which calls itself good, is the instinct of the herd animal, man: as such it has come to a breakthrough, preponderance and dominance over other instincts and will continue to do so more and more in line with a growing physiological approximation and assimilation of which it is a symptom. *Morality today in Europe is herd-animal morality*: – so only, as we understand it, one kind of human morality beside which, before which, after which many others, above all *higher* moralities are possible or ought to be. But this morality defends itself against such a 'possibility' or 'ought' with all its strength: stubbornly and relentlessly it says, 'I am morality itself, and nothing else is morality!' – yes, with the aid of a religion which indulged and flattered the most sublime herd-animal desires, we have come to a point where we find, even in political and social institutions, an increasingly visible expression of this morality: the *democratic* movement is the heir of the Christian movement. The increasingly mad howling, the increasingly undisguised grinding of teeth of the anarchist dogs who now roam the streets of European culture, indicates that the tempo of this movement is still much too slow and sleepy for those more impatient, for the sick and those addicted to the instinct referred to above: these anarchists, apparently in contrast to the peacefully industrious democrats and ideologues of revolution, still more to the foolish philosophasters and enthusiasts of fraternity who call themselves socialists and want a 'free society', are actually at one with them all in their fundamental and instinctive animosity towards every other type of society than that of the *autonomous* herd (to the point of denying even the concepts 'master' and 'servant' – *ni dieu ni maître* is how a socialist slogan runs –): at one in their tenacious resistance to every special claim, every special right and privilege, (so that means, in the final analysis, against *every* 'right': for when all are equal, nobody needs 'rights' any more –); at one in their mistrust of punitive justice (as though this were a violation of the weaker, an injustice against the *necessary* consequence of all earlier society –); but just as much at one in the religion of compassion, of suffering, in so far as simply felt, lived, endured (right down to the animal and up to 'God': – the excess of 'compassion with God' belongs to a democratic age –); at one, altogether, in the scream and impatience of compassion, in the lethal hatred against any kind of suffering, in the almost womanly incapacity to be able to remain a spectator, to be able to *let* suffering happen; at one in their involuntary gloom and mollycoddling, under the spell of which Europe seems threatened with a new Buddhism; at one in the belief in a morality of *communal* compassion, as though this were morality as such, as the height, the *attained* height of man, the sole hope of the future, the means for consoling people in the present, the great absolution of all former guilt: – at one in the belief in the community as the *saviour*, that is, in the herd, in 'themselves'. . . .

203

We who are of another faith –, we, to whom the democratic movement counts not just as a form of decay of political organization but as the form of decay, namely diminution, of man, as a way of levelling him down and lowering his value: where must *we* reach out with our hopes? – To *new philosophers*, there is no alternative; to spirits strong enough and primordially forceful enough to give an incentive for contrary valuations and for 'eternal values' to be valued another way round, turned another way round; to those sent on ahead, to men of the future who, in the present, tie up the knot of compulsion which forces the will of millennia on to *new* paths. To teach man that the future of mankind is his *will*, dependent on a human will, and to prepare him for great deeds of daring and comprehensive attempts at discipline and breeding, in order to put an end to that terrible domination of folly and accident hitherto known as 'history' – the folly of the 'greatest number' is just its final form –: for this, some time or other, a new type of philosopher and commander will be necessary, in comparison to whose image everything we have seen on earth by way of hidden, terrible and benevolent spirits will seem pale and dwarfed. It is the image of such leaders which floats before *our* eyes: – dare I say it out loud, you free spirits? The circumstances which one must partly create and partly take advantage of to bring this about; the probable ways and experiments by means of which a soul would grow to such height and power in order to feel the *compulsion* to these tasks; a transvaluation of values under the new pressure and hammer of which a conscience is steeled, a heart turned to iron, so that it can bear the weight of such a responsibility; on the other hand, the necessity of such leaders, the appalling danger that they might not materialize or that they might turn out badly or degenerate – these are *our* real worries and anxieties, you know, don't you, you free spirits? These are the heavy distant thoughts and thunderstorms that pass over the firmament of *our* life. There are few pains as deep as that of having seen, recognized and sympathized with an extraordinary man who has strayed from his path and degenerated: whoever has the rare eye for the absolute danger of 'man' himself *degenerating*, whoever, like us, has recognized the incredible contingency which has played its game with regard to the future of men – a game in which no hand participated, not even 'God's finger'! – whoever guesses at the calamity which lies concealed in the stupid naïvety and blind trust of 'modern ideas', still more in the whole Christian-European morality: he suffers from an anxiety which cannot be compared with any other, – he sees with one glance what, under a favourable accumulation and increase in forces and tasks could still *be bred from man*, he knows, with all the knowledge of his conscience, how man is still untapped for the greatest possibilities and how often the species, man, has already stood confronted with mysterious decisions and new paths: – he knows even better from his own painful memory what pathetic things have so far habitually shattered, snapped, sunk and made wretched an embryonic being of the highest potential. *The total degeneration of man* right down to what appears today, to socialist idiots and numbskulls, as their 'man of the future' – as their ideal! – this degeneration and diminution of man to the perfect herd animal (or, as they say, to the man in a 'free society'), this bestialization of man into a dwarf animal of equal rights and claims is *possible*, there is no doubt! Whoever has once thought these possibilities through to the end knows one form of nausea more than other people do – and perhaps also a new *task*!. . . .

229

There remains in those late epochs justifiably proud of their humaneness so much fear, so much *superstition* of fear of the 'wild, cruel animal', the mastering of which constitutes that very pride of those more humane epochs, that even palpable truths remain unspoken for centuries, as if by agreement, because they seem to help back to life that wild animal which has finally been killed off. Perhaps I take some risk in letting slip a truth like that: let others catch it again and give it so much 'milk of pious ways of thinking'[3] that it will lie quiet and forgotten in its old corner. – People should revise their notion of cruelty and open their eyes; they should finally learn impatience so that presumptuous fat errors like this, which have, for example, been fattened up by ancient and modern philosophers with regard to tragedy, should no longer parade around full of virtue and impertinence. Almost everything we call 'higher culture' is founded on the spiritualization and internalization of *cruelty* – that is my proposition; that 'wild animal' has not been killed off at all, it lives, it thrives, it has simply – made itself divine. What constitutes the painful ecstasy of tragedy is cruelty; what is pleasantly at work in so-called tragic pity, indeed, in basically everything that is sublime right up to the highest,

---

[3]   Schiller, *Wilhelm Tell* IV. 3. 2574. See also n. 68, p. 72.

most delicate thrills of metaphysics, attains its sweetness solely because the ingredient of cruelty is mixed into it. What the Roman in the arena, the Christian in the ecstasies of the cross, the Spaniard watching burnings or bullfights, the Japanese of today flocking to tragedy, the suburban Parisian worker hankering after bloody revolutions, the Wagnerienne who 'submits' to *Tristan and Isolde* with suspended will, – what they all enjoy and seek to imbibe with secret passion, are the spicy potions of the great Circe 'cruelty'. Here, of course, we must expel the foolish psychology taught previously, its only instruction on cruelty being that it arose at the sight of the suffering of *others*: there is also an abundant, superabundant enjoyment of one's own suffering, of making oneself suffer, – and wherever man allows himself to be talked into self-denial in the *religious* sense or to self-mutilation, as with the Phoenicians and ascetics, or to desensualization in general, decarnalization, contrition, to Puritanical spasms of penitence, conscience-vivisection and Pascalian *sacrifizio dell'intelletto*, he is secretly lured and propelled by his cruelty, by the dangerous thrills of cruelty turned *against himself*.

Finally, consider how even the knower, in forcing his mind to perceive *against* his inclination and often enough against his heart's desire – namely, to say 'no' where he would like to affirm, love and adore –, holds sway as artist and transfigurer of cruelty; indeed, every time something is given deep and thorough consideration is a violation of, and desire to hurt, the fundamental will of the mind, which ceaselessly strives for appearance and superficiality, – in all will to know, there is already a drop of cruelty.

260

On a stroll through the many finer and coarser moralities that have ruled on earth or still rule, I found certain traits regularly recurring together and closely linked: until I concluded that there were two basic types and a basic difference. There is a *master morality* and a *slave morality*; – I add at once, that in all higher and more mixed cultures attempts to mediate between the two moralities also appear, even more often a confusion of the same and mutual misunderstanding, even, on occasion, their harsh juxtaposition – indeed, in the same person, within one soul. The moral value-distinctions have either arisen among a ruling section that was pleasurably aware of being different from the ruled, – or among the ruled, the slaves and dependents of every degree. In the first case, when it is the rulers who determine the concept 'good', it is the exalted, proud states of the soul that are perceived as conferring distinction and ordering rank. The noble man distances himself from men in whom the opposite of such elevated, proud states finds expression: he despises them. We should immediately note that in this first kind of morality the antithesis 'good' and 'bad' means the same as 'noble' and 'despicable': – the antithesis 'good' and 'evil' is of different descent. Everyone who is cowardly, timid, petty and thinks only of narrow utility is despised; as is the mistrustful person with his unfree glances, the person who abases himself, the dog-like man who lets himself be maltreated, the fawning flatterer, above all, the liar: – it is a fundamental belief of all aristocrats that the common people are all liars. 'We who tell the truth' – is how the nobility in ancient Greece referred to itself. It is clear that the moral value-distinctions everywhere first referred to *people*, and only afterwards, derivatively and late, were they applied to actions: which is why it is a grave mistake for historians of morality to start from such questions as 'Why have acts of compassion been praised?' The noble type of man feels *himself* to be the determiner of values, he does not need to find approval, in his opinion, 'What harms me is harmful as such', he knows that he himself is the one to first confer honour on a thing, he *creates values*. He honours everything which he knows pertains to himself: a morality like this is self-glorification. To the fore is the feeling of richness, of power ready to overflow, the happiness of high tension, the consciousness of wealth which would like to give and share: – the noble man, too, helps the unfortunate, but not from compassion, or almost not, but more from an urge produced by the abundance of power. The noble man honours the powerful man in himself, as well as the one who has power over himself and knows when to speak and when to remain silent, who practises severity and harshness on himself with relish and honours everything that is severe and harsh. 'Wotan placed a hard heart in my breast,' is what an old Scandinavian saga says: the poet who said this caught correctly what springs straight from the soul of a proud Viking. Such a type of man is proud of the very fact that he has not been made for compassion: which is why the hero of the saga adds in warning, 'If a man does not have a hard heart when young, it will never harden'. The noble and the brave who think like this are the furthest from that morality that sees the badge of morality precisely in compassion or in doing things for others or in *désintéressement*; one's faith in one's self, one's pride in one's self, a basic animosity and irony towards 'selflessness' belongs just as definitely to noble morality as a mild contempt and wariness towards compassionate feelings and the 'warm heart'. – The powerful are the ones who *understand* how to honour, it is their art, their realm of invention. The deep reverence for age and ancestry – all law rests on this dual reverence –, the faith and prejudice in favour of the ancestors and against those to come is typical of the morality of the powerful; and when, on the other hand, the men of 'modern ideas' almost instinctively believe in 'progress' and 'the future' and show increasingly scant respect for age, the ignoble descent of these 'ideas' is clearly enough revealed. But mostly, however, a morality of the rulers is alien to contemporary taste and embarrassing in the severity of its fundamental principle that we have duties only towards our peers; that we have the right to behave towards beings of lower rank, towards everything alien, as we deem fit or 'as the heart dictates', at all events 'beyond good and evil' –: compassion and such like may belong here. The capacity for and duty of long drawn-out gratitude and revenge – both within the peer-group only –, finesse in retribution, a refined concept of friendship, a certain need to have enemies (as drainage-channels, as it were, for the emotions envy, quarrelsomeness, arrogance, – basically in order to be a good *friend*): all these are typical features of noble morality which, as indicated, are not the morality of 'modern ideas' and are therefore difficult to appreciate today, also difficult to unearth and uncover. – It is different with the second type of morality, *slave morality*. Assuming that the violated, the oppressed, the suffering, unfree, unsure-of-themselves and tired should moralize: what would their moral valuations have in common? Probably a pessimistic suspicion towards the whole human condition would find expression, perhaps a condemnation of man together with his condition. The slave looks at the virtues of the powerful with resentment: he has scepticism and mistrust, he has *refinement* of mistrust toward every 'good' that is honoured there –, he would like to convince himself that happiness is not genuine even there. Conversely, those qualities are stressed and highlighted which serve to ease the existence of the suffering: here compassion, the obliging helping hand, the warm heart, patience, diligence, humility, friendliness are honoured –, because here these are the most useful qualities and almost the only means of enduring the pressure of existence. Slave morality is essentially a morality of usefulness. Here is the source from which that famous antithesis, 'good' and '*evil*' emerged: – power and danger were projected into evil, a certain dreadfulness, finesse and strength that would not allow contempt to arise. According to slave morality, therefore, the 'evil person' arouses fear; according to master morality it is precisely the 'good person' who arouses and wishes to arouse fear, whilst the 'bad' man is felt to be contemptible. The antithesis comes to a head when, in accordance with the logic of slave morality, a whiff of contempt finally clings to the 'good people' in this morality as well – however slight and benign this contempt might be –, because the good person, to the slaves' way of thinking, must at any rate be the man who is *not dangerous*; he is good-natured, easy to deceive, perhaps a little stupid, *un bonhomme*. Wherever slave morality predominates, language shows a propensity for the words 'good' and 'stupid' to edge closer together. – A final basic difference: the longing for *freedom*, the instinct for happiness and the niceties of the feeling of freedom belong just as necessarily to slave morality and morality as the skill and enthusiasm in reverence, in devotion, is the regular symptom of an aristocratic way of thought and valuation. – This explains without further ado why love *as passion* – our European speciality – simply must be of noble provenance: as is well known, we trace its invention to the poet-knights of Provence, those magnificently inventive men of the *'gai saber'*, to whom Europe owes so much, itself almost included.

The Gay Science

344

To what extent even we are still pious. – In science, convictions have no citizens' rights, so people say with good reason: only when they decide to descend to the modest level of hypothesis, of provisional experimental standpoint, of a regulative fiction, can they be allowed the right of entry and indeed certain value within the realm of knowledge, – albeit with the proviso that they remain under police supervision, the police of mistrust. – But does that not mean, on closer inspection: only when conviction *ceases* to be conviction does it have the right to gain entry to science? Would it not be the beginning of the discipline of the scientific spirit to allow itself no more convictions? . . . This is probably true: it only remains to ask whether a prior conviction has to exist *in order for this discipline to begin*, such an imperative and unconditional conviction, indeed, that it sacrifices all others to itself. We see that science, too, rests on a faith, there is absolutely no science without 'presuppositions'. The question whether *truth* is what is required must not only be antecedently given an affirmative answer, but the affirmation in the answer must be so strong that it expresses this proposition, this faith, this conviction: '*Nothing* is *more* necessary than truth, and in relation to it everything else is of only secondary value'. – This unconditional will to truth: what is it? Is it the will *not to be deceived*? Is it the will *not to deceive*? The will to truth, namely, could also be interpreted in the latter way: provided that in the generalization 'I will not deceive', the special case of 'I will not deceive myself' is also included.

But why not deceive? Why not let oneself be deceived? – Note that the reasons for the first reside in a quite different area than for the second: one does not want to be deceived, on the assumption that it is harmful, dangerous, calamitous to be deceived, – in this sense, science would be a long process of prudence, caution, usefulness against which one could, however, justifiably object: What? Is not-wanting-to-be-deceived really less harmful, less dangerous, less calamitous: what do you know, in advance, of the character of existence, to be able to decide whether the greater advantage lies on the side of absolute mistrust or absolute confidence? But in case both should be needed, a great deal of confidence *and* a great deal of mistrust: where could science find its absolute faith, its conviction on which it rests, that truth is more important than any other thing, even than any other conviction? Precisely this conviction could not have come into being if both truth and untruth were continually to prove themselves useful: as is the case. So – faith in science, which now undoubtedly exists, cannot have taken its origin from such a calculation of utility, but rather *in spite of* the fact that the uselessness and danger of the 'will to truth', of 'truth at any price', are continually proved. 'At any price': oh, we understand that well enough, when we have brought one faith after the other to the altar and slaughtered it! – Consequently, the 'will to truth' does *not* mean, 'I will not be deceived', but instead – we have no choice – 'I will not deceive, not even myself': and *with this we are on the ground of morality*. Just consider thoroughly: 'why do you not want to deceive?', especially when it should appear, – and it does appear! – as though life were aimed at appearance, I mean at error, deception, dissemblance, delusion, self-delusion, and when, on the other hand, the great manifestation of life has, in fact, always shown itself to be on the side of the most unscrupulous *polytropoi*.[1] Such a resolve might, to give it a mild gloss, perhaps be a piece of quixotism, a small, enthusiastic folly; it could, however, also be something much worse, namely a destructive principle hostile to life . . . 'Will to truth' – that could be a hidden will to death. – In that way, the question: why science? leads back to the moral problem: *Why morality at all*, when life, nature, history are 'non-moral'? Without a doubt, – the truthful man, in that daring and final sense that faith in science presupposes, *thus affirms another world* from the one of life, nature and history; and inasmuch as he affirms this 'other world', must he not therefore deny its opposite, this world, *our* world, in doing so? . . . But you will have understood what I am aiming at, namely that our faith

---

[1] Literally 'many-turning', 'polytropos' in Homer is a usual epithet of Odysseus (for instance in the very first line of the *Odyssey* meaning 'versatile, wily, devious, cunning, resourceful'). 'Polytropoi' here are '[unscrupulous] men who know all the angles'.

in science is still based on a *metaphysical faith*, – that even we knowers of today, we godless anti-metaphysicians, still take *our* fire from the blaze set alight by a faith thousands of years old, that faith of the Christians, which was also Plato's faith, that God is truth, that truth is *divine* . . . But what if precisely this becomes more and more unbelievable, when nothing any longer turns out to be divine except for error, blindness and lies – and what if God himself turned out to be our oldest lie?' –

357

On the old problem: 'What is German?' – Add up for yourself the actual achievement of philosophical thought that can be attributed to Germans: can they, in any legitimate sense, also be attributed to the whole race? May we say: they are simultaneously the work of the 'German soul', at least a symptom of the latter in the sense in which we are used to taking Plato's ideomania, his almost religious mania for the forms, at once an event and testimony of the 'Greek soul'? Or would the reverse be true? Would they be so very individual, so very much an *exception* to the mind of the race as was, for example, Goethe's paganism with a good conscience? Or as was Bismarck's Machiavellism with a good conscience, his so-called *Realpolitik*, amongst Germans? Did our philosophers not, perhaps, even run counter to the *needs* of the 'German soul'? In short, were the German philosophers really – philosophical *Germans*? – I recall three cases. First, *Leibniz's* incomparable insight[2], which proved him right not only against Descartes but against everyone who had philosophized before him – that consciousness is just an accidental feature of representation, *not* the necessary and essential attribute of the same, in fact, that everything which we call consciousness only makes up one state of our mental and psychic world (perhaps a diseased state) and *by no means the whole of it*: – is there anything German about this idea, the profundity of which has not been exhausted even today? Is there any reason to suppose that a Latin could not easily have thought up this reversal of appearances? – for it is a reversal. Secondly, let us recall *Kant's* tremendous question mark which he placed after the concept 'causality'[3] – not that he, like Hume, at all doubted its legitimacy: on the contrary, he carefully began to mark out the

---

[2] Leibniz held that we had perceptions of which we were unaware ('perceptions dont on ne s'apperçoit pas'). Cf. *Monadology* §14.

[3] Cf. 'Preface' to Kant's *Prolegomena to any Future Metaphysics* (originally published in 1783).

boundaries within which this concept has any meaning (we are not yet done with the drawing of this boundary even today). Thirdly, let us take *Hegel's* astonishing stab which pierced through all logical usages and pamperings when he dared to teach that the concepts of species develop *from one another*:[4] a proposition that prepared the minds of Europe for the last great scientific movement, Darwinism – for without Hegel, no Darwin. Is there anything German about this Hegelian innovation, which first brought the decisive concept 'development' into science? – Yes, without a doubt: in all three cases we feel that something of us has been 'uncovered' and divined, and are thankful for this, and at the same time surprised, each of these three propositions is a considered piece of German self-knowledge, self-experience and self-understanding. 'Our inner world is much richer, more extensive, more concealed', this is what we feel, with Leibniz; as Germans, we doubt, with Kant, the ultimate validity of scientific knowledge and, in general, anything which can be known *causaliter*: the know*able* appears to us of *lesser* value simply because of that. We Germans are Hegelians, even if we had never had a Hegel, in so far as we (unlike all Latins) instinctively attach a deeper sense and higher value to becoming and developing than to what 'is' – we hardly believe in the legitimacy of the concept of 'being' –; similarly, in so far as we are not minded to concede that our human logic is logic as such, the only kind of logic (we would far rather persuade ourselves that it is just a special case and perhaps one of the most peculiar and stupid ones –). A fourth question would be whether *Schopenhauer* with his pessimism, that is, with his problem of the value of *existence*,[5] had to be a German. I do not think so. The event, *after* which this problem was to be expected with certainty, so that an astronomer of the soul could have calculated the day and hour for it, the decline of faith in the Christian God, the victory of scientific atheism, is a pan-European event in which all peoples should have their share of merit and honour. On the contrary, precisely the Germans could be blamed – those Germans with whom Schopenhauer lived contemporaneously –, for having *delayed* this victory of atheism most dangerously and for the longest period of time; Hegel, in fact, was a delayer *par excellence*, with his grandiose attempt to convince us of the divinity of existence by finally enlisting the help of our sixth sense, the 'historical sense'. Schopenhauer was, as a philosopher, the *first* avowed

---

[4] G. W. F. Hegel, *Encyclopedia of Philosophical Sciences* (1830 edn), §368 (especially *Zusatz*).
[5] Cf. A. Schopenhauer *The World as Will and Representation* vol. 1, Book IV, and vol. 2, chs 46 and 49.

and uncompromising atheist whom we Germans have had: his animosity towards Hegel had its motives here. He viewed the lack of divinity of existence as something given, palpable, indisputable; he lost his philosopher's calm and grew angry every time he saw somebody hesitate and deviate here. This is where his whole integrity is located: unswerving, straightforward atheism is, quite simply, the precondition for posing his problems, representing, as it does, a victory of the European conscience, won at last and with difficulty, the most momentous act of a two-thousand-year-long discipline in truth which ultimately forbids itself the *lie* of faith in God . . . You see *what* actually conquered the Christian God; Christian morality itself, the concept of truthfulness which was taken more and more seriously, the confessional punctiliousness of Christian conscience, translated and sublimated into scientific conscience, into intellectual rigour at any price. Regarding nature as though it were a proof of God's goodness and providence; interpreting history in honour of divine reason, as a constant testimonial to an ethical world order and ethical ultimate purpose: explaining all one's experiences in the way pious folk have done for long enough, as though everything were providence, a sign, intended, and sent for the salvation of the soul: now all that is *over*, it has conscience *against* it, every sensitive conscience sees it as indecent, dishonest, as a pack of lies, feminism, weakness, cowardice, – this severity makes us *good* Europeans if anything does, and heirs to Europe's most protracted and bravest self-overcoming!

As we thus reject this Christian interpretation and condemn its 'meaning' as counterfeit, the *Schopenhauerian* question immediately strikes us in a terrible way: *does existence, then, have any meaning at all?* – that question, which will need a few centuries to be even heard completely and in its full depth. What Schopenhauer himself answered to this question was – if you forgive me – something precipitate, youthful, just a compromise, a standstill and deadlock in precisely those Christian-ascetic moral perspectives, from which *faith had been withdrawn* along with faith in God . . . But he *asked* the question – as a good European, as I have said, and *not* as a German. Or have the Germans perhaps shown, at least in the way in which they appropriated Schopenhauer's question, their inner affiliation and kinship with, their readiness and *need* for his problem? The fact that even in Germany, people are pondering and publishing on the problem posed by him – albeit belatedly! – is certainly not enough to make us decide in favour of this closer affiliation; we could even count the peculiar *ineptitude* of this post-Schopenhauerian pessimism as a reason against, – the Germans obviously did not behave as though they were in their element in this matter. I am not in any way referring to Eduard von Hartmann here; on the contrary, my old suspicion remains to this day that he is *too canny* for us, or rather that, old rogue that he is, he was from the start poking fun, and not just at German pessimism, – only to end, perhaps by 'bequeathing' to the Germans in his will the extent to which they themselves could be made fools of in the age of foundations. But I ask: should we perhaps count the old humming-top Bahnsen as a credit to the Germans, who voluptuously spent his whole life revolving around his *real-dialectic* misery and 'personal bad luck', – would that, perhaps, be German? (by the way, I recommend his writings be used as I myself used them, as anti-pessimistic food, on account of their *elegantiae psychologicae*, suitable, I think, for the most constipated bowels and temperament). Or could we count such dilettantes and old maids as the sugary apostle of virginity, Mainländer, amongst the true Germans? In the final analysis, a Jew will turn out to be the only true German (– all Jews become sugary when they moralize). Neither Bahnsen nor Mainländer, to say nothing of Eduard von Hartmann, provide clear evidence for the question whether Schopenhauer's pessimism, his horrified glimpse into a world turned godless, stupid, blind, mad and questionable, his *honest* horror . . . was not just an exceptional case amongst Germans, but a *German* event: whereas everything else in the foreground, our bold politics, our cheerful patriotism that views everything, resolutely enough, relative to a not very philosophical principle ('*Deutschland, Deutschland über Alles*'), in other words *sub specie speciei*, namely the German species, proves the contrary with great clarity. No! The Germans today are *not* pessimists! And Schopenhauer was a pessimist, I repeat, as a good European and *not* as a German. –

'The Greek State' (1871/2)

Preface

We moderns have the advantage over the Greeks with two concepts given as consolation, as it were, to a world behaving in a thoroughly slave-like manner while anxiously avoiding the word 'slave': we speak of the 'dignity of man' and of the 'dignity of work'. We struggle wretchedly to perpetuate a wretched life; this terrible predicament necessitates exhausting work which man – or, more correctly – human intellect, seduced by the 'will', now and again admires as something dignified. But to justify the claim of work to be honoured, existence itself, to which work is simply a painful means, would, above all, have to have somewhat more dignity and value placed on it than appears to have been the case with serious-minded philosophies and religions up till now. What can we find, in the toil and moil of all the millions, other than the drive to exist at any price, the same all-powerful drive which makes stunted plants push their roots into arid rocks!

Only those individuals can emerge from this horrifying struggle for existence who are then immediately preoccupied with the fine illusions of artistic culture, so that they do not arrive at that practical pessimism that nature abhors as truly unnatural. In the modern world which, compared with the Greek, usually creates nothing but freaks and centaurs, and where the individual man is flamboyantly pieced together like the fantastic creature at the beginning of Horace's *Ars Poetica*,[1] the greed of the struggle for existence and of the need for art often manifests itself in one

---

[1] lines 1–5.

and the same person: an unnatural combination that gave rise to the need to excuse and consecrate that very greed ahead of the dictates of art. For that reason, people believe in the 'dignity of man' and the 'dignity of work'.

The Greeks have no need for conceptual hallucinations like this, they voice their opinion that work is a disgrace with shocking openness – and a more concealed, less frequently expressed wisdom, nevertheless alive everywhere, added that the human being was also a disgraceful and pathetic non-entity and 'shadow of a dream'.[2] Work is a disgrace because existence has no inherent value: even when this very existence glitters with the seductive jewels of artistic illusions and then really does seem to have an inherent value, the pronouncement that work is a disgrace is still valid – simply because we do not feel it is possible for man, fighting for sheer survival, to be an *artist*. Nowadays it is not the man in need of art, but the slave who determines general views: in which capacity he naturally has to label all his circumstances with deceptive names in order to be able to live. Such phantoms as the dignity of man, the dignity of work, are the feeble products of a slavery that hides from itself. These are ill-fated times when the slave needs such ideas and is stirred up to think about himself and beyond himself! Ill-fated seducers who have destroyed the slave's state of innocence with the fruit of the tree of knowledge! Now he must console himself from one day to the next with transparent lies the like of which anyone with deeper insight would recognize in the alleged 'equal rights for all' or the 'fundamental rights of man', of man as such, or in the dignity of work. He must be prevented at any cost from realizing what stage or level must be attained before 'dignity' can even be mentioned, which is actually the point where the individual completely transcends himself and no longer has to procreate and work in the service of the continuation of his individual life.

And even at this level of 'work', a feeling similar to shame occasionally overcomes the Greeks. Plutarch says somewhere,[3] with ancient Greek instinct, that no youth of noble birth would want to be a Phidias himself when he saw the Zeus in Pisa or a Polyklet when he saw the Hera in Argos: and would have just as little desire to be Anacreon, Philetas or Archilochus, however much he delighted in their poetry. Artistic creativity, for the Greek, falls into the same category of undignified work as any

[2] Pindar, *Pythian* VIII. 95.
[3] 'Life of Pericles', ch. 2.

philistine craft. However, when the compelling force of artistic inspiration unfolds in him, he *has* to create and bow to the necessity of work. And as a father admires his child's beauty and talent but thinks of the act of creation with embarrassed reluctance, the Greek did the same. His pleased astonishment at beauty did not blind him to its genesis – which, like all genesis in nature, seemed to him a powerful necessity, a thrusting towards existence. That same feeling that sees the process of procreation as something shameful, to be hidden, although through it man serves a higher purpose than his individual preservation: that same feeling also veiled the creation of the great works of art, although they inaugurate a higher form of existence, just like that other act inaugurates a new generation. *Shame*, therefore, seems to be felt where man is just a tool of infinitely greater manifestations of will than he considers himself to be, in his isolated form as individual.

We now have the general concept for categorizing the feelings the Greeks had in relation to work and slavery. Both were looked on by them as a necessary disgrace that aroused the feeling of *shame*, at the same time disgrace and necessity. In this feeling of shame there lurks the unconscious recognition that these conditions are *required* for the actual goal. In that *necessity* lies the horrifying, predatory aspect of the Sphinx of nature who, in the glorification of the artistically free life of culture [*Kultur*], so beautifully presents the torso of a young woman. Culture [*Bildung*], which is first and foremost a real hunger for art, rests on one terrible premise: but this reveals itself in the nascent feeling of shame. In order for there to be a broad, deep, fertile soil for the development of art, the overwhelming majority has to be slavishly subjected to life's necessity in the service of the minority, *beyond* the measure that is necessary for the individual. At their expense, through their extra work, that privileged class is to be removed from the struggle for existence, in order to produce and satisfy a new world of necessities.

Accordingly, we must learn to identify as a cruel-sounding truth the fact that *slavery belongs to the essence of a culture*: a truth, granted, that leaves open no doubt about the absolute value of existence. *This truth* is the vulture which gnaws at the liver of the Promethean promoter of culture. The misery of men living a life of toil has to be increased to make the production of the world of art possible for a small number of Olympian men. Here we find the source of that hatred that has been nourished by the Communists and Socialists as well as their paler descendants, the white race of 'Liberals' of every age against the arts, but also against classical antiquity. If culture were really left to the discretion of a people, if inescapable powers, which are law and restraint to the individual, did not rule, then the glorification of spiritual poverty and the iconoclastic destruction of the claims of art would be *more* than the revolt of the oppressed masses against drone-like individuals: it would be the cry of compassion tearing down the walls of culture; the urge for justice, for equal sharing of the pain, would swamp all other ideas. Actually, an over-exuberant compassion did break down the flood-gates of cultural life for a brief period now and then; a rainbow of compassionate love and peace appeared with the first radiance of Christianity, and beneath it, Christianity's most beautiful fruit, the Gospel of St John, was born. But there are also examples of powerful religions fossilizing certain stages of culture over long periods of time, and mowing down, with their merciless sickle, everything that wants to continue to proliferate. For we must not forget one thing: the same cruelty that we found at the heart of every culture also lies at the heart of every powerful religion, and in the nature of *power* in general, which is always evil; so we shall understand the matter just as well, if a culture breaks down an all too highly raised bulwark of religious claims with the cry for freedom, or at least justice. Whatever wants to live, or rather must live, in this horrifying constellation of things is quintessentially a reflection of the primeval pain and contradiction and must seem, in our eyes, 'organs made for this world and earth',[4] an insatiable craving for existence and eternal self-contradiction in terms of time, therefore as *becoming*. Every moment devours the preceding one, every birth is the death of countless beings, procreating, living and murdering are all one. Therefore, we may compare the magnificent culture to a victor dripping with blood, who, in his triumphal procession, drags the vanquished along, chained to his carriage as slaves: the latter having been blinded by a charitable power so that, almost crushed by the wheels of the chariot, they still shout, 'dignity of work!', 'dignity of man!' Culture, the voluptuous Cleopatra, still continues to throw the most priceless pearls into her golden goblet: these pearls are the tears of compassion for the slave and the misery of slavery. The enormous social problems of today are engendered by the excessive sensitivity of modern man, not by true and deep pity for that misery; and even if it were true that the Greeks were ruined because they kept slaves, the opposite is even more certain, that we will be destroyed by the *lack* of slavery: an activity which

---

[4] Goethe, *Faust* II line 11906.

neither the original Christians nor the Germanic tribes found at all objectionable, let alone reprehensible. What an elevating effect on us is produced by the sight of a medieval serf, whose legal and ethical relationship with his superior was internally sturdy and sensitive, whose narrow existence was profoundly cocooned – how elevating – and how reproachful!

Whoever is unable to think about the configuration of society without melancholy, whoever has learnt to think of it as the continuing, painful birth of those exalted men of culture in whose service everything else has to consume itself, will no longer be deceived by that false gloss the moderns have spread over the origin and meaning of the state. For what can the state mean to us, if not the means of setting the previously described process of society in motion and guaranteeing its unobstructed continuation? However strong the sociable urges of the individual might be, only the iron clamp of the state can force huge masses into such a strong cohesion that the chemical separation of society, with its new pyramidal structure, *has* to take place. But what is the source of this sudden power of the state, the aim of which lies far beyond the comprehension and egoism of the individual? How did the slave, the blind mole of culture, *come about?* The Greeks have given us a hint with their instinct for the law of nations that, even at the height of their civilization and humanity, never ceased to shout from lips of iron such phrases as 'the defeated belong to the victor, together with his wife and child, goods and blood. Power (*Gewalt*) gives the first *right*, and there is no right that is not fundamentally presumption, usurpation and violence'.

Here again we see the degree to which nature, in order to bring society about, uses pitiless inflexibility to forge for herself the cruel tool of the state – namely that *conqueror* with the iron hand who is nothing but the objectification of the instinct indicated. The onlooker feels, from the indefinable greatness and power of such conquerors, that they are just the means of an intention revealing itself through them and yet concealing itself from them. It is as though a magic will emanated from them, so curiously swiftly do weaker powers gravitate to them, so wonderfully do they transform themselves, when that avalanche of violence suddenly swells, and enter into a state of affinity not present till then, enchanted by that creative kernel.

If we now see how, in no time at all, the subjected hardly bother about the dreadful origin of the state, so that basically history informs us less well about the way those sudden, violent, bloody and at least in *one* aspect inexplicable usurpations came about than about any other kind of event: if, on the contrary, hearts swell involuntarily towards the magic of the developing state, with the inkling of an invisibly deep intention, where calculating reason can only see the sum total of forces: if the state now is actually viewed enthusiastically as the aim and goal of the sacrifices and duties of the individual: then all this indicates how enormously necessary the state is, without which nature might not succeed in achieving, through society, her salvation in appearance [*im Scheine*], in the mirror of genius. How much knowledge does not man's instinctive pleasure in the state overcome! One should really assume that a person investigating the emergence of the state would, from then on, seek salvation only at an awe-struck distance from it; and where we do not see monuments to its development, devastated lands, ruined towns, savage men, consuming hatred of nations! The state, of ignominious birth, a continually flowing source of toil for most people, frequently the ravishing flame of the human race – and yet, a sound that makes us forget ourselves, a battle-cry that has encouraged countless truly heroic acts, perhaps the highest and most revered object for the blind, egoistic mass which wears the strange expression of greatness on its face only at tremendous moments in the life of the state!

We must, however, construe the Greeks, in relation to the unique zenith of their art, as being *a priori* 'political men *par excellence*'; and actually history knows of no other example of such an awesome release of the political urge, of such a complete sacrifice of all other interests in the service of this instinct towards the state – at best, we could honour the men of the Renaissance in Italy with the same title, by way of comparison and for similar reasons. This urge is so overcharged amongst the Greeks that it continually and repeatedly starts to rage against itself, sinking its teeth into its own flesh. This bloody jealousy of one town for another, one party for another, this murderous greed of those petty wars, the tiger-like triumph over the corpse of the slain enemy, in short, the continual renewal of those Trojan battle-scenes and atrocities which Homer, standing before us as a true Hellene, contemplated with deep *relish* – what does this naïve barbarism of the Greek state indicate, and what will be its excuse at the throne of eternal justice? The state appears before it proudly and calmly: leading the magnificently blossoming woman, Greek society, by the hand. For this Helen, he waged those wars – what grey-bearded judge would condemn this[5]? –

---

[5] *Illiad* III. 146ff.

It is through this mysterious connection that we sense here between the state and art, political greed and artistic creation, battlefield and work of art, that, as I said, we understand the state only as the iron clamp producing society by force: whereas without the state, in the natural *bellum omnium contra omnes*,[6] society is completely unable to grow roots in any significant measure and beyond the family sphere. Now, after states have been founded everywhere, that urge of *bellum omnium contra omnes* is concentrated, from time to time, into dreadful clouds of war between nations and, as it were, discharges itself in less frequent but all the stronger bolts of thunder and flashes of lightning. But in the intervals, the concentrated effect of that *bellum*, turned inwards, gives society time to germinate and turn green everywhere, so that it can let the radiant blossoms of genius sprout forth as soon as warmer days come.

With regard to the political Hellenic world, I will not remain silent about those present-day phenomena in which I believe I detect dangerous signs of atrophy in the political sphere, equally worrying for art and society. If there were to be men placed by birth, as it were, outside the instinct for nation and state, who thus have to recognize the state only to the extent they conceive it to be in their own interest: then such men would necessarily imagine the state's ultimate aim as being the most undisturbed co-existence possible of great political communities, in which *they*, above all, would be permitted by everyone to pursue their own purposes without restriction. With this idea in their heads, they will promote that policy that offers greatest security to these interests, whilst it is unthinkable that, contrary to their intentions, they should sacrifice themselves to the state purpose, led perhaps by an unconscious instinct, unthinkable because they lack precisely that instinct. All other citizens are in the dark about what nature intends for them with their state instinct, and follow blindly; only those who stand outside this know what *they* want from the state, and what the state ought to grant them. Therefore it is practically inevitable that such men should win great influence over the state, because they may view it as *means*, whilst all the rest, under the power of the unconscious intention of the state, are themselves only means to the state purpose. In order for them to achieve the full effect of their selfish aims through the medium of the state, it is now, above all, essential for the state to be completely freed from those terrible, unpredictable outbreaks of war, so that it can be used rationally; and so, as

---

[6] 'War of all against all', cf. Thomas Hobbes, *De cive* 1. 12; *Leviathan*, ch. XIII.

consciously as possible, they strive for a state of affairs where war is impossible. To this end, they first have to cut off and weaken the specifically political impulses as much as possible and, by establishing large state bodies of *equal importance* with mutual safeguards, make a successful attack on them, and therefore war in general, extremely unlikely: whilst on the other hand they try to wrest the decision over war and peace away from the individual rulers, so that they can then appeal to the egoism of the masses, or their representatives: to do which they must in turn slowly dissolve the monarchical instincts of the people. They carry out this intention through the widest dissemination of the liberal-optimistic world view, which has its roots in the teachings of the French Enlightenment and Revolution i.e. in a completely un-Germanic, genuinely Romanesque, flat and unmetaphysical philosophy. I cannot help seeing, above all, the effects of the *fear of war* in the dominant movement of nationalities at the present time, and in the simultaneous spread of universal suffrage, indeed, I cannot help seeing those truly international, homeless, financial recluses as really those whose fear stands behind these movements, who, with their natural lack of state instinct, have learnt to misuse politics as an instrument of the stock exchange, and state and society as an apparatus for their own enrichment. The only countermeasure to the threatened deflection of the state purpose towards money matters from this quarter is war and war again: in the excitement of which at least so much becomes clear, that the state is not founded on fear of the war-demon, as a protective measure for egoistic individuals, but instead produces from within itself an ethical momentum in the love for fatherland and prince, indicating a much loftier designation. If I point to the use of revolutionary ideas in the service of a self-seeking, stateless money aristocracy as a dangerous characteristic of the contemporary political scene, and if, at the same time, I regard the massive spread of liberal optimism as a result of the fact that the modern money economy has fallen into strange hands, and if I view all social evils, including the inevitable decline of the arts, as either sprouting from that root or enmeshed with it: then you will just have to excuse me if I occasionally sing a pæan to war. His silver bow might sound terrifying; but even if he does swoop in like the night,[7] he is still Apollo, the just god who consecrates and purifies the state. But first, as at the beginning of the *Iliad*, he shoots his arrows at mules and dogs. Then he actually hits people and, everywhere, pyres with

---

[7] *Iliad* 1. 47–52.

corpses blaze. So let it be said that war is as much a necessity for the state as the slave for society: and who can avoid this conclusion if he honestly inquires as to the reasons why Greek artistic perfection has never been achieved again?

Whoever considers war, and its uniformed potential, *the military profession*, in connection with the nature of the state as discussed so far, has to conclude that through war, and in the military profession, we are presented with a type, even perhaps the *archetype of the state*. Here we see, as the most general effect of the war tendency, the immediate separation and division of the chaotic masses into *military castes*, from which there arises the construction of a 'war-like society' in the shape of a pyramid on the broadest possible base: a slave-like bottom stratum. The unconscious purpose of the whole movement forces every individual under its yoke, and even among heterogeneous natures produces, as it were, a chemical transformation of their characteristics until they are brought into affinity with that purpose. In the higher castes, it becomes a little clearer what is actually happening with this inner process, namely the creation of the *military genius* – whom we have already met as original founder of the state. In several states, for example in Sparta's Lycurgian constitution,[8] we can clearly make out the imprint of that original idea of the state, the creation of the military genius. If we now think of the original military state, alive with activity, engaged in its proper 'work', and picture for ourselves the whole technique of war, we cannot avoid correcting our concepts of 'dignity of man', 'dignity of work', absorbed from all around us, by asking whether the concept of dignity is appropriate for work which has, as its purpose, the destruction of the 'dignified' man, or for the man to whom such 'dignified work' is entrusted, or if, in view of the warlike mission of the state, those concepts do not rather cancel each other out as being mutually contradictory. I would have thought the war-like man was a *means* for the military genius and that his work was, again, just a means for the same genius; and that a degree of dignity applies to him, not as absolute man and non-genius, but as means of genius – who can even choose his own destruction as a means to the masterpiece which is war, – that dignity, then, *of being acknowledged as worthy to be a means for genius*. But what I have demonstrated here, with a single example, is valid in the most general sense: every man, with his whole activity, is only dignified

---

[8] For a brief, elementary discussion of the 'Lycurgian constitution', cf. ch. 5 of *The Emergence of Greek Democracy 800–400 BC* by W. G. Forrest (1966).

to the extent that he is a tool of genius, consciously or unconsciously; whereupon we immediately deduce the ethical conclusion that 'man as such', absolute man, possesses neither dignity, nor rights, nor duties: only as a completely determined being, serving unconscious purposes, can man excuse his existence.

Plato's perfect state is, according to these considerations, certainly something even greater than is believed by his warmest-blooded admirers themselves, to say nothing of the superior smirk with which our 'historically'-educated reject such a fruit of antiquity. The actual aim of the state, the Olympian existence and constantly renewed creation and preparation of the genius, compared with whom everything else is just a tool, aid and facilitator, is discovered here through poetic intuition and described vividly. Plato saw beyond the terribly mutilated Herm of contemporary state life, and still saw something divine inside it.[9] He *believed* that one could, perhaps, extract this divine image, and that the angry, barbarically distorted exterior did not belong to the nature of the state: the whole fervour and loftiness of his political passion threw itself onto that belief, that wish – he was burnt up in this fire. The fact that he did not place genius, in its most general sense, at the head of his perfect state, but only the genius of wisdom and knowledge, excluding the inspired artist entirely from his state, was a rigid consequence of the Socratic judgment on art, which Plato, struggling against himself, adopted as his own. This external, almost accidental gap ought not to prevent us from recognizing, in the total concept of the Platonic state, the wonderfully grand hieroglyph of a profound *secret study of the connection between state and genius*, eternally needing to be interpreted: in this preface we have said what we believe we have fathomed of this secret script. –

---

[9] Nietzsche conflates two things here: (a) the incident of the mutilation of the herms (reported in Thucydides VI. 27ff.), and (b) Alcibiades' panegyric on Socrates at the end of Plato's *Symposium* (221d1–222a6).

'Homer's Contest'

If we speak of *humanity*, it is on the basic assumption that it should be that which *separates* man from nature and is his mark of distinction. But in reality there is no such separation: 'natural' characteristics and those called specifically 'human' have grown together inextricably. Man, at the finest height of his powers, is all nature and carries nature's uncanny dual character in himself. His dreadful capabilities and those counting as inhuman are perhaps, indeed, the fertile soil from which alone all humanity, in feelings, deeds and works, can grow forth.

Thus the Greeks, the most humane people of ancient time, have a trait of cruelty, of tiger-like pleasure in destruction, in them: a trait which is even clearly visible in Alexander the Great, that grotesquely enlarged reflection of the Hellene, and which, in their whole history, and also their mythology, must strike fear into us when we approach them with the emasculated concept of modern humanity. When Alexander has the feet pierced of the brave defender of Gaza, Batis, and ties his live body to his chariot in order to drag him around to the scorn of his own soldiers:[1] this is a nauseating caricature of Achilles, who abused the corpse of Hector at night by similarly dragging it around; but for us, even Achilles' action has something offensive and horrific about it. Here we look into the bottomless pit of hatred. With the same sensation, we observe the bloody and insatiable mutual laceration of two Greek factions, for example in the Corcyrean revolution.[2] When, in a battle between cities, the victor, according to the *rights* of war, puts the whole male population to the sword

---

[1] Cf. Jacoby, F., *Die Fragmente der griechischen Historiker* (Leiden, 1940–1), 142.5.
[2] Thucydides III.70–85.

and sells all the women and children into slavery, we see, in the sanctioning of such a right, that the Greek regarded a full release of his hatred as a serious necessity; at such moments pent-up, swollen sensation found relief: the tiger charged out, wanton cruelty flickering in its terrible eyes. Why did the Greek sculptor repeatedly have to represent war and battles with endless repetition, human bodies stretched out, their veins taut with hatred or the arrogance of triumph, the wounded doubled up, the dying in agony? Why did the whole Greek world rejoice over the pictures of battle in the Iliad? I fear we have not understood these in a sufficiently 'Greek' way, and even that we would shudder if we ever did understand them in a Greek way.

But what lies *behind* the world of Homer, as the womb of everything Hellenic? In the *latter*, we are already lifted beyond the purely material fusion by the extraordinary artistic precision, calmness and purity of the lines: its colours, through an artistic deception, seem lighter, gentler and warmer, its people, in this warm, multi-coloured light, seem better and more likeable – but where do we look if we stride backwards into the pre-Homeric world, without Homer's guiding and protecting hand? Only into night and horror, into the products of a fantasy used to ghastly things. What earthly existence is reflected in these repellingly dreadful legends about the origins of the gods: a life ruled over by the *children of the night* alone, by strife, lust, deception, age and death. Let us imagine the air of Hesiod's poems, difficult to breathe as it is, still thicker and darker and without any of the things to alleviate and cleanse it which poured over Hellas from Delphi and numerous seats of the gods: let us mix this thickened Bœotian air with the dark voluptuousness of the Etruscans; such a reality would then *extort* from us a world of myths in which Uranus, Kronos and Zeus and the struggles of the Titans would seem like a relief; in this brooding atmosphere, combat is salvation and deliverance, the cruelty of the victory is the pinnacle of life's jubilation. And just as, in truth, the concept of Greek law developed out of *murder* and atonement for murder, finer culture, too, takes its first victor's wreath from the altar of atonement for murder. The wake of that bloody period stretches deep into Hellenic history. The names of Orpheus, Musaeus and their cults, reveal what were the conclusions to which a continual exposure to a world of combat and cruelty led – to nausea at existence, to the view of existence as a punishment to be discharged by serving out one's time, to the belief that existence and indebtedness were identical. But precisely these conclusions are not specifically Hellenic: in them, Greece meets India and the

Orient in general. The Hellenic genius had yet another answer ready to the question 'What does a life of combat and victory want?', and gives this answer in the whole breadth of Greek history.

In order to understand it, we must assume that Greek genius acknowledged the existing impulse, terrible as it was, and regarded it as *justified*: whereas in the Orphic version there lay the thought that a life rooted in such an impulse was not worth living. Combat and the pleasure of victory were acknowledged: and nothing severs the Greek world so sharply from ours as the resultant *colouring* of individual ethical concepts, for example *Eris* and *envy*.

When the traveller Pausanias visited the Helicon on his travels through Greece, an ancient copy of the Greeks' first didactic poem, Hesiod's *Works and Days*, was shown to him, inscribed on lead plates and badly damaged by time and weather.[3] But he still saw this much, that in contrast to the usual copies it did not carry that little hymn to Zeus at the head, but began straight with the assertion: 'There are *two* Eris-goddesses on earth'.[4] This is one of the most remarkable of Hellenic ideas and deserves to be impressed upon newcomers right at the gate of entry to Hellenic ethics. 'One should praise the one Eris as much as blame the other, if one has any sense; because the two goddesses have quite separate dispositions. One promotes wicked war and feuding, the cruel thing! No mortal likes her, but the yoke of necessity forces man to honour the heavy burden of this Eris according to the decrees of the Immortals. Black Night gave birth to this one as the older of the two; but Zeus, who reigned on high, placed the other on the roots of the earth and amongst men as a much better one. She drives even the unskilled man to work; and if someone who lacks property sees someone else who is rich, he likewise hurries off to sow and plant and set his house in order; neighbour competes with neighbour striving for prosperity. This Eris is good for men. Even potters harbour grudges against potters, carpenters against carpenters, beggars envy beggars and minstrels envy minstrels.'[5]

The two last verses, about *odium figulinum*,[6] seem to our scholars incomprehensible in this place. In their judgment, the predicates 'grudge' and 'envy' fit only the nature of the bad Eris; and for this reason they make no bones about declaring the verses not genuine or accidentally trans-

---

[3] Pausanias IX.31.4.
[4] In the received text, this is line 11.
[5] Hesiod, *Works & Days* 12–26.
[6] 'potters' hatred'.

posed here. But another ethic, not a Hellenic one, must have inspired them to this: for Aristotle makes no objection to referring these verses to the good Eris.[7] And not just Aristotle, but the whole of Greek antiquity thinks about grudge and envy differently from us and agrees with Hesiod, who first portrays one Eris as wicked, in fact the one who leads men into hostile struggle-to-the-death, and then praises the other Eris as good who, as jealousy, grudge and envy, goads men to action, not, however, the action of a struggle-to-the-death but the action of the *contest*. The Greek is *envious* and does not experience this characteristic as a blemish, but as the effect of a *benevolent* deity: what a gulf of ethical judgment between him and us! Because he is envious, he feels the envious eye of a god resting on him whenever he has an excessive amount of honour, wealth, fame and fortune, and he fears this envy; in this case, the god warns him of the transitoriness of the human lot, he dreads his good fortune and, sacrificing the best part of it, he prostrates himself before divine envy. This idea does not estrange his gods at all from him: on the contrary, their significance is made manifest, which is that man, whose soul burns with jealousy of every other living thing, *never* has the right to compete with them. In Thamyris' fight with the Muses, Marsyas' with Apollo, in the moving fate of Niobe,[8] there appeared the terrible opposition of the two forces that ought never to fight one another, man and god.

However, the greater and more eminent a Greek man is, the brighter the flame of ambition to erupt from him, consuming everyone who runs with him on the same track. Aristotle once made a list of such hostile contests in the grand style: amongst them is the most striking example of how even a dead man can excite a living man to consuming jealousy.[9] Indeed, that is how Aristotle describes the relationship of the Kolophonian Xenophanes to Homer. We do not understand the strength of this attack on the national hero of poetry unless we construe the root of the attack to be the immense desire to take the place of the fallen poet and inherit his fame, as later with Plato, too. Every great Hellene passes on the torch of the contest; every great virtue strikes the spark of a new grandeur. If the young Themistocles could not sleep at the thought of Miltiades' laurels,[10] his early-awakened urge found release only in the long rivalry with

---

[7] Aristotle, *Rhetoric* 1388a16, 1381b16–17: *Nicomachean Ethics* 1155a35–b1.
[8] Three cases of humans who tried unsuccessfully to compete with the gods, Thamyris and Marsyas in artistic accomplishment and Niobe in philo-progenetiveness.
[9] Aristotle, *Fragments*, ed. Ross, 7 (from Diogenes Laertius II.5.46).
[10] Plutarch, 'Life of Themistocles', ch. 3.

Aristides, when he developed that remarkable, purely instinctive genius for political action which Thucydides describes for us.[11] How very typical is the question and answer, when a notable opponent of Pericles is asked whether he or Pericles is the best wrestler in the city and answers: 'Even if I throw him he denies having fallen and gets away with it, persuading the people who saw him fall.'[12]

If we want to see that feeling revealed in its naïve form, the feeling that the contest is vital, if the well-being of the state is to continue, we should think about the original meaning of *ostracism*: as, for example, expressed by the Ephesians at the banning of Hermodor. 'Amongst us, nobody should be the best; but if somebody is, let him be somewhere else, with other people.'[13] For why should nobody be the best? Because with that, the contest would dry up and the permanent basis of life in the Hellenic state would be endangered. Later, ostracism acquires a different relation to the contest: it is used when there is the obvious danger that one of the great contending politicians and party leaders might feel driven, in the heat of battle, to use harmful and destructive means and to conduct dangerous *coups d'états*. The original function of this strange institution is, however, not as a safety valve but as a stimulant: the preeminent individual is removed to renew the tournament of forces: a thought that is hostile to the 'exclusivity' of genius in the modern sense, but assumes that there are always *several* geniuses to incite each other to action, just as they keep each other within certain limits, too. That is the kernel of the Hellenic idea of competition: it loathes a monopoly of predominance and fears the dangers of this, it desires, as *protective measure* against genius – a second genius.

Hellenic popular teaching commands that every talent must develop through a struggle: whereas modern educators fear nothing more than the unleashing of so-called ambition. Here, selfishness is feared as 'evil as such' – except by the Jesuits, who think like the ancients in this and probably, for that reason, may be the most effective educators of our times. They seem to believe that selfishness, i.e. the individual, is simply the most powerful *agens*, obtaining its character of 'good' and 'evil' essentially from the aims towards which it strives. But for the ancients, the aim of agonistic education was the well-being of the whole, of state society [*der staatlichen Gesellschaft*]. For example, every Athenian was to develop

---

[11] Thucydides I. 90ff.
[12] Plutarch, 'Life of Pericles', ch. 8.
[13] Heraclitus, Fragment 121.

himself, through the contest, to the degree to which this self was of most use to Athens and would cause least damage. It was not a boundless and indeterminate ambition like most modern ambition: the youth thought of the good of his native city when he ran a race or threw or sang; he wanted to increase its reputation through his own; it was to the city's gods that he dedicated the wreaths which the umpires placed on his head in honour. From childhood, every Greek felt the burning desire within him to be an instrument of bringing salvation to his city in the contest between cities: in this, his selfishness was lit, as well as curbed and restricted. For that reason, the individuals in antiquity were freer, because their aims were nearer and easier to achieve. Modern man, on the other hand, is crossed everywhere by infinity, like swift-footed Achilles in the parable of Zeno of Elea: infinity impedes him, he cannot even overtake the tortoise.

But as the youths to be educated were brought up competing with one another, their educators in their turn were in rivalry with each other. Full of mistrust and jealousy, the great music masters Pindar and Simonides took their places next to each other; the sophist, the advanced teacher of antiquity, met his fellow sophist in contest; even the most general way of teaching, through drama, was only brought to the people in the form of an immense struggle of great musicians and dramatists. How wonderful! 'Even the artist has a grudge against the artist!'. And modern man fears nothing so much in an artist as personal belligerence, whilst the Greek knows the artist *only in personal struggle*. Where modern man senses the weakness of a work of art, there the Hellene looks for the source of its greatest strength! What, for example, is of particular artistic importance in Plato's dialogues is mostly the result of a competition with the art of the orators, the sophists, the dramatists of his time, invented for the purpose of his finally being able to say: 'Look: I, too, can do what my great rivals can do; yes, I can do it better than them. No Protagoras has written myths as beautiful as mine, no dramatist has written such a lively and fascinating whole as the *Symposium*, no orator has composed such speeches as I present in the *Gorgias* – and now I reject all of that and condemn all imitative art! Only the contest made me a poet, sophist and orator!' What a problem reveals itself to us when we enquire about the relationship of the contest to the conception of the work of art! –

On the other hand, if we take away the contest from Greek life, we gaze immediately into that pre-Homeric abyss of a gruesome savagery of hatred and pleasure in destruction. Unfortunately, this phenomenon appears quite often when a great figure was suddenly withdrawn from the contest through an immensely glorious deed and was *hors de concours*[14] in his own judgment and that of his fellow citizens. Almost without exception the effect is terrible; and if we usually draw the conclusion from these effects that the Greek was unable to bear fame and fortune: we should, perhaps, say more exactly that he was not able to bear fame without further competition or fortune at the end of the contest. There is no clearer example than the ultimate fate of Miltiades.[15] Placed on a lonely pinnacle and carried far beyond every fellow competitor through his incomparable success at Marathon: he feels a base lust for vengeance awaken in him against a citizen of Para with whom he had a quarrel long ago. To satisfy this lust, he misuses his name, the state's money and civic honour, and disgraces himself. Conscious of failure, he resorts to unworthy machinations. He enters into a secret and godless relationship with Timo, priestess of Demeter, and at night enters the sacred temple from which every man was excluded. When he has jumped over the wall and is approaching the shrine of the goddess, he is suddenly overwhelmed by a terrible, panic-stricken dread: almost collapsing and unconscious, he feels himself driven back and, jumping back over the wall, he falls down, paralysed and badly injured. The siege must be lifted, the people's court awaits him, and a disgraceful death stamps its seal on the glorious heroic career to darken it for all posterity. After the battle of Marathon he became the victim of the envy of the gods. And this divine envy flares up when it sees a man without any other competitor, without an opponent, at the lonely height of fame. He only has the gods near him now – and for that reason he has them against him. But these entice him into an act of hubris, and he collapses under it.

Let us also mention that even the finest Greek states perish in the same way as Miltiades when they, too, through merit and fortune have progressed from the racecourse to the temple of Nike. Both Athens, which had destroyed the independence of her allies and severely punished the rebellions of those subjected to her, and Sparta, which, after the battle of Aegospotamoi,[16] made her superior strength felt over Hellas in an even harder and crueller fashion, brought about their own ruin, after the example of Miltiades, through acts of hubris. This proves that without envy, jealousy and ambition in the contest, the Hellenic state, like

---

[14] Out of the competition or contest.

[15] Herodotus VI 133–6.

[16] Decisive Athenian naval defeat at the hands of the Spartans in 405 BC. Cf. Xenophon, *Hellenica* II. 1.10–32.

Hellenic man, deteriorates. It becomes evil and cruel, it becomes vengeful and godless, in short, it becomes 'pre-Homeric' – it then only takes a panicky fright to make it fall and shatter. Sparta and Athens surrender to the Persians like Themistocles[16] and Alcibiades[17] did; they betray the Hellenic after they have given up the finest Hellenic principle, the contest: and Alexander, the rough copy and abbreviation of Greek history, now invents the standard-issue Hellene and so-called 'Hellenism'. –

[16] Thucydides I. 135ff.
[17] Thucydides VIII. 45ff.

Index of names

Index of subjects

Cambridge Texts in the History of Political Thought

Titles published in the series thus far

Aquinas *Political Writings* (edited by R. W. Dyson)
  0 521 37595 9 paperback
Aristotle *The Politics* and *The Constitution of Athens* (edited by Stephen Everson)
  0 521 48400 6 paperback
Arnold *Culture and Anarchy and other writings* (edited by Stefan Collini)
  0 521 37796 X paperback
Astell *Political Writings* (edited by Patricia Springborg)
  0 521 42845 9 paperback
Augustine *The City of God against the Pagans* (edited by R. W. Dyson)
  0 521 46843 4 paperback
Augustine *Political Writings* (edited by E. M. Atkins and R. J. Dodaro)
  0 521 44697 X paperback
Austin *The Province of Jurisprudence Determined* (edited by Wilfrid E. Rumble)
  0 521 44756 9 paperback
Bacon *The History of the Reign of King Henry VII* (edited by Brian Vickers)
  0 521 58663 1 paperback
Bagehot *The English Constitution* (edited by Paul Smith)
  0 521 46942 2 paperback
Bakunin *Statism and Anarchy* (edited by Marshall Shatz)
  0 521 36973 8 paperback
Baxter *Holy Commonwealth* (edited by William Lamont)
  0 521 40580 7 paperback
Bayle *Political Writings* (edited by Sally L. Jenkinson)
  0 521 47677 1 paperback
Beccaria *On Crimes and Punishments and other writings* (edited by Richard Bellamy)
  0 521 47982 7 paperback
Bentham *Fragment on Government* (introduction by Ross Harrison)
  0 521 35929 5 paperback
Bernstein *The Preconditions of Socialism* (edited by Henry Tudor)
  0 521 39808 8 paperback
Bodin *On Sovereignty* (edited by Julian H. Franklin)
  0 521 34992 3 paperback
Bolingbroke *Political Writings* (edited by David Armitage)
  0 521 58697 6 paperback
Bossuet *Politics Drawn from the Very Words of Holy Scripture* (edited by Patrick Riley)
  0 521 36807 3 paperback
The British Idealists (edited by David Boucher)
  0 521 45951 6 paperback
Burke *Pre-Revolutionary Writings* (edited by Ian Harris)
  0 521 36800 6 paperback

Leibniz *Political Writings* (edited by Patrick Riley)
   0 521 35899 X paperback
The Levellers (edited by Andrew Sharp)
   0 521 62511 4 paperback
Locke *Political Essays* (edited by Mark Goldie)
   0 521 47861 8 paperback
Locke *Two Treatises of Government* (edited by Peter Laslett)
   0 521 35730 6 paperback
Loyseau *A Treatise of Orders and Plain Dignities* (edited by Howell A. Lloyd)
   0 521 45624 X paperback
Luther and Calvin on Secular Authority (edited by Harro Höpfl)
   0 521 34986 9 paperback
Machiavelli *The Prince* (edited by Quentin Skinner and Russell Price)
   0 521 34993 1 paperback
de Maistre *Considerations on France* (edited by Isaiah Berlin and Richard Lebrun)
   0 521 46628 8 paperback
Maitland *State, Trust and Corporation* (edited by David Runciman and Magnus Ryan)
   0 521 52630 2 paperback
Malthus *An Essay on the Principle of Population* (edited by Donald Winch)
   0 521 42972 2 paperback
Marsilius of Padua *Defensor minor* and *De translatione Imperii*
   (edited by Cary Nederman)
   0 521 40846 6 paperback
Marsilius of Padua *The Defender of the Peace* (edited and translated by Annabel Brett)
   0 521 78911 7 paperback
Marx *Early Political Writings* (edited by Joseph O'Malley)
   0 521 34994 X paperback
Marx *Later Political Writings* (edited by Terrell Carver)
   0 521 36739 5 paperback
James Mill *Political Writings* (edited by Terence Ball)
   0 521 38748 5 paperback
J. S. Mill *On Liberty*, with *The Subjection of Women* and *Chapters on Socialism*
   (edited by Stefan Collini)
   0 521 37917 2 paperback
Milton *Political Writings* (edited by Martin Dzelzainis)
   0 521 34866 8 paperback
Montesquieu *The Spirit of the Laws*
   (edited by Anne M. Cohler, Basia Carolyn Miller and Harold Samuel Stone)
   0 521 36974 6 paperback
More *Utopia* (edited by George M. Logan and Robert M. Adams)
   0 521 52540 3 paperback
Morris *News from Nowhere* (edited by Krishan Kumar)
   0 521 42233 7 paperback

Nicholas of Cusa *The Catholic Concordance* (edited by Paul E. Sigmund)

   0 521 56773 4 paperback

Nietzsche *On the Genealogy of Morality* (edited by Keith Ansell-Pearson)

   0 521 69163 X paperback

Paine *Political Writings* (edited by Bruce Kuklick)

   0 521 66799 2 paperback

Plato *The Republic* (edited by G. R. F. Ferrari and Tom Griffith)

   0 521 48443 X paperback

Plato *Statesman* (edited by Julia Annas and Robin Waterfield)

   0 521 44778 X paperback

Price *Political Writings* (edited by D. O. Thomas)

   0 521 40969 1 paperback

Priestley *Political Writings* (edited by Peter Miller)

   0 521 42561 1 paperback

Proudhon *What is Property?* (edited by Donald R. Kelley and Bonnie G. Smith)

   0 521 40556 4 paperback

Pufendorf *On the Duty of Man and Citizen according to Natural Law*

   (edited by James Tully)

   0 521 35980 5 paperback

The Radical Reformation (edited by Michael G. Baylor)

   0 521 37948 2 paperback

Rousseau *The Discourses and other early political writings* (edited by Victor Gourevitch)

   0 521 42445 3 paperback

Rousseau *The Social Contract and other later political writings* (edited by Victor Gourevitch)

   0 521 42446 1 paperback

Seneca *Moral and Political Essays* (edited by John Cooper and John Procope)

   0 521 34818 8 paperback

Sidney *Court Maxims* (edited by Hans W. Blom, Eco Haitsma Mulier and Ronald Janse)

   0 521 46736 5 paperback

Sorel *Reflections on Violence* (edited by Jeremy Jennings)

   0 521 55910 3 paperback

Spencer *The Man versus the State* and *The Proper Sphere of Government*

   (edited by John Offer)

   0 521 43740 7 paperback

Stirner *The Ego and Its Own* (edited by David Leopold)

   0 521 45647 9 paperback

Thoreau *Political Writings* (edited by Nancy Rosenblum)

   0 521 47675 5 paperback

Tonnies *Community and Civil Society* (edited by Jose Harris and Margaret Hollis)

   0 521 56119 1 paperback

Utopias of the British Enlightenment (edited by Gregory Claeys)

   0 521 45590 1 paperback